Stepfamilies:

A Guide to Working With Stepparents and Stepchildren

Stepfamilies:

A Guide to Working with Stepparents and Stepchildren

EMILY B. VISHER, Ph.D.

and

JOHN S. VISHER, M.D.

Stepfamily Association of America, Inc.

BRUNNER / MAZEL, Publishers • New York

FOURTH PRINTING

Library of Congress Cataloging in Publication Data

Visher, Emily B   1918-
    Stepfamilies: a guide to working with stepparents and stepchildren.
    Bibliography: p.
    Includes index.
    1. Stepparents—United States. 2. Stepchildren—United States. I. Visher,
John S., 1921-   joint author. II. Title. [DNLM: 1. Counseling. 2. Mar-
riage. 3. Divorce. 4. Parent-child relations. HQ728 V829s]
HQ777.7.V57   301.42'7   78-25857
ISBN 0-87630-190-1

Published by
BRUNNER/MAZEL, INC.
19 Union Square, New York, New York 10003

MANUFACTURED IN THE UNITED STATES OF AMERICA

With Appreciation and
Deep Affection for
Our Stepfamily

Foreword

The past several decades have been marked by growing clinical interest in the family and by an expansion of family research. Both areas of endeavor have led to the conclusion that some of the psychological distress in family systems previously dealt with through individual treatment can be better understood and more effectively approached by family therapy.

In these exciting times, with the appearance of many new books and papers, a "family" is usually assumed to be the intact or "nuclear" family, since the overwhelming proportion of research and clinical publications deal with such families. But fully one-third of American children under age 18 do not live in intact or nuclear families, and one out of every seven children is a stepchild.

Unfortunately, the clinical insights and therapeutic techniques derived from work with nuclear families cannot be applied blindly to stepfamilies. Partly because they live in a type of family with important cultural and structural differences, stepparents and stepchildren have to deal with special problems. Their coping styles may be quite different from those in a nuclear family, and as a result we need to examine stepfamilies in order to develop a sensitive, clinical understanding of what is more-or-less typical stepfamily behavior, and what leads to success or failure for these families. Without such insight, the clinician often fails to understand and may attempt to intervene in family processes in unhelpful ways. Publications designed to assist therapists and counselors in their efforts to understand and to help stepparents and stepchildren who consult them have been lacking—the literature cupboard is almost bare.

Into this informational void come Emily and John Visher, bringing to their task experience gained in uniting their own two families, as well as years of interest in working professionally with remarried parents, stepparents and stepchildren. Drawing upon their personal and professional experiences, they have brought together in this volume a wealth of clinical insights about stepfamilies. Individuals who work with families will find here not only a clear presentation of the manifold and diverse problems which arise in stepfamilies, but also detailed guidelines and suggestions for dealing with these problems. Readers will become aware of different norms, tensions, conflicts and stages that are, at least in part, related to stepfamily status. They will find here a comprehensive overview of current knowledge about one type of family, the stepfamily, as well as clinical interventions which have proven useful with such families.

Twenty-five million adults face the previously uncharted complexities of stepparenthood every day. The knowledge, perspective, understanding, support and courage the Vishers bring come none too soon for these husbands and wives, and for those who are attempting to assist them in their efforts to achieve successful stepfamily integration.

JERRY M. LEWIS, M.D.
Timberlawn Psychiatric Research Foundation
Dallas, Texas

Preface

This book began to materialize in the late fifties when we joined together two families and began the task of stepfamily integration. We had anticipated that our personal enthusiasm about our new relationship and our "blended" family, together with our professional awareness of individual emotions and interpersonal dynamics, would provide the necessary ingredients for making the new venture instantly successful.

In what proved to be both a complicated and a rewarding process, we gradually became aware that we were personally involved in a passage or transition from one stage to another, and we became familiar with the complexity of remarriage. Widespread divorce, single parenting, and remarriage are relatively new developments in American society, and we found that there are few models and traditions. There is much to be learned and as yet there are few systematic studies of the joys and sorrows along the way.

In addition to our personal experience we have become aware professionally that counselors and therapists need to know more about the characteristics of divorce, single parenting and remarriage if they are to be successful in their efforts to assist individuals seeking their help for difficulties with these particular phases of life.

Transition and change are difficult for human beings, and each individual copes with stresses in personally determined ways. Physiological factors and cultural characteristics, together with specific life experiences, will determine each person's responses.

Acceptance and support are valuable in times of change. With understanding and guidance as well, stress may become a growth-promoting challenge rather than a regressive emotional overloading of the individual. With a sustained interpersonal relationship, human beings have tremendous potential for adaptation and change (Vaillant, 1977).

Thus this book is the result of both our personal and professional experiences with persons attempting to cope successfully with the challenges of remarriage. It is hoped that the information in it will aid therapists and counselors in their understanding of stepfamilies and their work with adults and children living in such families. There are strengths and positive values in remarriage with children. The invincibility of the human spirit demands respect and admiration. We believe that counselor and therapist understanding, guidance, acceptance and support will enable more stepfamilies to find the life satisfactions which they seek.

Acknowledgments

We wish to thank our own stepfamily as well as many other stepfamilies we have met for their contribution to this book. Our typist, Esther Pollex, has been good natured and accommodating throughout this endeavor, and, although she is not a member of a stepfamily herself, we appreciate the interest she has shown in the content of the manuscript as well as in the task of decoding the scrambled pages she received from us.

A portion of Chapter 13 on working with stepfamilies is from a paper written by Marjorie Daehler, R.N. and Robert Daehler, M.D., family therapists at the Family Psychiatric Center in Phoenix, Arizona. We appreciate their willingness to allow us to include their material.

Many clinicians have provided information and clinical examples which are contained in the book. While it is impossible to separate and acknowledge the many sources contributing to our present understanding, we would like to express our special appreciation to the following: Joan Allen, M.S.W., William Ayres, M.D., Gregory Bellow, M.S.W., Ruth Berlin, M.S.W., L.C.S.W., Gloria Sax Burk, M.D., Robert Green, Ph.D., Joan Haller, M.S.W., Robert Herman, M.D., Marilyn R. Hershenson, M.S.W., L.C.S.W., E. Walton Kirk, Ph.D., Carolyn McClenahan, M.S., Irene Sardanis-Zimmerman, Ph.D., Charles Walton, M.D., and Mary Taylor Warmbrod, Ph.D.

EMILY B. VISHER
JOHN S. VISHER
Palo Alto, California

Contents

Introduction

Stepfamilies as they exist in America today are relatively new on the scene. They are not going to disappear in the foreseeable future and they need to be understood, valued, and supported in their attempts to achieve their potential. While many such families work out their destinies themselves, countless others are seeking professional guidance for the problems that arise. As mental health professionals become more knowledgeable with regard to stepfamily structure and dynamics, they will become more skillful in their efforts to provide assistance to this new population of stepparents and stepchildren. Not only professionals but also individuals living in stepfamilies are seeking information to aid them in their respective tasks. In this volume we will present general background information as well as clinical material to provide guidelines for therapists and counselors as they work with an ever-increasing number of stepfamilies.

Many professionals have looked puzzled when we asked if they see stepparents or stepchildren in their practice. Sudden recognition comes when they consider from this perspective whom they are seeing and they realize they are, indeed, involved with remarried families. Differences between nuclear families and stepfamilies have often been overlooked and we hope this book will be helpful in clarifying them. Special issues which arise for remarried parents and their children will also be discussed.

At the beginning of the twentieth century, stepfamilies resulted primarily from remarriage following the death of a parent, while today contemporary stepfamilies result primarily from remarriage following the divorce of the natural or biologic parents. The divorce rate in America continues to escalate, and since 80 percent of these divorced persons remarry, and 60 percent of these remarriages involve an adult with physical custody of one or more children, it is estimated that over 15 million children are now living with a remarried parent.

A stepfamily is here defined as a family in which at least one of the adults is a stepparent. With this definition, the number of stepfamilies is unknown and much larger than that indicated by the census data which include only the family with whom the children live. Remarriages in which the children of one of the spouses may "visit" rather than "live" experience many problems similar to those in a remarriage involving "live-in" stepchildren. In addition, many similar situations are experienced by couples who have long-term relationships but are not legally married. Because of experiential similarities, the term "stepfamily" as used in this book includes:

1. Families in which children *live* with a remarried parent and a stepparent. (National census data for 1977 indicate that 13 percent of children under 18 are living in this type of family.)

2. Families in which children from a previous marriage *visit* with their remarried parent and stepparent. (In many instances the parent with physical custody has not remarried and therefore these children appear in the census data as members of a single-parent family.)

3. Families in which the couple is not married and children from a previous marriage either live with or visit with the couple. (Since similar problems often arise in these long-term relationships involving children, these families are included even though the terms "remarriage" and "spouse" may be used in the written text.)

These three family patterns are similar in that there is an adult couple in the household with at least one of the adults having a child by a previous marriage.

It has been said that 40 percent of second marriages end in divorce within four years. This is one indication of the need for more understanding of and help for these families. To date there has been little research done on remarriage, and practical guidelines for remarried parents and their partners have only recently found their way into the popular literature. Guidelines for therapists and counselors are practically nonexistent—providing such information is one purpose of this book. Current knowledge regarding the cultural, structural, and emotional aspects of stepfamilies is also included since this is the basis from which guidelines emerge.

Research data indicate that socioeconomic differences may be associated with different stepfamily dynamics. Private practitioners and private, state, and county clinics see primarily middle-class families of American society. Except for certain research data, the information contained here is drawn from this core population.

The first two chapters are concerned with contemporary American culture, followed by a chapter on research relating to remarriage. The next four chapters deal with women in mother/stepmother relationships and with men in father/stepfather relationships. In each case there is, first, a chapter devoted to common problems and conflicts and, next, there is a chapter concerned with methods and techniques that counselors and therapists have found helpful in working with persons in that category.

Chapters 8 and 9 consider the problems of the remarried couple and the types of help available to them. The following two chapters deal with children's difficulties and ways in which the needs of the children can be met.

Finally, Chapters 12 and 13 focus on stepfamilies as a family unit and the application of family therapy to stepfamilies. Then Chapter 14 provides a brief summary or overview of the subject. The appendices list guidelines which stepfamilies have found helpful and references to books and articles which have been helpful to stepfamilies.

Successful counseling and therapy spring from many theoretical backgrounds. A major element needed for success, however, is a good relationship between the person seeking help and the individual who is providing the assistance. Warmth and understanding are crucial ingredients in this relationship. The more familiar the counselor or therapist is with the life situations, both internal and external, of the client or patient, the more likely the relationship between them will be satisfying and productive. In addition, many therapeutic contacts involve some form of "restructuring" or "reframing" of experience for the client or patient, which depends upon adequate therapist or counselor knowledge of the individual's life experiences. We have attempted to provide adequate background material to facilitate an appreciation for and a familiarity with the stresses and conflicts faced by individuals in stepfamilies. While interactional and dynamic material is accurate, names and background information have been altered to protect the identity of the individual.

A number of therapeutic approaches have been used with stepfamilies, e.g., individual therapy, couples groups, and family counseling. These and other methods are discussed in chapters dealing with the practical aspects of providing services to this population.

We are not suggesting that new therapeutic skills are needed to work with stepparents, stepchildren, and stepfamilies. We have found, however, that therapists and counselors often feel overwhelmed with stepfamily complexity, and we are suggesting that a general familiarity with the subject is needed by therapists and counselors if they are to be effective in designing therapeutic services, in restructuring stepfamily experiences, and in establishing therapeutic rapport.

Stepfamilies:

A Guide to Working With Stepparents and Stepchildren

1

Cultural characteristics of stepfamilies

The pattern of American family life is changing rapidly. No longer is the average American family a mother, a father, and two children. These families remain in our society, but now standing beside these families are the single-parent families, mother and children, and, in growing numbers, fathers and children. And behind them in the shadows are the stepfamilies, mother/stepmother, father/stepfather, children/stepchildren and the ghosts of former relationships. The cultural position and structure of these new stepfamilies are different from the familiar nuclear families, and the joys and sorrows of these new families are also different.

While the terms "stepmother," "stepfather" and "stepchildren" appear in standard American dictionaries, the term "stepfamily" is not included. The "step-" prefix comes from the middle and old English prefix "steop-" meaning "bereaved" or "orphaned." The term "step-" came into use at a time when it was basically the death of a natural or biologic parent rather than parental divorce that led to the eventual remarriage of the other parent.

The "step-" relationship designations remain in use, but various terms have been coined to refer to the resultant family: "remarried," "reconstituted," "recoupled," "blended," or "stepfamily."

The simplest definition of a stepfamily is the one used here: "a family in which at least one of the couple is a stepparent." Adults living in stepfamilies with or without custody of their children, as well as unmarried parents living in long-term couple relationships, are seeking professional help for a similar range of problems. Therefore, a simple and broad classification seems the most useful in this mental health context.

In 1964 Simon estimated that there were eight million children in the United States living with a stepparent; by 1975 Roosevelt and Lofas (1976) reported that there were 15 million children under 18 living in stepfamilies, and that there were a minimum of 25 million husbands and wives who were stepfathers and stepmothers. In this country at present, one million children and a half a million adults each year become members of stepfamilies.

Using statistics obtained from the Population Reference Bureau for 1977, the living arrangements for children under 18 are shown in Diagram A.

Many stepfamilies are families in which there are no children under 18, or families in which the children under 18 only visit. Therefore, the 13% figure does not represent the total number of

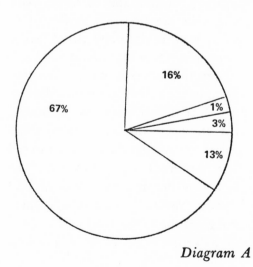

67% Nuclear or intact families
17% Single-parent families
    16% living with mother
    1% living with father
3% Foster and other living arrangements where the adults are not biological parents.
13% Families in which one of the two adults is not the biologic parent.

Diagram A

stepfamilies in the population. It is clear, however, that there are three common family patterns in America today—namely, nuclear or intact families, single-parent families, and step-, blended or re-married families.

Only recently has attention been given to these latter families. Studies of stepparenting are beginning to appear, and organizations for stepfamilies are being founded. Throughout the years there has been a trickle of stepparents into the offices of mental health professionals, and with the increasing number of such families, the trickle is becoming a steady stream. However, help has not always been forthcoming, not because of bad intentions on the part of the counselor or therapist, but because of unfamiliarity with the "stepfamily culture."

In the past, children of divorce and of remarriage and not the adults have been the focus of professional and educational attention. Recently, a few stepparents have shown a willingness to "come out of the closet," and greater acceptance and understanding of this family pattern will, it is hoped, lead more to do so. Little concern has been given to the functioning of stepfamilies, although the functioning of "nuclear" or intact families has received considerable attention for a number of years. Research on stepfamilies is in its infancy, and to wait until hard statistical data are available for therapists and counselors would in the meantime deprive many individuals of much needed assistance.

Stepfamilies are culturally disadvantaged families. Down through the ages, in all societies, tales of wicked stepmothers are a part of the literary heritage, while at intervals a cruel stepfather appears in the literature. The term stepchild also carries with it a less than favorable image. As Simon states in *Stepchild in the Family* (1964, p. 17), "If you want to indicate neglect, say step-child and everyone will know what you mean."

In a recent book, Bruno Bettelheim (1977) sees fairy stories as a necessary part of the culture. He believes that Cinderella and similar tales give children a vehicle to use in dealing with their ambivalent feelings about their mother. There is the good mother and the bad mother, with the stepmother serving as the bad mother. Now that stepmothers have become a numerically large reality in our society continuation of such tales only perpetuates the negativity that envelopes a stepfamily.

In a paper questioning Bettelheim's conceptualization, Michel Radomisli (1978) expresses the belief that by age six children can learn to differentiate and deal with "bad" and "good" without needing to polarize the experience and split the two apart. Radomisli postulates that the tenacity of the Cinderella myths has to do with the needs of parents rather than with the needs of children. To Radomisli the Cinderella myth protects the mother's authority and therefore benefits only indirectly the child because the mother feels more secure. The message to the child is "the best thing you have going for you is your mother. Do not leave a mother who loves you because no one else will care for you and look after you."

Fairies do not exist, and witches do no exist, but stepmothers do exist, and therefore certain fairy tales are harmful rather than helpful to large segments of the population. The presumption is that step relationships will not be good; that the stepfather will be cruel and the stepmother wicked; and that the stepchildren are poor maligned waifs. To walk around and interact in the middle of such a dark cloud is crippling to many stepfamilies.

Sociologists and anthropologists at times study a culture by examing its art or literature, its comic strips, or its garbage cans. The greeting card industry in America has become big business, and reflects the trends of this society. There are combine-it or do-it-yourself cards, mix-and-match cards, Peanuts cards, and cards bordering, or not-so-bordering on pornography. All these and many more are in addition to the conventional and traditional flowery messages for close relatives and friends and standard greetings for more distant friends and relations. There are cards for all occasions, and for all classifications of people—friends, postman, teacher, grandson, daughter, mother, father, sister, brother-in-law, and so on. But there are no cards for stepmother, stepfather, stepchild.

Since there are many millions of individuals in the "step" classification, the absence of greeting cards for these categories is not without psychological meaning. If Hallmark thought such cards would sell, it seems likely that they would appear with the other cards for relatives. Perhaps such cards die in the planning stage as the artist contemplates suitable drawings to accompany "For My Stepmother." This year one greeting card company did produce a card "For My Other Mother." This appears to be recognition that there is an area that needs attention, and an attempt is being made to fill the gap.

Human flexibility exceeds institutional flexibility, and it is only very gradually that the institutions in American society are making provision for the existence of stepfamilies. Schools, for example, at all levels produce conflicts and hurts for a number of their families. Little children are given materials and instructions to make Mother's Day cards for one mother each, or invitations to a school function for one set of parents only. The P.T.A. may send flyers to one parent, and not to the other parent living at a different address in the same locality. There is no way for the P.T.A. to know how divorced parents wish to work out attendance at such functions. Not providing similar information to all the parental figures involved with the child is a rejection of at least one parent and may prevent the individuals involved from working out such matters in the most comfortable way for their particular situation.

Very often the families involved are more comfortable than the school personnel. Recently a young child chided her stepmother for not being at a school performance by saying, "Why weren't you there? Some of my friends have two mothers and they both were there. I have two mothers and *none* of you were there."

Another stepmother of a five-year-old stepson, Rick, who lived with her and her husband, received a call from the P.T.A. asking for her husband. When she replied that he was at work, very tentatively and somewhat apologetically the caller inquired of Rick's stepmother, "Oh . . . we need some help with the P.T.A. . . . Would *you* be willing to help?" As this stepmother remarked, "It made me really feel like an outsider. And another thing, on the kindergarten forms there was a line for the natural mother, a line for the natural father, and somewhere my name went in a little box on the form as the person Rick's father was living with."

It is often important for the school to be in touch with a child's parents. When the child's natural parents are no longer living together, school personnel very often make their job more difficult by depriving themselves, the child, and the child's families, of an opportunity to share school progress and concerns with all the responsible adults. Some ex-spouses and partners feel comfortable in working together in regard to their child's school program. However, several parents and stepparents have reported that schoolteachers and administrators become anxious and even visibly shaken when natural parents and stepparents all arrive at the same time for the parent-teacher conference. If teachers can be more relaxed with this pattern there will be less time required on their part to interact with the adults important in the child's nonschool life. For many other individuals, however, this much interaction between ex-spouses is not the pattern of choice. In fact, the school conference could become a disaster if all parental figures were involved. So flexibility is the key to successful school-stepparent relationships.

As awareness of new patterns of family structure grows, innovative ways of acknowledging such families can emerge. One common task given to young children in school is to draw a picture of their family. This may become a traumatic experience for children who are a part of two separate households. Before asking her students to do such a drawing, a sensitive teacher talked for some time with her pupils about the different family constellations represented by her and by her students. There was a discussion in the classroom that grew more comfortable as the various patterns were shared. Then the children settled down to drawing their family or families, with some children receiving two sheets of drawing paper rather than the customary one sheet. No longer did these children have to choose to acknowledge only one household, when in reality they were members of two family units living in two separate homes.

One other problem area involving schools and colleges mentioned many times by parents, stepparents and children is the discomfort and hurt feelings at graduation time. Often due to space restrictions, students receive only two tickets—"one for each parent." Whom does the graduate invite? Divorced mother and father? Mother and stepfather? Father and stepmother? There seems no way to go. No satisfactory choice, including everyone, is possible.

The consciousness of society needs to be sharpened in the area of stepfamily life. As this happens many customs and ways of doing things will appear inappropriate. Some areas will require major shifts, while in others only minor alterations will be necessary to adapt to the new family patterns. For example, there is a scouting ceremony in which a son receives his Eagle Scout award. The custom in this event is that the parents are included in the ceremony, and the son at one point pins on his mother a small replica of his own Eagle Scout pin. In a growing number of families, after a divorce takes place, the boy's father enters into or continues with his son in the Scouting program. Under these circumstances it is appropriate that the natural father be a part of the ceremony. If the divorced father has remarried, who receives the mother's pin, and how? Even if the two ex-spouses would be comfortable participating jointly, it may produce a situation confusing to the participants and others present at the service. With thought a more appropriate procedure could be adopted.

There are numerous articles appearing in newspapers and magazines devoted to the premise that the American family is not dead. However, there is often a failure to recognize that the forms taken by the American family have altered greatly. The stepfamily is one of the new patterns. It has crept slowly into the American social scene, and it is time to examine its characteristics so that members of stepfamilies will meet with understanding and empathy and thus become a more comfortable segment of modern America.

THE INVISIBILITY OF STEPFAMILIES

It is clear that members of stepfamilies often go to great lengths to hide their step-status. It has been noted that many stepparents even lie verbally and on printed forms so that it will not be public knowledge that they are stepparents.

In a recent conversation with Owen Spann, KGO (San Francisco) radio personality and author with his wife Nancie Spann of a book about their stepfamily, *Your Child? I Thought It Was My Child!*, Owen spoke of the lack of response to the topic of stepparenting on his radio talk show. "If we're talking about divorce, remarriage, marital problems, or parent-child problems all ten telephone lines light up at once. There are hundreds of calls, and we don't know how many aren't able to get through. For parent-child problems it's Gang Busters! The calls come in: 'My child sucks his thumb.' 'My child wets his bed.' 'My child has this problem.' 'My child has that problem.'

"If you get into the area of stepfamilies, there's absolute silence. You know they're out there, all 20 million of them, but they don't call in. For all other areas of parent-child, parent-parent, or adult-adult relationships the telephone board lights up like a Christmas tree. We know that in stepfamilies there are problems, but they just don't want to talk about them. Perhaps we get six calls an hour. My experience is that other talk shows have the same experience" (Spann, 1977).

It is a common experience for workshops and lectures to be planned for stepparents and publicized to as many as 20,000 to 30,000 families; yet only a handful of people may respond—even when there is no fee.

There is little information on the reasons for stepfamily invisibility. The limited information available indicates that the following cultural and personal factors may be operating.

1. If the stepparent has been married and divorced there is often a feeling that there has been one failed marriage, and therefore to admit difficulties in a second marriage is admitting that there must be something very wrong with oneself. In fact, trying to defend oneself against the anxiety that accompanies such a negative self-concept may lead to denial that any difficulties exist in the present marriage, either with the children or with the spouse.

2. Parent-child problems are part of the cultural norm. There have been many books written and talks given on the subject. There are parental stress hot lines, and "Parent Effectiveness Training" courses. Much research has

been done in the area of parent-child relationships. Everyone is well aware that parents can be burdened with many difficulties.

Stepparenting, however, has not been studied. Few books on the subject have been written, and speakers have not identified themselves to the public as being stepparents with stepparent-stepchild problems. Recognition and public awareness of these problems are only in the embryonic stage, and as a result stepfamilies feel uncomfortable and outside the accepted cultural patterns. For this reason they may keep a very low profile.

3. One of the remarks made to stepparents by friends and neighbors—and all too often by mental health professionals—is, "Well, you knew what you were getting into." These reassuring words usually follow some expression of anger or discouragement made by a stepparent, and they leave the stepparent feeling even more frustrated, more discouraged, and more helpless and alienated than before.

In a job situation careful inquiry may give an applicant a good idea of what will be entailed in filling the position. However, it is almost impossible to assess the interpersonal aspects of a job before actually accepting the position and experiencing personal relationships over a period of time. Similarly, most stepparents are aware of the objective job requirements: four children to house and feed, $20,000 yearly income, $200 alimony going out, $300 child support going out, $150 child support coming in, shared household chores, two weeks in the mountains every summer. But the interpersonal interactions, crucial elements in family functioning, usually cannot be assessed in advance. There is no way for individuals "to know what they are getting into."

So when stepparents voice some of their negative feelings and are not understood, many react by keeping their feelings to themselves, at times even hiding the fact that they are stepparents, thus joining the invisible multitude.

4. Stepparents' expectations of themselves are usually unrealistically high; since they may not be able to live up to these expectations, they often consider that there is something wrong with their feelings and with themselves. For example, they may feel guilty at having angry feelings about a stepchild. It is not acceptable to be angry at your

stepchild because you are not sure you care about this little creature who has suddenly entered your life. So there is anger, guilt, and low self-esteem—and a need to conceal these feelings. Present models depicted on television appear to hinder rather than help in this regard. The program "Eight Is Enough" is somewhat more realistic than is the "Brady Bunch," but even in the former stepparents are portrayed as having the patience of Job and the wisdom and understanding of Solomon. In addition, the programs give the impression that all problems that arise can be solved in 28 to 56 minutes.

5. When individuals have a feeling of security they are able to acknowledge problems and discuss areas of interpersonal functioning they may wish to improve. Parents may seek groups in which they can discuss problems within their family, knowing in general what society expects of them as parents and having a degree of confidence in their ability to fulfill their own and other's expectations. On the other hand, the role of stepparents or stepchildren has not been defined, so that individuals in stepfamilies often have little confidence that they can meet their own and others' expectations.

   Adult partners may have widely differing expectations. These differences can lead to arguments and feelings of disappointment. The partners may criticize each other and consequently become very insecure in the stepparenting area. Children may also be confused as to how they are supposed to "feel" and "act" toward stepparents and stepsiblings; they may, too, become overwhelmed by feelings that they are bad, and as a result become very unsure of themselves. The rules of the game are not available, but the game is already underway. Keeping "silent" seems to be the best course of action to many people.

6. For most individuals in stepfamilies there are counterparts with whom there is competition. It is difficult for stepmothers and natural mothers not to feel competitive, for stepfathers and natural fathers not to feel competitive, and for stepchildren and their stepsiblings not to feel competitive.

   Children question their position in the family relative to stepsiblings and/or to half siblings, the basic question being, "Who is loved the most?" For the adults, where custody issues are often matters of concern, to admit to stepfamily difficulties seems unwise. Protection from criticism by an ex-spouse becomes important, and the adults struggle along as best they can without seeking outside understanding and support. Even when no custody issues are involved, fear of criticism by ex-spouses coming either directly or indirectly through the children appears to account for the reluctance of many adults to acknowledge the difficulties they find in remarriage situations.

7. Often stepchildren do not reveal that they are members of stepfamilies. They pick up the discomfort around them and may feel that something is wrong with *them* so they keep secret the fact that they have stepparents. In addition, stepchildren frequently cling to the fantasy, even after a remarriage, that they natural parents will re-unite. Not acknowledging the existence of a stepparent helps to keep that fantasy intact, and sometimes also creates a public impression that the original nuclear family is still together.

8. Invisibility breeds invisibility. When individuals feel different from the people around them, the usual tendency is to try to hide the difference. If one feels in a "one-down" position because of the difference, the need to hide becomes all the more important. Stepfamilies have been unacknowledged and different, and in a "one-down" position in society. Therefore their reticence to become recognized is easy to understand.

Fortunately there is a gradual shift in America, and an increasing number of popular articles and books about stepparents have appeared. These publications have been welcomed by stepparents and have given them an awareness that there are others with similar feelings and situations. Stepfamily visibility is growing.*

Sociologists who have studied family patterns worldwide recognize that the nuclear family is an anomaly. Extended families of many different structures are predominant throughout the world,

---

* Organizations specifically concerned with meeting the needs of stepfamilies are also being formed: Stepfamily Foundation of America, Inc., 900 Welch Road, Suite 400, Palo Alto, California 94304; Duet Again, Des Moines, Iowa; Remarried, Inc., (an organization affiliated with Parents Without Partners).

and existed in America until relatively recently. If stepfamilies can be recognized as one of many acceptable family patterns, the adults in these families will have more opportunity to be comfortable with their roles and with themselves, and their children will have more opportunity to make better use of the variety offered to them by the increased number of interpersonal contacts within their extended stepfamily structures.

2

Structural

characteristics

of stepfamilies

COMPARISON OF AMERICAN FAMILY PATTERNS

A basic difficulty for stepfamilies arises from the question of what constitutes a family. In America people grow up knowing that a family is a mother, father, and one or more children. This group of people live together in one house or apartment, and in some cases other related individuals such as grandmothers or grandfathers come to live with them for awhile.

Television programs tell you this. In first grade "Dick and Jane" tell you this. And until recently, the experience of growing up in America told you this. Now the message is changing, but there is confusion rather than clarity as to what is the new message.

To the individuals involved in alternate family patterns one thing is clear. Their family is not a nuclear or intact family. Just what it is remains ambiguous and disturbing. Among stepfamilies themselves there is disagreement even to what members belong "in the family." One couple considers that they, plus all the children from previous marriages (the "blending" of two families) constitute a stepfamily unit. Another couple is adamant that only the children who live with them are members of their family. The husband's children who visit are not family members; they are

15

merely guests. One stepchild considers that the parent with whom he or she lives, an ex-spouse, is a member of the stepfamily unit along with the other natural parent, stepparent, siblings and stepsiblings. Another stepchild delineates the family by splitting groups apart so that stepparents and stepsiblings are not included in the family.

To those not involved this confusion often appears superficial and not too important. To those involved there is a fundamental, often unconscious discomfort that can influence even the simplest interchanges. Family introductions are strained, and many stepparents are upset when the first question following introductions is, "Which children are yours?" Even when only casual interest is being expressed in the question, to the parent/stepparent the sense of complexity and fragmentation in the family structure is underlined and produces a certain uneasiness. According to many adults in stepfamilies, they protect themselves from uncomfortable feelings by not letting it be known that theirs is a stepfamily.

Society continues to react disapprovingly to divorce and remarriages. Thus, the insecurity felt by many members of stepfamilies may be the result of negative feelings sensed in others, as well as personal and intrapsychic determinants. To avoid "the hassle of trying to explain the family relationships" many stepfamily couples become guarded with their answers to what seem to be simple questions about their family.

Fast and Cain (1966), in their paper on stepparenting state, "The strong tendency in the major professions dealing with interpersonal relationships to use a health-illness model in understanding behavior makes it tempting to see the stepfamily in terms of pathology. Inevitably then, the 'cure' for its disturbance will be sought in the best possible approximation of the normative pattern of the nuclear family in this society. We think this is a tactical error. If our analysis is generally correct, attempts to reproduce the nuclear family in the step situation are doomed to failure in any case."

A stepfamily is not a nuclear or intact family because there is a biological parent somewhere else. Even if the biological parent is dead, this parent did exist, and very often is still very much alive in a psychological sense. There are other family patterns such as foster families in which there is a biological parent elsewhere, and these will be compared later. The common tendency for stepfamilies to be viewed as comparable to intact or nuclear families leads to many difficulties, including strong feelings of isolation and alienation on the part of stepfamilies.

Stepfamily structure is more varied than intact family structure, and role definition for individuals in such families has not been established in this society. This ambiguity, together with the "negative aura" which still surrounds divorce and remarriage involving children, makes for considerable misunderstanding and lack of empathy from sources external to the stepfamily, as well as within the stepfamily.

In an intact or nuclear family there is a mother, father, and their children. In a stepfamily there can be a stepmother with no children and a father and his children. There can be a stepfather with no children and a mother and her children. There can be a couple, each of whom is both a parent and a stepparent. These structural elements alone produce complicated sets of emotions which even individuals within the families often find difficult to accept and understand.

In regard to understanding from outside of the family unit, much of the advice offered in newspaper columns such as "Dear Abby" treat stepfamily situations as though the original nuclear, intact family is still the family unit, even after a divorce and the establishment of a stepfamily has taken place. Mental health professionals often continue to think in terms of the nuclear family, and hence be concerned with the children's relationship with their two biological parents while the importance of the relationship between stepchildren and stepparents is unrecognized and neglected. And when the individuals remain in the geographic location in which they have previously lived, the community tends to consider stepparent and stepsiblings as somehow attached to the original nuclear family unit. It is easy to see why stepfamilies have difficulty establishing their identity.

There is confusion as to the characteristics of stepfamilies, adoptive families, and foster families. Brenda Maddox (1975, p. 26) writes, "Time and time again, people confuse stepparenthood with adoption. A typical comment was offered to me enthusiastically by a radio broadcaster sophisticated enough to know better: 'Stepparents—what a fascinating subject! My sister was a stepmother. She and her husband couldn't have any children of their own and then they got this Korean war orphan. That was 15 years ago and now are they having problems.' "

Recently an attorney who deals with domestic relations in his practice commented, "I thought a man was a stepfather only when the natural father was dead." And many times, mental health professionals, or stepparents themselves, ask, "Oh, is a stepfamily a family in which there is a foster child?"

While there are similarities between different types of family constellations, there are also fundamental and important differences. Diagram B indicates in summary form six major structural similarities and differences between stepfamilies, nuclear families, single-parent families, adoptive families, and foster families. It appears that the most important characteristic listed is the existence of a biological parent elsewhere. Even when this parent is dead, the psychological impact usually continues. From the diagram it is clear that the most structurally dissimilar families are stepfamilies and nuclear families.

While Brenda Maddox (1975, p. 27) outlines many differences between stepfamilies and adoptive families, there is one basic similarity that is important to consider, and that is the fact that there is at least one biological parent outside the family unit in both cases. In adoptions, where both biological parents are outside the adoptive family unit, the outside existence of both biological parents is a major similarity between a foster family and an adoptive family.

It is estimated that more than one-third of all adoptions in the United States are adoptions of stepchildren (Maddox, 1975, p. 167). In these "adoptive stepfamilies," since one of the couple is the biological parent of the adopted child, there has been a relationship between the adult and the child prior to the present marriage. The two adults do not start at the same place in their relationship to the adopted child. This is true also for stepfami-

Diagram B

Comparison of American Family Patterns
Major Structural Characteristics

	Stepfamilies	Nuclear families	Single-parent families	Adoptive families	Foster families
	Biological parent elsewhere.	—	Biological parent elsewhere.	Biological parent elsewhere.	Biological parent elsewhere.
	Virtually all members have recently sustained a primary relationship loss.	—	All members have recently sustained a primary relationship loss.	The children have sustained a primary relationship loss.	The children have sustained a primary relationship loss.
	An adult couple in the household.	An adult couple in the household.	—	Usually an adult couple in the household.	Usually an adult couple in the household.
	Relationship between one adult (parent) and child predates the marriage.	—	—	Relationship between one adult (parent) and child predates the marriage *where stepchildren are adopted.*	—
	Children are members in more than one household.	—	Children may be members in more than one household.	—	Children may be members in more than one household.
	One adult (stepparent) not legally related to a child (stepchild).	—	—	—	The adults have no legal relationship to the child.

Biological parent }
Natural parent } used synonymously

Nuclear family }
Intact family } used synonymously

lies, but not for nuclear, single-parent, or foster families. A difference in bonding, which is a function of duration of the relationship, does at times cause difficulties. The non-biological parent in the unit may feel left out, the biological parent often feels very protective of the child, and if the child is not an infant, the child has stronger ties to one of the two adults.

Only in nuclear or intact families are there two biological parents. In other types of family units, the fact that there are biological parents elsewhere creates a situation which can be stressful for all the individuals concerned. Primary interpersonal relationships have been disrupted and dealing with these losses is one of the most difficult readjustments human beings have to make.

The subjective experience of therapists, adoption counselors, and foster family agencies is that there is a positive correlation between the degree of acceptance and understanding by the present parental figures of the absent biological parents and the emotional well-being of the child. Restated, children are affected either positively or negatively by the positive or negative feelings the second parental adults have about the biological parents.

It is very difficult for the adults involved not to feel competitive, and for the children not to feel torn in two directions. Indeed, even in happy and relaxed adoptive families, when the child has been adopted in infancy, there is often a strong pull for the adopted individual to seek his or her biological parents many years later. Each year newspaper and magazine stories appear telling of the emotional reunion of blood siblings or children and biological parents, and in 1978 the California legislature considered a law making it legal for adopted children to contact their biologic parents when they reach the age of 18. While there are numerous long-lost princes and princesses in the fantasies of children in intact or nuclear families, these childhood adoption fantasies do not have the emotional impact that is caused by the actual existence of biological parents outside the family unit.

In stepfamilies and single-parent families, and occasionally in foster families, the fact that the children are members of two households may cause considerable strain for both the children and the adults. As a rule, children live with one parent and visit with the other parent. To many not involved in such matters, visitation sounds simple enough. To parents involved with stepfamilies, or with single-parent families, visitation rights often become a bitter battleground. Children may be tossed back and forth by angry parents using the children as a vehicle for expressing their anger at the other parent. Even when visitation is smooth and amicable, children often find themselves swinging from one type of living situation to a very different pattern of living, as they go from one household to another. Children do not find this easy.

Only recently have attorneys become aware of their need to be more sensitive to the emotional complexities of such situations. Goldstein, Freud, and Solnit in *Beyond the Best Interests of the Child* (1973) advocate that in contested situations the parent with custody be the person to define the visitation rights for the child. However, many attorneys, mental health professionals, and noncustodial parents are unhappy with this solution, and attempts are being made to devise alternative plans.

A group of attorneys and mental health professionals in San Francisco are studying various visitation and custody alternatives, and Persia Woolley, the author of *Creative Survival for Single Mothers* (1975), is preparing a book on custody arrangements with a particular focus on innovative and alternative concepts of custody. While such interest is directed primarily at the problems created at the time of the divorce, remarriage of a parent does not alter the emotional aspects of visitation and custody arrangements. In many cases remarriage brings with it added emotional difficulties and often the desire for an alteration in custody and visitation agreements.

In nuclear families, single-parent families, and adoptive families, adults have legal rights in regards to the children. Because there is no legal ambiguity there are clear lines of responsibility, and a feeling of permanence to the relationships. In stepfamilies, a stepparent has no legal relation to a stepchild. Most often the relationship lasts only as long as the marriage lasts. Such impermanence certainly affects the psychological welfare of stepchildren and makes it important to offer stepfamilies preventive as well as therapeutic help. It is also to be hoped that legal attention will be directed towards the matter of the legal rights and relationship between stepparent and stepchild. As the law now stands in most states, if a parent in a stepfamily dies or a divorce occurs the stepparent has no legal rights to custody of the stepchildren. For example, a mother and her two children and the children's stepfather have been a family unit for over ten years. The children are now 14 and 12, and during a month in the summer they visit with their natural father in another state. Suddenly the mother dies. Legally the children cannot stay in the home in which they have grown up, with the man with whom they have had a primary relationship, even if that is his desire and the wish of the children. Recently there have been a few exceptions to this situation in rulings of courts which have awarded custody of the child to non-blood relatives (Woolley, 1978). But, in general, agreement of the biological father or nearest relative would be necessary.

The nuclear family has become the "standard" American family. As a result variations from this standard are suspect and individuals in other types of families often feel that their family is a "substandard" family. Adults in stepfamilies frequently comment, "We're working hard to become a nuclear family."

Stepfamilies are often considered to be similar to nuclear families. Single-parent families are not so considered. As can be seen from Diagram B, there is one similar structural characteristic shared by both nuclear and stepfamilies; both have an adult couple in the household. By definition it is a characteristic not present in single-parent families. Thus it seems possible that this is the characteristic primarily responsible for the impression that nuclear families and stepfamilies are similar. If the other factors are considered, however, the similarity between stepfamily structure and the structure of nuclear families disappears.

There are important similarities between stepfamilies and single-parent families: the need to deal with separation and loss, a biological parent elsewhere, and children who may be members of two separate households. With the addition of a new parental figure as a result of a remarriage, the single-parent family becomes a stepfamily and the children's loyalty conflicts and feelings of loss may escalate, and so may rivalries, jealousies, and feelings of aienation and isolation for both children and adults.

In stepfamilies a child is part of the "remarriage package." In adoptive families the couple jointly decides to adopt a child and there are equal bonds between the child and both adults. When stepparents adopt their stepchildren there is then an important added similarity between adoptive families and stepfamilies in that some parent-child bonds have pre-dated the couple relationship. However, the children no longer have a membership in two households, and both adults are legally related to the children; thus the lines of responsibility and belonging are clear-cut. The adoption of a stepchild does not alter the fact that, except in the case of an infant, the child has relationships of differing duration with the two adults. Hence, adoptions of stepchildren do not necessarily reduce stepfamily tensions arising from this source.

Structurally, stepfamilies and foster families are the most similar. There are two major differences, however, that need to be considered. The foster child stands at the same distance from both of the adults since there are no previous relationship bonds, and both adults have chosen to have a foster child. In addition, if the arrangement is not satisfying to the adults they are free to relinquish the foster child and return to the status of a nuclear family, or a couple, as the case may be. A stepfamily does not have this freedom of choice.

Thus stepfamilies share certain structural elements with other family types, but appear to be structurally the most complex of all the families. The emotional components also appear to be the most complex. Structure combined with cultural and personality characteristics produces specific stepfamily dynamics and interactions, hence the importance of considering more carefully the structural elements of these families.

THE STRUCTURE OF STEPFAMILIES

A stepfamily is a family which is formed as the final phase of a process beginning with the disintegration of a marriage, either by death or divorce. Following death or divorce there is a period of single parenting, then a courtship and/or living together phase, and eventually for many couples, the remarriage itself.

Except for adults who have not been previously married and who are marrying a parent, all individuals in a stepfamily have had to deal with total or partial loss of a primary relationship. The particular circumstances surrounding the loss, together with individual differences in ability to deal with such losses, make for wide variations in adaptation and subsequent acceptance of the new stepfamily. These previous relationships result in ambiguity in stepfamily boundaries, with an emotionally and, at times, legally important adult living elsewhere. The presence of these ex-spouses creates what Messinger (1976) has called "permeable boundaries" for stepfamilies. Obviously, many emotional conflicts for both adults and children can result from the existence of a previous marriage relationship.

In stepfamilies there are many variations in custody arrangements, in visiting arrangements, and in financial arrangements. These structural variations tend to cause specific types of situations and reactions, many examples of which will be discussed in subsequent chapters.

The most common term used to describe stepfamilies seems to be the word "complex." Diagrams C, D, and E illustrate graphically why this family structure is so complex. In these diagrams two separate figures are given; namely, the number of two-person interactions that are possible, and the number of all possible interactions. All possible interactions include all possible groups of three, four, five, etc. Individuals in stepfamilies find these figures overwhelming, and also comforting, because emotionally they have realized the complexity, and adding intellectual recognition is satisfying. This overall complexity, together with a unique combination of stepfamily structures can make for difficulties as the family attempts its reorganization.

In an attempt to describe stepfamily structure in terms familiar enough to convey conceptual and emotional understanding, Dr. Richard Fisch (1977) of the Mental Research Institute in Palo Alto uses the analogy of the "merging of two organizations." Like

Nuclear Family

John's Parents   Mary's Parents

John   Mary

John and
Mary's Children

Possible Interactions
Pairs 28
All 247

Diagram C

Courtesy of Carolyn McClenahan, M.S.

Remarriage of Mary

John's   Mary's   Bill's   Betty's
Parents   Parents   Parents   Parents

Mary's   Mary   New husband   Bill's
Ex-husband   Bill   Ex-wife
John   Betty

John and   Bill and Betty's
Mary's   Children
Children

Possible Interactions
Pairs 136
All 131, 054

Diagram D

Courtesy of Carolyn McClenahan, M.S.

Remarriage of Mary and John

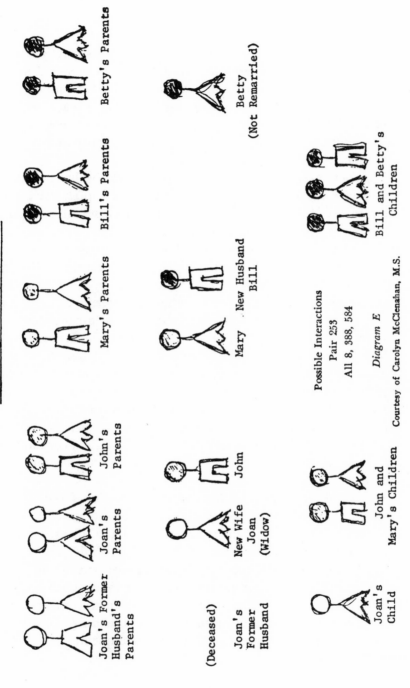

Joan's Former Husband's Parents

Joan's Parents

John's Parents

Mary's Parents

Bill's Parents

Betty's Parents

(Deceased)

Joan's Former Husband

New Wife Joan (Widow)

John

Mary

New Husband Bill

Betty (Not Remarried)

Joan's Child

John and Mary's Children

Bill and Betty's Children

Possible Interactions
Pair 253
All 8, 388, 584

Diagram E

Courtesy of Carolyn McClenahan, M.S.

all analogies there is a limitation to the comparison, but within these limits valuable concepts can be communicated.

To elaborate, two corporations, each with its own personnel and operational procedures, are brought together and an attempt is made to merge the two into a successfully functioning unit. Mergers in the business world do not usually take place smoothly. High officials are dropped and continue outside the new organization in a new position, with feelings of insecurity and rejection affecting their behavior and decisions.

The new executives of the merged corporation have a difficult task before them. Employees are insecure and apprehensive about their future. One group may be used to a laissez-faire corporate atmosphere, while the other group is accustomed to considerable structure and bonus incentives. There is loyalty to one's own group, and distrust of the new group. Attachment of the employees to the officials that have been ousted by the merger pose a problem. Morale declines, the employees begin to confide in the officer with whom they worked in the original organization, and friction develops between the two high company officials.

Too radical and too quick changes, lack of communication at the top, and unrealistic expectations for the new company will lead to frustration and anger. The future of the new organization looks shaky. On the other hand, if the two leaders are able to form a cohesive unit, establish some workable policies somewhere in between the characteristics of each of the original corporations, and deal together directly and fairly with all employees, the new merger may begin to stabilize.

In an inexact way this describes the situation faced by stepfamilies. The fact that power also continues to reside with the natural parent outside of the stepfamily unit and the usual pattern of children going back and forth from the household of one parent to the household of the other further complicate the picture. Looking at the number of communication units in an intact family of mother, father, their parents, and two children, as contrasted with the number of communication units in the diagrammed stepfamilies, makes the magnitude of the complexity clear (Diagrams C, D, E).

Stepparents are responsible for the decision to continue their relationship and thus the life of the stepfamily. The fact that many stepfamilies "make it" attests to the dedication and determination of the couple to work at solving complicated problems. Many parents in intact families are highly motivated to succeed as parents. Because of stepfamily complexity, it usually requires even higher motivation, particularly on the part of the adults, to bring about adequate family cohesiveness to retain viability as a stepfamily. Increased understanding of the situation, recognition of the difficulties, and opportunities to share experiences are proving to be most helpful to these families.

PROBLEM AREAS RESULTING FROM STEPFAMILY STRUCTURE

Individuals in stepfamilies tend to forget that many of the problems they deal with are problems found in all family relationships: sibling rivalry, friction between parents and children, attempts by children to play one parent off against the other, disobedience, lack of understanding by spouse, etc. Many of these common family difficulties are exaggerated in stepfamilies due to the complexity of the family structure, while other difficulties arise because of unique stepfamily characteristics:

1. *There is a biological parent outside of the stepfamily unit and a same-sexed adult in the household.* Even when the natural parent has died, very often this absent parent continues to exert a strong psychological force within the stepfamily.

One man said, "It took me a number of years after my first wife died to be able to act without first thinking about what she would have said to do in the situation."

Another man commented, "My children thought of their mother as a saint. My new wife had a lot of trouble competing with this image. But now my first wife's halo is slipping and things are going better."

Pictures of a dead spouse often hang in places of honor in the home even after a second marriage. The new spouse moving into the home of the widow or widower may feel very much an outsider.

When the other parent, the ex-spouse, is still alive, the power exerted by this individual can be very great. If the relationship between the ex-spouses is amicable there tends to be cooperation between all the adults. On the other hand, cooperation between ex-spouses may diminish when an ex-spouse remarries. Feelings of insecurity and competition often arise when a same-sexed adult enters the picture. Further, an unhappy marriage frequently results in an unhappy divorce, and remarriage brings increased feelings of having been rejected on the part of the ex-spouse, competition for the children's affection, and fear of further loss of the children. Power struggless become common.

To illustrate: A stepfamily consisting of a woman and her three children, and a father and his two children have difficulty forming relaxed and satisfying relationships because the ex-spouses insist on maintaining visitation patterns set up prior to the marriage These require the husband's children to visit their mother every weekend and holiday. Therefore, the stepmother, who is working outside the home, has very little non-task-oriented time to relax with and develop her relationships with her step-children, and the new stepfamily unit has little time to pursue any leisure time activities together.

Another stepfamily plans to take a ski trip together. The equipment is rented and the reservations made. At the last minute the phone rings and the husband's ex-wife says that she has decided to have the children remain with her for the weekend instead of going on the ski trip with their father and stepmother. In such situation the helplessness and lack of control over the functioning of the family are a source of much emotional distress.

2. *Most children in stepfamilies hold membership in two households.* This leads to considerable discomfort and ambiguity for the children. As one stepchild stated to his father and stepmother: "The culture shock coming to visit you is bad. I have to get used to new rules. Everything here is different and I feel strange. Then I go back to my mother and she makes it okay again."

What is the role of a visiting stepchild in the stepfamily? As one psychologist expressed it, the visting children are caught in a double-bind situation with no way to win. "If the visiting children are considered to be full members of the family, this doesn't work because they aren't; if the visiting children are considered to be visitors in the family, this doesn't work because they aren't." The lack of clear role definition, the conflict of loyalties that such children experience, the emotional reaction to the altered family pattern, and the loss of closeness with their parent who is now married to another person create inner turmoil and confused and unpredictable outward behavior in many children.

3. *The role definition for stepparents is also ill defined.* The abstract of an article written by Fast and Cain (1966) outlines the problem: "Stepparent role-related difficulties in developing stable patterns of feeling, thinking and acting toward their stepchildren are discussed in terms of contradictory pressures on them to act as parent, nonparent, and stepparent; the sharing of role functions of parent with the previous parent in ways not clearly established in the society; weakened social mores (e.g., the incest taboo), and anomalies in role learning opportunities."

Stepparents do not know what to expect of themselves, other family members do not know what to expect of stepparents, and society has no idea what to except. Can a school teacher expect a stepmother to come for a parent-teacher conference? Will a stepfather be upset when his stepson is hurt in an automobile accident? Many such questions do not arise in reference to natural parents, but arise repeatedly in reference to stepparents.

Some stepparents have a clear idea of the role they wish to play in their new family, and when this choice meets the needs of the other family members, no particular conflict results. Most stepparents, however, try one role after another, unsuccessfully seeking to establish a pattern acceptable to themselves and to the rest of the family. A study of successful patterns is needed to develop models for effective stepparenting.

4. *The fact that "blended" families come together from diverse historical backgrounds accentuates the need for tolerance of differences.* As with the merger of two corporations, two groups with different values and needs, procedures and interactions, come to-

gether and need to establish a working relationship. Even when there is only one person "joining" an existing group, if this person is one of the two adults in charge of the stepfamily, clashes may occur because the patterns established by the other adult and the children seem so alien to those expected by the new stepparent. Patterns in families may grow unconsciously and unnoticed until an outside observer arrives on the scene.

One large stepfamily consisting of the two parents who each brought three children to the marriage spoke of their first six months together as constant "group therapy." The mother and her three children were very clear in their perceptions of how they saw the group of father and his three children, and vice versa. One group was an academically-oriented, organized and relatively "straight" group, while the other group was interested in sports rather than academics, somewhat disorganized, and espoused more "radical" leanings. In intact families a family milieu develops slowly with continuous compensation for individual differences. The need to suddenly deal on a day-to-day basis with intrafamily diversity can be very stressful.

One mother and stepmother voiced one of their many dilemmas this way: "My children were used to saying grace before meals, using pretty good table manners when the ate, and staying at the table until everyone was finished eating. My stepchildren, on the other hand, although they were similar in age to my own children, thought that saying grace was for the birds, mushed around in their food, couldn't wait to gulp it down and then rushed off to watch TV. At least that's the way I saw it. My husband and I got into arguments about this all the time at first. After a while I guess we worked it out pretty well though I'm not sure any of us felt too comfortable with the compromises."

A stepfather who married a widow expresses the general difficulty well when he says, "I'm living with a very alive fact that these children and their mother had a way of life and I had a way of life and we're having trouble merging them."

5. *Step-relationships are new and untested, and not a "given" as they are in intact families.* The new couple may have a rela-

tionship which they have developed slowly, but suddenly the relationship with children is a part of the picture too. To quote a stepmother, "On bad days all I can think of is the fact that all I wanted was to be married to Jim. But now I have his daughter as part of my life whether I want her or not."

A stepfather laments, "I'm not sure I would ever have wanted children, and here I am spending my life having to plan everything around my stepdaughter. My wife and I can't do anything spontaneously. We always have to get a babysitter for Julie. I didn't ask for Julie but she's always with us."

As for the children, they find themselves needing to relate to a stepparent, and perhaps stepsiblings, through no choice of their own. Siblings certainly have their abysmal moments, but basically it is a "given" that there is a relationship. In stepfamilies there is a sudden requirement that relationships be formed.

Children feel squeezed out as their natural parent begins relating to stepchildren, and they may find their stepsiblings individuals they would not choose as friends. "And there's Rob under foot all the time, wanting me to play with him and go places with him when I want to see the kids I've been playing with for years. It's not fair," yells a stepchild to his father.

Even when the new groups are in tune with each other there is never the comfort of just deep down "knowing" that there is a bond of caring and love. Outward signals and signs are continuously needed in many stepfamilies to demonstrate that caring and love really exist.

6. *The children in stepfamilies have at least one extra set of grandparents.* For one of the couple, one set is a pair of ex-in-laws, while for at least some of the children, the new set is a pair of stepgrandparents. Suddenly grandparents are asked to incorporate into their lives a new set of children, or at least a new parental-type adult. Many grandparents do not find themselves able to accept stepgrandchildren, or a new spouse. Grandparents and grandchildren may form a tight unit to exclude all others. Destructive coalitions can occur in all types of families, but stepfamilies are families at particular risk in this regard.

7. *A final important characteristic has to do with the stepfamily financial arrangements.* Conflicts over money are a frequent cause of tension in all families. In stepfamilies, however, money can take on many emotional overtones. There may be alimony payments to an ex-spouse, child support payments going out to an ex-spouse, and child-support payments coming in from an ex-spouse. Stepfamilies incomes may shift but usually the payments remain the same unless changed in court. If there is an increase in income this works well for the stepfamily, although there is often the fear that the ex-spouse will take legal action to receive more money. If the stepfamily income drops, then the burden of this falls on the stepfamily since the payments going out routinely are not tied to a change in income. Changes in the income of the ex-spouse do not automatically alter alimony or child support payments. If the income of the ex-spouse is reduced it is helpful to the stepfamily that it does not have to make up the difference; conversely, if the income of the ex-spouse is increased, the stepfamily often feels deprived as it continues to pay out the same amount as before. Alimony and child support are often painful areas. Having an alive and unmarried ex-spouse sometimes makes those areas more difficult.

Money is often used as the battleground between ex-spouses. Unfortunately, it is a convenient vehicle for this. The exchange of money ties the ex-spouses together and may continue to fuel the feelings of rejection and guilt and anger. A mother tells her children she cannot buy them a new game because their father, her ex-husband, does not give her enough money so that she can do so. An ex-husband is late with his child support payments so that those waiting for the payment are anxious about running into debt. An ex-wife receives a sizeable inheritance and resists attempts by her ex-husband to reduce the payments he is making to her. An ex-husband gets a new job but keeps it a secret so that he will not run the risk of having to share some of the increased income with his ex-wife.

Because of disagreements over money during the post-divorce period, remarried couples work out a variety of solutions to the stepfamily financial problem. Some husbands and wives agree to keep their funds separate, with the husband paying for his children and the wife paying for hers. For some this plan can work, while for other stepfamilies it appears to work poorly since it tends to create a wedge between the two merging groups, and may even prevent a satisfactory merger.

A stepfather recently spoke of how easy he felt it had been to work out his stepfamily situation. He commented that the family had been very well off financially from the time of their marriage. For that reason, he and his wife had been able to go out to dinner, take weekend trips and travel as they wished. They had help at home to do many of the household chores, and they had no anxiety in the area of money. He and his wife had agreed that their easy financial situation had been largely responsible for the smoothness with which they were able to integrate their large stepfamily. Unfortunately, in most stepfamilies there is a financial crunch, with many emotional ramifications.

Past experiences in a family of origin and in a former marriage influence feelings and behavior in a subsequent stepfamily, and as a result individuals in a stepfamily bring with them personal ways of reacting to spouses, parents, and children. Some adults and children who have coped throughout their lives in a marginal way may find the stress inherent in a stepfamily too difficult. However, even previously relaxed parents may become tense and troubled stepparents or partners of stepparents, and many comfortable and well behaved children may become upset and disagreeable stepchildren. It is apparent that stepfamily culture and structure can produce stressful life situations and consequent emotional conflicts in individuals who have coped and can cope successfully with the other aspects of their lives.

3

Research
in stepfamily
relationships

When one considers that each year in the United States one-half million adults become stepparents of one or more children, and that there may be upwards of 15 million children under 18 living in stepfamilies, it is somewhat surprising that a social phenomenon of this magnitude has not received more attention from those concerned with research in child development and family dynamics. A search of the literature has revealed only a limited number of serious scientific studies with direct applicability to some aspect of stepfamily relationships. Those studies with particular relevance to stepfamily relationships will be discussed in this chapter.

DEMOGRAPHIC STUDIES

In recent years there have been studies resulting in demographic data concerning the prevalence and incidence of stepfamilies in the United States. Bohannan and Erickson (1977, p. 2), at the Western Behavioral Sciences Institute in La Jolla, California, studied a stratified random sample of residents of San Diego, California. Of the some 2000 families contacted with children under 18, 74 percent were natural parent households, 16 percent were mother-headed households, 1 percent were father-headed households, and 9 percent were stepfather families. Bohannan defines stepfather families as those in which the husband is a stepfather with his stepchildren living in the household.

Another interesting demographic finding of the Bohannan and Erickson study was that out of 190 natural and stepfamilies from the total sample who were interviewed in depth (106 stepfather families and 84 natural father families) almost all of the natural families turned out to have at least one stepparent a generation back. They commented, "In fact, most people today appear to have some (personal) experience with a step-relationship" (p. 2).

Since Bohannan and Erickson define a stepfather family as a unit living together in one dwelling at the time of his survey and interviews, he does not include as members of the family children who may have a step-relationship, but do not reside with the family studied. The most common pattern in stepfamilies is for the new stepfather to join a unit in which the children have been living with their natural mother in a mother-headed household. Only 2 percent of his families had the father's natural children living in the family unit, thus conferring the designation of stepmother on the wife. But she might well be the stepmother of other children not living with them. It appears that confusion about family definitions may result in statistics which are not comparable.

As previously indicated, in this book a stepfamily is defined as a family in which at least one of the couple is a stepparent. The stepchildren need not be living in the household. Clinically, the problems may be somewhat different, but the existence of children from a previous marriage creates a complex family pattern irrespective of whether or not the children live in the household.

Glick and Norton (1971, 1973) and Carter and Glick (1970) have published findings which indicate that every year in the United States nearly one million children under the age of 18 see a parent remarry, and well over half a million adults suddenly find themselves in the stepparent role. One in every three American marriages is a remarriage for one or both partners. For British marriages the figure is one of every four. While the rate of marriage has been declining because of a trend toward marriages at an older age, remarriage rates have risen by 40 percent during the 1960s and 1970s, and the annual number of divorces during the same years has risen by 80 percent (Maddox, 1975), p. 7).

Well over half of all divorces are among couples who have children, and in the United States the average number of children per divorce decree has risen from less than one in the fifties to three in the seventies (Maddox, 1975, p. 8). But precise totals are hard to come by. The Census Bureau seems reluctant to ask pointed questions.

Brenda Maddox (1975) has estimated that close to one million American children are involved in divorces every year:

> If three-quarters of their mothers remarried (as they usually do, within three years), that would make nearly 750,000 stepchildren a year created by divorce alone. But divorce is not the only cause of children acquiring a stepparent. In the United States each year upwards of 400,000 children lose a parent through death . . . at the time of the 1970 census, 50,000 children under the age of ten were living with a widowed father. . . . If even half of these widowers remarry their new marriages would produce about 200,000 stepchildren a year. There are about 400,000 out of wedlock babies born each year, and some of these mothers keep their babies and marry a man who is not the father of the child. Therefore, it is safe to estimate that the yearly crop of new stepchildren in America is somewhere around one million (pp. 8-9).

The National Center for Health Statistics, in a 1970 report on Children of Divorced Couples, stated that in recent years over one-half million children, about nine out of every 1,000, have been involved each year in divorce. Since 1922 the number of children so involved has increased six times; since 1950 the number has doubled. Since the child population under 18 in 1970 was 66 million and there were eight million stepchildren, this means that roughly one in every eight children was a stepchild, and by 1977 the number has risen to one in every six children. These figures are cold, objective measures of the change in American family patterns during the last decades (Maddox, 1975, p. 9).

OVERVIEWS AND CRITIQUES OF RESEARCH LITERATURE

Mona McCormick (1974) of the Western Behavioral Sciences Institute has reviewed all available literature on stepfathers to 1974. She also cites papers on the legal aspects of the step-relationship, and the available literature on stepchildren. The second half of her book discusses each significant paper in a brief but succinct paragraph.

More than 71 books, papers, and articles have been listed in an annotated bibliography prepared by Clifford Sager and the staff of the Remarriage Consultation Service of the Jewish Board of Family and Children's Services (1978). This list also contains materials which can be given to clients with therapeutic intent. Each reference is followed by a commentary indicating its importance or usefulness in the field of remarriage studies.

In a literature review and critique, Kenneth N. Walker, Joy Rogers and Lillian Messinger (1977) summarize the present state of knowledge about the field and update McCormick's work, including material which is also relevant to divorce law. They point out that, unlike a first marriage, there are legal encumbrances concerning custody, visiting rights, and support payments which cause problems for each remarried family. The child has no rights in the situation.

Walker and colleagues comment that very few of the many research studies they reviewed are "based on procedures which permit a clear assessment of their validity, reliability, and generalizations." Most reported findings are "suggestive—possibly valid, but unproven." According to Walker et al., there are basically four types of research studies in the literature:

1. Studies of samples of stepfamilies which are not random or representative of the population, such as the Bernard study (1956) which used 2,009 informants who were students, colleagues and friends of the author, a sociologist, and resulted in a book-length study which was informative but not valid from a research point of view.

2. Studies of large random samples conducted at one point in time, of persons who were or are children of remarried

parents. These studies are limited in that all data are obtained from one member of the remarriage family, whose report is based upon recall of experiences from a distant time.

3. Studies of small-scale random samples which focus on one aspect of the remarriage family; Duberman's work (1975) is an example. Her cases are drawn from the files of a marriage license bureau in Cleveland, Ohio, and she focuses primarily on the quality of relationships among members of remarriage families.

4. Studies based on nonrandom samples, such as those drawn from clinic populations, who obviously are highly self-selected and may present special, nontypical problems.

The report of Walker et al. is especially helpful in its discussion of the kinds of research which are needed:

Better information is needed about 1. the demographic characteristics of remarriage families and 2. the most significant stressors within remarriages for their members . . . The second need can be met by both large- and small-scale studies designed to test hypotheses concerning stress in remarriage. Perhaps the greatest need here is for longitudinal studies which permit analysis of the remarriage family organization over time. . . . There also is a need for case studies of families which have successfully adapted to the special difficulties of remarriage, . . . to provide guidelines for therapeutic intervention as well as suggestions for institutional change beneficial to remarriage, as Burchinal (1964) suggests (p 285).

RESEARCH IN STEPPARENT-STEPCHILDREN RELATIONSHIPS

Fast and Cain (1966) studied 50 families in a child guidance center, and made a number of points which apply equally to stepmothers and stepfathers when they discussed the difficulties of stepparent roles:

1. A number of role-learning opportunities available to natural parents are not available to stepparents.

2. Stepparents have difficulty in developing stable patterns of feeling, thinking and acting toward stepchildren. They

do not know whether to act as a parent, stepparent or even a nonparent.

3. Uncertainty about appropriate role and behavior of the stepparents may lead to "intrapsychic and interpersonal difficulties which often appeared to augment problems based on the stepparent's uncertainties about their appropriate roles as parents" (p. 487).

Stepfamily relationships cannot be patterned after those of the traditional nuclear family. Fast and Cain proposed that the stepfamily should be considered as a structurally different type of child-rearing unit. They further stated that the stepparent's success in assuming the parent role was largely dependent on mutual acceptance by the spouse and by the stepchild, and that efforts to reproduce the nuclear family in the stepfamily unit are doomed to failure. "However strong the stepparent's determination to be a substitute parent, however skillful his efforts, he cannot succeed totally" (p. 488). They believe that organizational disturbance in stepfamilies is inevitable.

In her study (1947), "The Wicked Stepmother in a Child Guidance Clinic," Janel Pfloger found that a number of stepmothers expressed a view of themselves as being "on the spot," continually fearing and expecting criticism and blame from friends and relatives. The majority expressed the view that "it would be different" if the child were her own.

A study by Warner (1958) indicated that mothers and stepmothers have many of the same attitudes toward their difficulties in marriage and child-rearing. A group of ten mothers and ten stepmothers were chosen from the clients of a child guidance center. They were compared in their recognition of their children's problems and need for help, and in their attitudes toward responsibility for obtaining that help. Both groups came to the clinic hoping that more effective child-rearing practices would improve their relationships with their husbands. Both mothers and stepmothers perceived their children as threatening to their marriages but they did not recognize that their children had problems and also needed help. Six of the ten stepmothers gave as a reason for her marriage the need of the man and his children for her help. In summary, Warner's study seemed to show that in their family attitudes, these stepmothers react no differently than the natural mothers who came to the clinic for help.

Margaret Draughon (1975) has proposed three models of identification for the stepmother which might clarify and consequently ease her interactions with her stepchildren. These are the "primary" mother, the "other mother," and the "friend." Selection among these could be made on the basis of the child's mourning of the biological mother. If the child's mourning is incomplete and the mother is still psychologically alive, then the role of "friend" seems to have advantages. However, if the child's mourning of the biological mother is complete, i.e., she is psychologically dead for the child, then the stepmother's adopting the "primary" mother model seems to fit the needs of the situation best. Draughon feels that the "other mother" model does not appear to have advantages over the other models under any circumstances considered.

Draughon further comments that one of the most difficult aspects of the stepmother role is that there are no social guidelines with the resulting ambiguity in the stepmother's relationship with her stepchild. The child has difficulty relating to both his or her biological mother as well as to his/her stepmother as the "primary" mother. When the child has two or more mothers at the same time, the child may be pulled in different directions, and be confused that two persons can be "mother" at the same time. In the role model of the stepmother as "friend," the child does not see nor is seen by the stepmother as needing her for psychological survival. The stepchild can either become very close to her or develop a more superficial relationship with her over a period of time.

Duberman (1973) studied aspects of step-relationships among 88 stable stepfamilies in the Cleveland area. She taped interviews of the adults in the families, and gave each participant an opportunity to rate familial relationships and to evaluate the closeness of the family. She found that stepfathers achieve better relations with stepchildren than do stepmothers. Neither age nor sex of stepchild seemed to influence stepfather relationships, but stepmothers had better relations with stepchildren under age 13 than with teenagers. Sixty-four percent of the families rated themselves as having excellent relationships, while 18% rated themselves as having poor relationships.

Duberman's study attempted to identify social factors which might account for varying self-rating scores. The age of the stepfather was not a factor, but the age of the stepmother seemed to be correlated with the quality of her relationships to stepchildren. Seventy percent of stepmothers who were 40 years old or less had excellent relations with their stepchildren, while only 52 percent of stepmothers over 40 had similarly good relationships. Duberman also studied the effect of social and demographic factors on the relationships between the stepsiblings in the family. These will be discussed later in the section on research on adjustment of children to remarriage.

There have been a few studies attempting to measure intrafamily feelings and conflicts. One such study was done by Bowerman and Irish (1962), who concluded that stepfamilies have "more stress, ambivalence and low cohesiveness" than intact families. They found that "stepfathers appear to fare better in comparison with the real fathers . . . than do stepmothers in contrast with mothers in normal homes." They added, "The reactions of adolescent children indicate that stepmothers have more difficult roles than do stepfathers with the consequent implications for interactions within the family."

Lillian Messinger of the Clarke Institute in Toronto, Canada, reported on a study of couples who were married for the second time (1976). In her study, couples expressed surprise at their underestimation of the emotional upheaval involved. They were unprepared for the specific problems and stresses they had to face. Children were the biggest source of difficulty, followed closely by financial problems. Messinger believes, as do other researchers, that part of the difficulty arises from the fact that divorced-remarried people with children have not been assigned a clear status in society—one that "recognizes the differences in roles and functions between members of a first family and members of a remarried family" (p. 195). She also stated, "Our interviews with re-married couples frequently revealed guilt feelings about lack of positive emotions or, frequently, negative feelings toward their partner's children" (p. 196).

"Similarly, the children who were required to respond to the parent's new mate as though they were the child's 'real' parents often reacted with feelings of guilt, hostility, rebellion, or with-drawal," Messinger reported (p. 196). Some couples felt the link with the previous marriage through the children was divisive to the present marriage. The new mates often reported feeling the previous marriage of their spouses was like the "real" marriage and they were the outsiders. Another point in the study discussed moving from one residence to another. If the reconstituted family moved into one of the previously occupied houses, the new resi-dents felt like invaders and the old residents felt displaced and resisted sharing their territory.

Irene Sardanis-Zimmerman (1977) compared 35 stepmothers (with and without their own children) and 35 natural mothers. There were no significant demographic or socioeconomic differ-ences between the two groups. Stepmothers tended to be slightly more self-confident than natural mothers. They also were more ambivalent toward their children and stepchildren than were nat-ural mothers, who tended to feel closer to their children. Step-mothers reported feeling more jealousy toward their children and stepchildren than do natural mothers.

Janice Horowitz Nadler has completed a study on the subject of the psychological stress of the stepmother (1976). Three groups (part-time, full-time, and natural mothers) were compared. It was found that part-time and full-time stepmothers experienced more intrapersonal conflict than do natural mothers; had more feelings of anxiety, depression and anger regarding family rela-tions; and had more interpersonal conflict within the stepfamily than natural mothers. They also tended to have more negative in-volvement in their family relations, more conflict over family life, more conflict regarding their role, more conflict regarding finances, and more conflict regarding relatives and the community. Causes for the stepmother's psychological stress were hypothecated to be in her failure to find support within the stepfamily or within society for the effective enactment of her role, for the satisfaction of major personal needs, and for the affirmation of a favorable self-image.

The literature that exists has presented a rather conflicted picture of the stepfather family and its difficulties. Fast and Cain (1966) represent the negative, pessimistic approach about remarriage and its chances of success. Other authors also have emphasized the problems: E. M. Rallings (1976) pointed out, "The 'instant' father has no place to turn for explicit information and guidance about stepfathering, nor is he likely to have a model or models to pattern after." Mowatt (1972) observed group therapy of stepfathers and their wives who had problem children. The wives often viewed the stepfathers as rescuers, a role the stepfathers found hard to live up to, and there was evidence that the remarried couples used the previous spouse as a weapon in marital disagreements. Discipline and rule enforcement claimed the largest portion of the group's discussion time.

Phyllis Noerager Stern (1978) has written on the results of her inductive research on stepfather families and what she has learned about discipline. She points out that integration of a stepfather into the ongoing system of mother and child is complicated by problems involving the discipline of children. Her comments and suggestions were derived from interviews of 30 stepfather families. She contrasted integrative with disintegrative methods of discipline in stepfather families, finding that stepfathers who came in and attempted to discipline stepchildren before first establishing a bond of friendship failed to be integrated into the family unit.

In 1977 Bohannan reported research which showed that ". . . stepchildren view themselves as being just as happy as natural children, and are found to be just as successful and achieving as natural children. Children in stepfather households get along as well with their stepfathers as children in natural family households get along with their natural fathers. When mothers were asked the question, the results were the same. . . . In contrast, natural fathers rated their children as significantly happier than the stepfathers rated their stepchildren, and natural fathers rated themselves as significantly better fathers than the stepfathers rated themselves. In other words, stepfathers view themselves and their children as less successful and happy even though the children and their mothers did not feel that way" (p. 1). Perhaps these findings reflect the fact that stepfathers become more aware of their role within the family unit, and try harder than do natural fathers to be effective in this role.

ADJUSTMENT OF CHILDREN TO REMARRIAGE

There have been a number of attempts to assess the effects of divorce and remarriage on the adjustment of children. Although there have been several different opinions expressed in the literature, the consensus appears to be that there is not much long range effect, at least as measured by various research techniques to date. On the negative side, Langner and Michael (1963) reported that mental health consequences for children living in a remarriage family are worse than living in a family broken by bereavement or divorce without remarriage. Both situations are worse than living in an unbroken family. In contrast, a study by Nye (1957) reported that the unbroken, unhappy home is more stressful than the broken home. Children from lower-class families find remarriage more stressful.

More positively, Bernard (1956) applied the Bernreuter Personality Inventory to a sample of university students, of whom 89 were from remarriage families (66 males and 23 females). There were no significant personality differences between students from the remarriage families and those from intact families. Bernard cautiously concluded that stepfamily relations may in many cases be mutually supportive and healthy overall—healthier than the problem-filled family situation associated with disruptive first marriages. Goode (1964) drew the same conclusions from remarried women he studied who evaluated the effects of their remarriages on the lives of their children.

In 1964, Lee G. Burchinal conducted a study of 1500 Iowa high school students in order to determine whether the marital status of their parents had had any effect on their personal adjustment. The Minnesota Multiphasic Inventory was used. Five different family constellations were compared. Generally speaking, the conclusion was that there were no findings which suggested that divorce or remarriage had had any significant detrimental effects.

More recent studies have also shown that, in spite of the difficulties involved in reconstituted families, most stepchildren seem to fare quite well. As previously stated, Lucile Duberman (1973) found that the relationships in 64 percent of the homes she studied were rated as "excellent" by the family members. Duberman asked parents to rate their own child's relationship with each stepsib on a continuum from "Very Close" to "Very Distant." In addition, each parent was asked, during the oral part of the interview, to evaluate the relationships between the two sets of children. These four scores were combined, resulting in a score which indicated that 24 percent of the 45 reconstituted families with two groups of children rated the relations between the stepchildren as excellent, 38 percent "good," and 38 percent rated them "poor." She also analyzed various factors associated with the different rating groups. "It was found that when both sets of children live in the same house, the relations between them are more likely to be excellent than if they live in different houses. Furthermore, when the remarried couple have a child together, their children from former marriages are more likely to have harmonious relations. . . . Stepsibling Relationship Scores were higher when the father had less education than when he had more; and younger stepfathers seem to have children and stepchildren who get along better than older stepfathers . . ." (p. 190). Other findings were that when the oldest child was less than 13, especially the father's child, there was a greater probability of good stepsibling relationships.

Three studies of stepchildren indicate that the socioeconomic status of the family is related to the ease with which the children react to being a member of a stepfamily (Bowerman and Irish, 1962; Bernard, 1956; Langner and Michael, 1963). The higher the socioeconomic bracket, the more positive are the stepfamily interactions and functional characteristics. In commenting on these studies, Simon (1964, p. 234) considers that the differences lie in the reasons for the remarriage; individuals in lower socio-economic groups remarry to fill the role of the absent parent (a mother for the children, or a breadwinner for the family), while individuals in higher socioeconomic groups remarry for a satisfying couple relationship. The children do not want a new parent, so there is discord in the lower socioeconomic groups, with intra-psychic difficulties for the children in the stepfamily.

Wilson et al. (1975) performed a complicated statistical analysis of two national surveys in order to determine whether the children involved in divorce and remarriage with a stepfather in the family do indeed pay a heavy price in social terms, as some of the literature would seem to indicate. They studied key phenomena such as socialization, social interaction, and subsequent adult behavior, and found no evidence that there were differences between individuals who had experienced stepfather families, as compared to other types of family arrangements. They concluded that there appeared to be no reason why children in stepfather families could not experience a range of positive and negative relationships similar to those of children in natural families.

SUMMARY

The basic research findings may be summarized as follows:

1. At the present time one half million adults become stepparents each year in the United States.

2. One of every six American children under 18 is a stepchild.

3. There is a positive correlation between socioeconomic status and stepfamily success.

4. Studies of adults indicate that individuals growing up in stepfather families do not differ in measures of social functioning from individuals growing up in nuclear families.

5. Stepmother-stepchild relationships are much more tentative and difficult than stepfather-stepchild relationships.

6. Stepsibling relationships are relatively good, especially when there is a half-sibling to join the two groups together.

7. Stepfamilies experience more psychological stress than do intact families.

8. Stepmothers have difficulties with the negative "Stepmother" image.

This survey of the literature demonstrates how limited the research is on stepfamily realtionships. Family research is always difficult because of the profusion of variables, and objective or "counting" research often fails to get at the more subtle, emotional conflicts. The unhappiness and tension, the striving and failing, the joys and successes can be approached primarily through perceptions obtained from intensive studies over extended periods of time. Systematic inquiry is needed to test the validity of clinical impressions and resultant assumptions. Such studies have not yet been done.

4

Women in remarried relationships involving children

Women in remarriages involving children, or in long-term second or subsequent relationships involving children, commonly have unrealistic expectations of themselves—expectations often reinforced by their partners, by their relatives, and by society in general.

To varying degrees, depending on their personality and particular stepfamily constellation, mothers/stepmothers expect themselves to:

1. Make up to the children for the upset caused by the divorce or death in the original family.

2. Create a close-knit happy family in an attempt to return to square one (the nuclear family).

3. Keep all members of the family happy and contented.

4. Be living examples that the wicked stepmother myth is untrue.

5. Love their stepchildren instantly and equally to their natural children, and receive love from their stepchildren instantly.

In intact families, to have analogous expectations would be questionable; in stepfamilies such expectations are so unrealistic that they cause many difficulties which jeopardize the life of the stepfamily.

The first three expectations can be found in stepfamilies where the women are mothers only, stepmothers only, or both mother/stepmother, but the last two expectations are not applicable to stepfamilies in which the women are mothers only, and not stepmothers as well.

Since these expectations are widely encountered they will be discussed in general, while difficulties more specific to women with children and no stepchildren, women with stepchildren and no children of their own, and women with both children and stepchildren, will be outlined separately. The fact that there are so many different parent-child combinations in stepfamilies points once again to the complexity of stepfamily structure.

1. *Attempts to make up to the children for previous upset in their family*

The mother and/or stepmother in a stepfamily is usually very aware of the upset the child has experienced because of the death of a parent or because of the divorce of one of the child's parents. There is a desire to make up to the child for this hurt. If the mother has died or has disappeared the wish to make up for the child's loss usually is even greater. Such needs, however, can produce difficulties for the individuals in the new family as illustrated by the following situations.

A mother of two little girls, living for several years with a man not previously married, says:

> I know it was hard on my girls when my marriage to their father broke up, so I want to make it up to them now. But Jack gets upset because he says he'd like more time alone with me. I'm torn and discouraged and I can't see anything I can do to make it work out. Jack needs me, and the girls need me. How can I be sure my girls have had enough of my time? I'd like to be with Jack alone more too. He doesn't

spend much time doing things with all of us, so I keep having to choose between them and I feel all alone in the middle.

Another mother and stepmother anguishes about her adolescent stepdaughter who is having problems with the law because of truancy at school and petty theft:

> I knew when I married Charles that Lena was a disturbed child. She always had been hyperactive and a behavior problem. Then her mother died and she had a difficult time dealing with that. Then Charles and I met and I just knew I could help Lena. I was going to make up to her for all the upset. She'd never been happy, but seeing her father and me getting along well would be one difference. So Charles and I got married and I tried and tried, and then tried harder and harder, but Lena kept right on behaving the way she always had. I sent my own daughter back to live with her father because the friction between the two girls was so horrible. But that didn't help, and I got more and more angry, and I began to hate Lena, and Charles got mad at me and we fight. ... I don't know where to turn.

While fathers often attempt to make up to their natural children for pain caused in the loss of the nuclear family, fathers do not generally feel responsible in this way to their stepchildren. Society still gives women the responsibility for nurturing the family and maintaining its smooth emotional functioning. Thus it is the woman in the stepfamily who tends to feel the burden of "making up" for the child's past upset. She expects this of herself, and wants to give this to the child. Indeed, the more warm and loving the woman is, the more she may attempt to give to her children and stepchildren and the more problems may arise as a result. For example, the husband may feel left out and deprived, or the children may not respond as the mother or stepmother had envisioned. Stepchildren may experience the stepmother's attention as a desire to "replace their natural mother," and both children and stepchildren may react to the woman's concern as being intruded upon.

It is not possible to "take away" or "make up" for past pain.

Individuals experience anxiety and hurt as they deal with the stress of family disintegration through death or divorce. Further relationships can provide positive and warm interactions which can be deeply meaningful as and when they occur. The pain, however, did exist and cannot be made nonexistent. To accept its existence and understand the individual's need to mourn the loss and come to terms with the hurt is certainly helpful, but to expect to eradicate, replace, or somehow make up for the feelings sets up many disastrous, vicious circles for women in remarried relationships.

2. *Attempting to create a close-knit happy stepfamily*

Men apparently feel more responsibility for family functioning in subsequent family relationships than they do in first families (Bohannan and Erickson, 1977). Even so, usually it still falls to women to create the emotional climate for stepfamilies, and the expectation is that the stepfamilies will mirror effective nuclear families in cohesiveness, stability and interpersonal warmth. While for women in nuclear families this is often a difficult task, for stepmothers it is often an impossible one.

In America the fact that the structure of the nuclear family is seen as the "way it ought to be" seems to underlie the desire for adults and children in remarriages to return to square one, namely the nuclear family model. The children see the reuniting of their biologic parents as the means to achieving this goal, while the adults in the stepfamily attempt to close ranks within the new unit to form a solid core of togetherness. Many women in remarriages feel this to be their prime mission in life, a mission reinforced very frequently by their husbands and at times by friends and relatives. In trying to meet this challenge, women in stepfamilies often begin to feel drained and discouraged, then frustrated and angry, and finally trapped, confused and totally alone. In retrospect many women lament, "I tried too hard, altogether too hard."

A mother and stepmother speaking of the first years of her marriage stated the situation this way:

> I think that we would have had a much easier time if some-
> how Don (her husband) and I hadn't cared so much. If
> somehow it hadn't been so important to have one happy fam-
> ily or whatever you want to call it. If we had felt less strongly
> about that, I think that things would have been much easier.
> I've decided it's better to back off. The parents just have to
> back up. I cannot speak for Don, but I certainly had the
> expectations that we all could be close. One big happy
> family.

Until there is acceptance of new family models as viable alternatives to American nuclear families, many adults, particularly
women, in stepfamilies will continue their frustrating attempts
to create pseudo-nuclear stepfamilies. In *Stepchild in the Family*,
Anne Simon (1964, p. 235) mentions the study done by Bowerman and Irish in which stepfamilies were found to have "more
stress, ambivalence, and low cohesiveness" compared to intact
families. Simon's comment is that while these characteristics are
considered negative ones for children in nuclear families, they are
positive findings for children in stepfamilies. It seems likely that
the low cohesiveness is a particularly positive element, since stepchildren need psychological space in which to move back and
forth from one household to another.

If therapists and counselors can remain open to recognizing the
creative potential of new family patterns, they can do much to
help stepfamilies relinquish the often unconscious belief that productive nuclear families define functioning families. Mental
health professionals can help stepfamilies work out new models of
operation as a family system, and in this way not only relieve stepfamily tension, but also contribute to stepfamily adjustment in
general by reducing the commitment to the nuclear family as the
one productive family model.

3. *The need to keep all family members happy and contented*

In talking with women in stepfamilies, they state over and over
again that they feel responsible for the emotional well-being of all
members in the family. Since at least one family has been disrupted prior to the existence of the present family, the fear of

another break adds strength to the woman's desire to keep the situation running smoothly. Often these mothers and/or stepmothers negate their own feelings in their attempts to keep everybody else happy.

One mother describes her disastrous attempts at pleasing everyone.

> Mealtime was a terrible time. After their mother died, Len and the kids lived on macaroni and cheese. So I married Len and came into the family and spent every afternoon cooking up a storm. I'd always given my previous family meat, vegetables, potatoes and salad—so now I'd serve broccoli, potatoes, steak, and make big, beautiful desserts and serve these every night. And the kids hated every minute of it. Len would sit there and beam and say we're living like kings. Every night we're eating like kings. He was going bananas over the meals, and I was making them more and more elaborate because I loved him and liked the praise and wanted everyone to be happy. And the kids were fighting every inch of the way and the meal was one continuous hassle, hassle, hassle. What a way to live!

In intact families similar interactions occur in which the mother sees her role as that of giving to other family members even at considerable cost to herself. However, she usually receives more rewards for her efforts since the patterns have grown up slowly over many years, and she has learned ways in which to please. In stepfamilies, as Owen and Nancie Spann (1977) comment, such attempts to please can result in "instant chaos." The task of meeting the needs of the stepfamily members is fraught with unsuspected difficulties because of the tentativeness of the new stepparent-stepchild relationships and the lack of knowledge about each other's reactions. Trial-and-error is required to learn even the basic food idiosyncrasies of a stepchild or a new mate. When a child reacts to a meal with, "Ugh, this tastes awful! I've never had this before," a new mother/stepmother/family cook must be fortified with great security in regard to her culinary skills to retain a degree of calmness and self-acceptance.

A mother/stepmother may need help in accepting her own

needs and in counting her needs as equal to the needs of others in the stepfamily. In new stepfamilies, she needs to recognize the impossibility of satisfying such a diverse, unknown, and newly related group of individuals in many of the areas of interaction.

4. *Trying to escape the wicked stepmother myth.*

In *The Half Parent,* Brenda Maddox (1975) talks about a personal experience:

> I felt so guilty. Wasn't motherhood what I said I wanted during all those years of waiting? True, I did not think of myself as the children's real mother, but I did think of myself as "a mother." It took one of stepdaughter's small friends to tell me what I really was. I was driving the two girls home from a birthday party and was deep in my fantasy of myself as a suburban matron, chauffeuring a carload of kids, while they were silent in the back. Suddenly the friend asked, in a crystal English voice, "Is that your stepmother?" The answer came, slightly shaky: "Yes." There was a pause. "Oh. I always thought a stepmother was something like a witch" (p. 16).

Children learn at a very early age just what a stepmother is like. As an attorney said recently, "If you were to ask my seven-year-old daughter about stepmothers, she'd say they were very bad people because she knows Cinderella's stepmother." And little girls grow up to be women, and mothers, and stepmothers. And if they do become stepmothers, deep inside themselves they carry the stereotypes of the culture. They vow to themselves that they will not become "wicked stepmothers," and as a result they try to be super-perfect stepparents. And, unfortunately, these efforts very frequently lead to frustration—and to a perpetuation rather than an evaporation of the myth.

Anne Simon (1964) comments that "it is more than haphazard coincidence that almost all stepmothers seem to share the legendary traits; they come to resemble the stepmother stereotype because they become stepmothers. Behavioral science now allows us to understand that the situation has little to do with the character of the woman, or, for that matter, the child. It is the relationship between them that sparks the fire. . . . There is a kernel of truth in the stepmother fiction, but it is the result of interaction, a generic, not a personal truth" (p. 139).

Recent studies by Irene Sardanis-Zimmerman (1977) and Janice Horowitz Nadler (1976) corroborate the clinical impression that stepmothers experience considerably more intrapersonal stress than natural mothers regarding relationships with their children and stepchildren, as well as regarding all stepfamily interactions. Both authors consider that the existence of the wicked stepmother myth, and the difficulty that stepfamily and community at large have in escaping from the psychological effects of the myth, contribute to the stress reported by stepmothers.

Clear messages from therapists and counselors that the role of being a stepmother is a difficult one because of the situational complications and strength of conflicting emotions can do much to restore a stepmother's self-esteem. This may then enable her to cope much more effectively with her stepfamily interactions.

5. The expectation of instant love.

Closely related to the difficulties experienced by stepmothers as a result of the wicked stepmother myth are problems arising from expectations that all members of the new stepfamily will love each other. Simon (1964) and Schulman (1972) refer to this as the myth of "instant love." The adults in the stepfamily very frequently expect quick acceptance and love from the children, and the inability of the children to live up to these expectations produces strong negative feelings in the adults.* Stepmothers tend to feel rejected and unappreciated and very often anger and withdrawal follow, expressed as, "who needs this?"

The converse of the expectation of love from the stepchild is the expectation that the stepmother will love the stepchild. A young stepmother, married for the first time to Anthony, who had recently won custody of his young son, Bobby, illustrates the psychological difficulties when she says:

---

* The reactions of the stepchild will be discussed later in the chapter on stepchildren.

I have a very strong husband and he expects a lot of me. Before we were married he said, "If you take me, you take my son too!" And he expects me to really love his son. I feel guilty about having Bobby. Bobby's mother lost her husband, Anthony, lost her home which was important to her, and now we were taking her child away from her. At times I want Bobby to really love his mother, and at other times I don't want him to.

Sometimes I don't know where my feelings for my husband leave off and my feelings for Bobby begin. Am I doing this or that for Bobby because it's what I want to do for him, or am I doing it because it will please my husband?

Bobby is such a darling boy and nice to me, which makes me feel all the more guilty that I don't love him. I think Bobby may feel the same pressure, too—that *he* should love *me*. My husband doesn't understand how I can possibly feel the way I do, and I'm afraid to tell anyone my feelings because I'm sure I'd get their moral condemnation for resenting the charming, loveable little boy they all know. (Visher and Visher, 1978, p. 253).

Most mental health professionals do not expect love to happen overnight. They realize that love will mature slowly, if at all, and that many satisfactory relationships can exist in a atmosphere of respect without a deep feeling of love and commitment. However, many stepmothers continue to condemn themselves by holding fast to their expectations of "instant love."

One source of difficulty in this regard is the conflicting messages given to stepmothers by the community. At one and the same time the community conveys the message that stepmothers are cruel and do not love their stepchildren, and that they are supposed to love their stepchildren. It is a Catch 22 situation. Stepmothers are in a double bind. They must not act as parents, and they must love the child as their own. This attitude is illustrated by the friend who said to a stepmother, "Oh, how cold you are!" when this stepmother mentioned that her stepdaughter called her by her first name.

The lack of clear role definition in stepfamilies may lead to confusion and upset. Roosevelt and Lofas (1976) outline clearly how the expectation of instant love can lead to the birth of yet another wicked stepmother, even when the stepmother is a warm and giving person:

Feeling obliged to love a stepchild and getting withdrawal sprinkled with hostility, a stepmother may tend to resolve the discrepancy by constructing an emotional brief of stepchild unlovableness. She lists and relists her stepchild's faults and inadequacies. Who, her thinking goes, could ever be expected to love this child? And she cancels her debt. . . . The source of cruelty is the situation and not the person. How not to become the cruel stepmother is hard. How to become the cruel stepmother is easy. . . .

Simply put, here's how it can work. The stepmother offers interest and attention to the child. The child responds with coldness, indifference. The stepmother tries, keeps trying for a period, then finally withdraws. She takes a fixed position— a distant one. The stepchild finds his original negative assumption confirmed ("I always knew she was mean"). The child may attempt to break up the marriage. The stepmother retaliates. Through all kinds of actions, or inactions, a child may force choices to be made by his father. If the father sides with the child over the stepmother, the family is in trouble. The stepmother tries to win the father over to her side. At any rate, she wants to have the stepchild around less and less. Here she usually succeeds. Sooner or later, everybody gets into the act, and the scene is set for a traditional wicked stepmother play—sticky, mean, and heartbreaking (pp. 47, 69-70).

REMARRIED MOTHERS WITH NO STEPCHILDREN

As a group, it is likely that remarried mothers with no stepchildren have fewer conflicts than other women in stepfamilies. Usually these mothers have their children living with them, and since the man in the household has no children, there are fewer combinations and permutations than in stepfamilies where both adults have children. There is no competitiveness between groups of children, and the stepfather can relate to the children more as natural children. As one mother in such a family said, "My husband has no ambivalence in relating to my kids. The relationship is clear and so he can be very involved with them."

Since the mother and her children have worked out their relationship over a number of years, and there are no visiting or live-in stepchildren, there is little conflict over different sets of values. It is easier for the couple to work out any differences in values when there are not two sets of children acting out two different value systems.

One other positive aspect pointed out by a mother in this step-family situation was that she and her husband had time to themselves whenever her children were visiting their natural father. This time was considered to be very precious time by both the adults, and they felt fortunate to have such a noncomplicated stepfamily structure.

While there are these positive aspects, difficulties often arise in the area of discipline. Although the mother may want help with disciplining of the children, when the stepfather attempts to do so, she may suddenly become an angry mother bear defending her cubs, and the whole situation deteriorates. The stepfather's lack of experience with children adds to the problem. He has no period of accommodation to parenting, and very often incurs the anger of his stepchildren and their mother whenever he asserts himself. The stepfather then may withdraw and the mother feels let down and abandoned by her husband.

One strong feeling that remarried mothers have when they do not have stepchildren is that there is no balance in the family. There is "no trade-off." Although she has married only one person, her husband has married a family. He does things for her children, while she does not need to reciprocate by doing things for stepchildren. As a result, such a mother may carry a heavy load of guilt, and try to act as a buffer between her husband and her children. She may feel that to keep his love and affection she must protect her husband from the strain of relating to her children more than is absolutely necessary. Another difficulty arising from this lack of balance is that since the mother is not a step-mother as well, she may have more difficulty understanding the feelings of her husband toward his stepchildren.

If a remarried mother and her present husband have a child of their own, at times this upsets a previous balance. One professional man outlined his situation by saying:

I guess this is something you're heard a lot before. I have a young stepdaughter who I like a lot, and always did. I never had any children and I had fun with my stepdaughter, Jody. But now we have our own daughter and my marriage is going to hell. I never knew until my own daughter was born what the gut level feeling about a child could be. But my wife thinks that I'm rejecting her daughter now, and we've started fighting all the time, and I think our marriage won't last much longer.

While parents in nuclear families may have their favorites as far as their children are concerned, both parents stand at the same biologic distance from the children and differences in feelings are tolerated. The fact that some of the children in a stepfamily do not share their biology equally with both of the adults may lead to the bitterness just described. When the stepfather felt that he loved his own child more than his stepchild the mother, because of the very close mother-child bond, may have felt this as a rejection of herself and a wedge was driven between the couple. Parents in intact families do not expect to feel similar love for all their children. The expectation that adults will feel similarly about natural children and absent stepchildren is even more unlikely to match reality, and the relationship of many remarried couples is eroded by this unreasonable expectation. Where differences in feelings are acceptable, a new child in the family can bring satisfaction to the mother and stepfather, now father.

STEPMOTHERS WITH NO CHILDREN OF THEIR OWN

Duberman's study (1973) has indicated that in stepfamilies, stepmothers who have no children of their own tend to have a more difficult time than mothers, stepmothers with children of their own, or fathers and stepfathers. Although there has been no formal research to study the reasons for this finding, impressions resulting from work with stepmothers suggests that one important aspect is that women who have had no children of their own have no experience to aid them in the task of being a stepmother. They do not know what to expect from their stepchildren, since they have not been around children unless their vocation has been

child oriented. Not knowing what to expect in a situation leads to
anxiety and indecision, and stepmothers who are not mothers
certainly do express these feelings:

> I lived with my husband for a couple of years, then we
> were married two months ago and his ten-year-old son came
> to live with us. I've never been around children and I don't
> know what is normal for a ten-year-old boy to do. He inter-
> rupts, and he throws his clothes around and the place is a
> mess. If I insist he put his clothes away, am I being too
> strict? I can never make up my mind what is all right. Some-
> times I panic.

Many times a stepmother who is not a mother herself looks forward to being a mother to her husband's children. One father, a
widower, described his experience in marrying a woman who had
no children of her own.

> When Becky and I got married and shortly before it,
> Becky was very excited about the family. To have two chil-
> dren was a very exciting thing. Even before our marriage she
> spoke to others about her children, and I remember telling
> her, you know, Becky, they are not really your children. The
> children were initially just really enthusiastic about Becky
> and me marrying. Then it didn't take too long for them to
> feel a real competitive threat. And it didn't matter who Becky
> was.

A mother of a 15-year-old boy spoke of the remarriage of her ex-
husband to a woman without children:

> My son lived with his father until his father remarried.
> His second wife sailed in saying to my son, "I'm going to be
> your new mother." But he already had a mother! So now
> he's moved back with me. That was sure the wrong way for
> her to come on.

From these quotations it is easy to see the pitfalls for a woman
coming into a household as a stepmother and anticipating that
now she will have the family that she has not yet had herself. A
woman with no children of her own is in the position of being a

single person joining a preexisting group. She is the outsider trying to find a place for herself within a group that has already formed. It is a difficult task to break into an existing group, particularly so if the bonds between the group members are such that no space for a new member seems available. Being the only "outsider" is a lonely position indeed.

It is contact regarding the children that tends to create a continuing relationship, however minimum, between ex-spouses. Even if they have been previously married, women with no children tend to have no contact with their former husband after a short period of time following the divorce. This means, then, that in a stepfamily in which only the husband has children, there may be considerable contact with his ex-wife, with no corresponding contact with an ex-husband. As a result, there may be a triangular situation with three involved adults, with the stepmother feeling jealous of the continuing contact between her husband and his ex-wife.

If a woman is a stepmother only and not a mother as well, she does not enjoy the advantage of having the positive self-image of "mother," as well as the negative image of "stepmother." If she is rejected by her stepchildren or considered to be an inadequate stepmother by her husband, she has no basic mothering experiences to call on to feel adequate in this role. As a result, the feelings of insecurity and inadequacy can be very profound. As one such stepmother said:

> I always have the feeling of a stepmother being a second-class citizen. Maybe I put myself down; I was never able to see myself as a mother, and I never expected to be a full mother and I feel I missed out on a lot. I know that the most painful experiences of my life were experiences of being rejected as a stepmother. I feel like I more or less accept it now, but it was really hard. So maybe being a stepmother isn't really being second-rate and second-class. It just seems like there's something about blood relationships that is different."

As in stepfamilies where the wife has children and the husband does not, the feelings of the two adults toward the child may be

very, very different. This can cause serious problems between
the couple, because they may find it difficult to understand how
the other person can feel so differently, having no similar experience of their own with which to compare the other's emotions.

A mother's relationship to her children tends to be more involved and involving than a father's relationship to his children.
This may account for some clinical evidence that for a couple to
have a child of their own when the stepmother has not previously
been a mother may bring much happiness to the stepfamily. Since
many women grow up with a strong desire to be a mother, it may
mean a great deal to a stepmother to have a child of her own. To
be a stepmother and not a mother often leaves her feeling unfulfilled and jealous of the fact that her husband has had children
with another woman. As Brenda Maddox (1975) says, "new
babies can help. They certainly did for us. My stepson, who smiled
at none of us, turned out to be the best of us all at making our
first baby smile. And when the third one was born—another boy,
a healthy one this time—I could honestly say my stepparenthood
had ended" (p. 121).

REMARRIED MOTHERS WITH STEPCHILDREN

There is no more disunited a nation than the stepfamily
which assembles his and her children under one roof (Simon,
1964, p. 201).

Research, as well as anecdotal material, underlines the inherent
complexity when children from two families are joined together
by the marriage of their respective parents. While this complexity
makes possible a seemingly infinite number of difficulties, the
fact that both adults are parents and stepparents gives each of
them experience as parents and a shared involvement in being
stepparents. Each adult may have a range of feelings toward children and stepchildren, and as a result these feelings may be better
understood by each spouse. In addition, each adult will have a
previous spouse, which gives a sort of balance to the whole stepfamily structure.

Because of the bonds between each adult and his or her children which pre-date the marriage, there may be many competing groups within the stepfamily. It can be his versus hers, he and his versus her and hers, children versus adults, his children and his parents versus her children and her parents, etc. The intricacies involved in planning a holiday with the couple, children, step-children, and ex-spouses all having individual needs, which many times are mutually exclusive and crying for consideration, may discourage even the most enthusiastic stepparents. If the mother/stepmother is overcome by the confusion and ambiguity, her life may be unbearable to her.

Not having time alone with a spouse may seem a minor annoyance to women not trying to have some newlywed togetherness in the midst of stepfamily chaos. With two sets of children, the opportunity to be alone is elusive and fickle. To quote Owen Spann:

> You'll soon find that you cannot get rid of everybody, all at the same time. It's impossible.
> Consider school vacations, a grand time for your wife's ex-husband to take his kids for a week or two. But that's exactly the time you inherit yours from your ex-wife. Peace and quiet? Hardly . . . there's never *nobody* (Spann and Spann, 1977, pp. 152-153).

VARIATIONS ON THE STEPFAMILY THEME

A mother/stepmother talked of her situation, commenting that the number of variations within stepfamilies is very great. Because she agreed it was a good idea for her boys to live with their father, she had one of her children living with her, while two of her children lived with her ex-husband. Her husband has two of his children living with him, and one living with his ex-wife. The greater the number of children, the greater the number of variations. The guilt, the anxiety, and the mixture of parental feelings stirred up by separation from some of one's children before they are grown, combined with the guilt, the anxiety, and the mixture of parental feelings of one's spouse, who may be in a similar situation, hardly make for a household characterized by serenity and soft music. This woman wrote in response to a question about her stepfamily:

Some of our children live together with us and some live away. Some special stepparenting problems we have are a tendency to resent doing "time-consuming projects" for and with my stepchildren, that I would happily do for my own children. I would love to and wish I could be spending that same kind of time with my children. The same resentment crops up when I provide special opportunities like music lessons, and maternal advantages like the use of my car, for my stepchildren. I would expect to provide them for my children, but when I hear my stepchildren expecting me to provide them, I resent it. I also think that my impatience with my stepchildren's shortcomings is intensified because I have children with more "familiar" shortcomings living elsewhere. I would much prefer to have them living with us because I am more comfortable with their "shortcomings." In short, I enjoy my children and much prefer living with them to living with my stepchildren. It becomes easy to idealize the natural children's behavior and relationship, and easy to exaggerate the frustrations in the stepchildren's relationship. If we were all under one roof, reality would soon return!

There is also the variety resulting from the patterns of visiting stepchildren and live-in stepchildren. Simon (1964) has said in reference to stepmothers, "When her stepchildren live with her, her jealousy is often transformed into hostile feelings towards them. But when they are remote, it transforms into anxiety . . ." (p. 189). The sense of helplessness and lack of control are greater when the stepchild is a visitor, with feelings "going up and down like a yoyo." When the stepchildren are living in the family there is more constancy to the feelings, but rejection and hostility often characterize the step-relationships.

Stepmotherhood certainly sounds as though it has little to recommend it. Adults do not realize what lies ahead in the remarriage of a parent, feeling that now that there is a happy couple the family will live "happily ever after." The blindness of this faith no doubt is the reason many parents enter blithely into new marriages. However, many couples are becoming more cautious and are living together before considering marriage. They are trying to work out relationships between adults and children who are not related by blood; the situations they encounter are very similar to the ones being discussed.

There are many ways, however, in which the course of step-mothering can be made smoother. As more is learned about successful stepmother roles, guidelines can be presented. New books on stepparenting are providing understanding and support to stepparents. Further, as therapists and counselors become more sensitive to the issues and more knowledgeable about ways to help individuals in stepfamilies, there will be more effective help for stepmothers in coping with the psychological stresses of their role.

Many women in stepfamilies find satisfaction in the family very quickly, while many others arrive at a warm and friendly place only after a number of months or years. Some never find step-family satisfaction. Ways in which to help more women find gratification within this new type of family structure will be presented in the next chapter.

5

Working with women in stepfamilies

It is mothers, for the most part, who seek help when there are strains within their families. Similarly, in general it is stepmothers who seek help when there is stepfamily stress.

For mothers there are conversations between friends over a cup of coffee. There are P.T.A. meetings. There is Dr. Spock. There are Parent Effectiveness Training classes. There are parental stress hot lines. There are Family Service Agencies. There are ministers and pediatricians with skilled listening ears. There are therapists and counselors with a great deal of helpful knowledge about intact family functioning. These resources and more supply support, information, and therapeutic assistance to mothers. Women in stepfamilies do not feel they have similar support systems.

While many stepfamily issues are parenting and couple issues occurring in all types of families, familiarity with stepfamily structure and dynamics dramatically increases the trust stepparents have in the helpfulness of friends, neighbors, or professional persons with whom they interact. And, indeed, the understanding and effectiveness of the helpful individuals are increased manyfold by knowledge of the types of situations and dynamics commonly encountered in stepfamilies.

It is difficult to draw a line between counseling and therapy, and the approach used by a mental health professional will reflect individual training and personal style. In the following chapters, comments, case histories and vignettes may be utilized in a variety of ways to suit individual patients or clients and individual therapists or counselors. All illustrate common situations presented by individuals and stepfamilies who seek help.

INDIVIDUAL COUNSELING AND THERAPY

Eleanor

An attractive 31-year-old woman came to a therapist complaining of depression. She had been married for two years to a man who had a six-year-old son from a previous marriage. For the past year, Andy, her stepson, had been living with Eleanor and her husband, Bob. Bob and Eleanor now had a six-month-old son of their own.

After five appointments during a two-month period, Eleanor had little anxiety or depression, and reported changes at home that were bringing joy and satisfaction into her life. A telephone call on another matter four months after her last appointment prompted Eleanor to comment that she did not feel depressed, and that her stepfamily situation was continuing to be personally rewarding both in her relationship with her husband and with her son and stepson. During the two months time in which Eleanor met with her therapist the following significant discussions took place.

Initial appointment: When Bob and Eleanor had first been married they had had a good and easy relationship. Andy, four, lived with his mother and visited Bob and Eleanor several times a month. These visits went well and Andy accepted the new situation easily.

Bob became upset about the care his son was receiving and sought custody of Andy. Bob's ex-wife was reluctant to give up her custody of Andy, but the court awarded custody to Bob. So Andy moved in with Bob and Eleanor about a year prior to Eleanor's seeking help.

Eleanor quoted her husband as having said, "If you marry me, you take my son also. If you love me, you'll love him too." Eleanor continued, close to tears, "Andy's a darling little boy and likes me, but I don't love him. I feel so guilty. It's been worse since our son was born. I love him so much and it's not fair to Andy. Andy wants me to read stories to him, and I'm so tired and down that I don't, and Bob gets angry at me and wants to know what's wrong with me.

"Bob's so busy at his job that he hasn't time to do things with Andy or help me with the baby, and I fall into bed exhausted every night. Then on most weekends Andy's with his mother and things are very much better. But sometimes Andy doesn't want to visit his mother and Bob calls his ex-wife and says Andy's not coming over. Then he spends most of the weekend doing what Andy wants to do. I don't think Bob loves our son as much as he loves Andy. He never pays much attention to our son."

Eleanor was a warm, soft spoken woman who was clearly aware of her guilt feelings at not loving her stepson as much as she did her own son. She also felt particularly guilty about "taking Andy away from his mother" when she didn't love Andy as she felt she ought to. It seemed clear that Eleanor felt rejected by her husband because he criticized her for having the feelings she had about Andy and did not show the same concern for their son as he did for his son, Andy. However, Eleanor showed no awareness of her anger at her husband. Indeed, she kept extolling Bob's virtues and putting herself down for her inadequacy in handling the situation.

The therapist commented on the complexity of relationships and feelings in stepfamilies, and on the common, but usually unrealistic, expectations of instant love between stepparent and stepchild. Eleanor was relieved and was eager to come again in a week.

Second appointment: Eleanor began to talk at once about her and Bob's sexual relationship. Slowly they were drifting apart emotionally and sexually. She considered that their sexual relationship during the first year of their marriage had been excellent, but in the past year she had lost interest in sex and this was causing more and more difficulties between Eleanor and her husband. She felt pushed by Bob in the sexual area, stated that she had to have an orgasm or Bob felt there was something inadequate about his lovemaking, and that she found herself being too tired to want or enjoy sexual intercourse.

At this point it appeared that stepfamily issues might be quite secondary to a disturbed relationship between the couple. Eleanor was able to acknowledge that she felt frustrated and annoyed with Bob's sexual pushing, and she agreed that the pressure she felt to have an orgasm stopped her from accepting any affection from her husband because she felt that he would want to continue touching and caressing to the point of sexual intercourse.

Eleanor was not sure if her husband would be willing to come to an appointment with her to discuss her sexual relationship, and she felt that she would be able to talk to him about it herself. The therapist suggested that with individual differences in sexual needs, a man's sexual ability is not in fact related to his wife having an orgasm every time they have intercourse. Eleanor agreed that the pressure she felt "to perform right" angered her and resulted in her having virtually no sexual desire. She also decided that she would talk to her husband about her feelings, and suggest that they have intercourse when they both felt like it, with no expectation that she would be more active than she felt she wished to be. She knew she enjoyed affection and believed that she would be able to persuade Bob that her lack of orgasms was not related to his skill as a lover. In fact, she recognized that her anger, plus the fact of feeling more tired now that she had two children to care for, certainly worked against being an active sexual partner at all times.

Third appointment: This was a very emotional session occurring three weeks after the second appointment. The family had been out of town, and sexually the situation between Eleanor and Bob had improved greatly. She had been able to talk to her husband about the content of the previous therapy hour, and Bob had responded very positively. Eleanor was amazed to find that with the pressure gone she was more relaxed about sex, and was actually enjoying sexual intercourse again and participating actively most of the time.

Then, a few days before her appointment, Eleanor and Bob had a big fight. Bob had come home and told Eleanor that Andy would not be spending a month with his mother during the summer as had been planned. Bob had stopped at his ex-wife's condominium on his way home from work, and they had agreed to no more visitation at all by Andy since Andy had said he didn't want to spend a month in the summer with his mother.

Eleanor became very angry and told Bob that her summer had been wrecked. She had been looking forward to summer but now that Andy was going to be there all summer she was very upset. Bob and Eleanor had remained distant ever since and Eleanor was tearful and depressed.

The following dynamics emerged in this session. Eleanor felt very guilty about her lack of love toward her stepson. Because she did not love him she considered that she had no right to reprimand him for anything he did. In addition, she felt that she had no right to enter into any of the planning involving Andy. Plans concerning Andy were made by Bob and his ex-wife, and because of Bob's guilt about the pain of the divorce for Andy, he tried to keep Andy happy—even when it meant changing plans three times on a Saturday when Andy kept changing his mind as to whether or not he wanted to visit his mother for the day. Plans concerning the new baby were made by Bob and Eleanor together.

It became clear that Andy was in a very powerful position. His father catered to his every whim, and his stepmother said nothing. Around home, even when Andy was being annoying, no adult voiced disapproval. Eleanor withdrew, and Bob became more and more resentful of her withdrawal. Bob criticized Eleanor, tried to "make up" to Andy for his stepmother's lack of attention, and showed little concern for the baby.

Eleanor tearfully agreed that she was feeling increasingly helpless, and that anger that she felt toward Bob got displaced to Andy. When the therapist pointed out that Eleanor was counting herself out in the household in which she lived, Eleanor stopped crying and recounted many ways in which this was true. She recognized that there were, indeed, four members in that household —herself, Bob, Andy, and the baby—and they all had needs. Difficulties and resentments were going to build up if one person's needs were not considered, and that was what had been happening. One might not love a "boarder" in a household, but, even, so, the needs of all members living together must be considered in the working out of the overall domestic situation.

Eleanor began to talk of her resentment at the amount of time her husband spent talking to his ex-wife on the telephone and stopping to see her to visit and make plans for Andy. Eleanor did not discuss with Bob situations involving Andy. Suddenly Eleanor recognized the consequences of her not considering herself an integral part of her own household and she exclaimed "My God, I've set it up so Bob is a husband to two women."

Very quickly Eleanor began talking about her own needs—her need for some time to herself on the weekends, her need for some recreation, her need for Andy to be quiet in the house when the baby was sleeping. Eleanor began to realize that she didn't need to love Andy to have a say in the plans, even when it included Andy and his mother. She and Bob, as a couple, could decide about Andy's plans and their plans. The adults together could talk to Bob's ex-wife about Andy's visiting with her. And Eleanor could suggest to Bob various summer plans she might like, and try to work out a satisfactory vacation with him.

Fourth appointment: Eleanor fairly danced into this session, two weeks after the third session. During the interval her life had practically turned around. She had been able to talk at some length with her husband about her last therapy hour and he had listened intently. Although Bob had been somewhat reluctant, Eleanor had left the two children with him while she did some things she had wanted to do for a long time. Even though pangs of guilt crept in, she continued to think of her own needs as well as of those of the others, and her resentment at Andy had virtually disappeared as she curbed him when he became disruptive at home. He had calmed down, and Eleanor had been surprised to find that she was really beginning to enjoy her stepson. She had read him several stories at bedtime, and the two of them were doing more things together. Now that Eleanor was relating to his son, Bob was no longer angry at her and Bob and Eleanor were enjoying each other.

The summer plans were still unclear, and Eleanor was questioning the advisability of changing plans whenever Andy changed his mind about visiting his mother. With the therapist's help she began to consider that it might be better for Andy to know that once he made a decision about visiting his mother that decision would stand as a matter of course. Eleanor was clear that such a policy would certainly be helpful to the other individuals involved.

Following the session, Eleanor was to have a conference with Andy's teacher. Previously, Bob had always gone to the school for the teacher's conferences, but today he was unable to go. Eleanor felt very uncomfortable about this meeting because she felt that Andy's teacher had been rather distant with her and knew that she didn't really love Andy. Eleanor also said that she kept feeling that "everyone is watching me as a stepmother to see if I screw up."

Once again Eleanor's guilt about her feelings for Andy was making difficulties. The therapist suggested that Eleanor may have herself held back from Andy's teacher, and that her guilt might be playing a part in her feeling of being watched by friends and neighbors. Eleanor considered that this might indeed be at least part of the situation. Once again expectations of love for a stepchild were discussed, and Eleanor recognized that she had felt considerable pressure from Bob in this area. She now felt angry at being told by him how she was to feel about his son.

Eleanor left the session accepting that she *did* care about Andy's welfare, and that the quality of the stepfamily relationships would help determine what feelings she might have in the future.

Fifth appointment: Two weeks later Eleanor returned for a final appointment. Her interview with Andy's teacher had gone very well. Eleanor had felt relaxed and found that Andy's teacher was very warm and friendly. This had let Eleanor know that it had been largely her own sense of guilt at not measuring up to expectations of love for Andy that had colored the relationship previously.

Eleanor felt easy with her neighbors now, and was enjoying both her son and her stepson more and more. She no longer felt drained and tired in the evening, and she and Bob were having a good sexual relationship. Eleanor was full of ideas of things she wanted to do in the future. She felt adequate as a person and, even though it temporarily disrupted her relationship with Bob, she was standing up for things that were important to her. The situation with Bob and his ex-wife had been altered so that together Eleanor and Bob dealt with her. This shift had changed the structure so that Eleanor and Bob felt some control within their own household. There were still awkward times with Andy's mother, but Eleanor felt secure in her relationship with her husband and found that painful times did not continue to affect her and Bob as they had previously. She left feeling that she was adequate and could cope with whatever situations would arise in the future.

Eleanor was a warm and giving person, who was able to recognize and acknowledge her feelings. Insecurity at becoming a stepmother had undermined her sense of personal security, and her anger at her husband's expectations had been focused on her stepson. Eleanor felt understood and validated within the therapy hours. Her situation was restructured by the therapist, and very quickly Eleanor was willing to take considerable responsibility for dealing differently with her life. Bob appreciated the lifting of her depression and, although he initially shifted his behavior reluctantly, as the home situation became more rewarding for him, he was willing to work with Eleanor toward necessary changes.

Eleanor may represent the many women who have good basic self-confidence and could deal easily with nuclear family situations, but find themselves unable to handle effectively the complicated expectations and interpersonal relationships in stepfamilies.

June

June was an attractive 28-year-old woman married for a few
months to a man who had one daughter, Celia, from a previous
marriage. Celia's mother had walked out on her husband and
daughter, and Celia had been cared for by her grandparents. After
about three years Celia's father, Carl, and June were married.

June was determined to make up to Celia for not having a
mother, and she quit her job as a dancing teacher to bake cookies
and play with her eight-year-old stepdaughter. June had enjoyed
her job a great deal, but Carl felt that his daughter needed to have
a stepmother who was at home, and June herself saw her role as
being a full-time mother for the little girl.

By the end of four months June was in counselor's office, crying
hysterically and feeling "at the end of her rope." She spoke of
attempting day after day to talk with Celia, to invite Celia's
friends over to play, to do fun things with her stepdaughter. And
the harder June tried, the more Celia retreated, until June felt as
though she didn't exist.

Celia would relate with all the women in the neighborhood and
with her friends. Then she would come into the house, go directly
to her room without a word, and remain there until Carl came
home. By this time June was in tears and Carl was upset and angry
at June. June had begun yelling at Celia more and more, and Carl
started yelling at June and upbraiding her for being so mean to
his daughter. By the time June sought help, she and Carl were
talking about divorce.

June told the counselor she had read several books on being a
stepparent, but they hadn't helped. As the counselor empathized
with the difficulties of moving into a situation with another person's child, June stopped crying. Together they talked about how
much personal satisfaction June had lost in giving up her dancing
job. June, however, was not willing to consider even a part-time
dancing job when Celia was in school. Her whole being was directed toward becoming a successful, full-time stepmother.

The counselor pointed out that Celia was probably afraid to
trust a relationship with her stepmother because of the loss of her

natural mother when she was four, and then another loss when she moved from her grandparents' home. For a few minutes June was able to see Celia's withdrawal as not being directed at her personally, but rather the result of fear of another loss. June agreed that it might take Celia a number of months to warm up to her, and that she would approach Celia more slowly. But by the end of the hour June had returned to talking about her need to follow Celia into her bedroom and demand that Celia talk to her.

June left the appointment still feeling hopeless about receiving affection from Carl or from Celia. She agreed to return for another appointment, but called a few days later to cancel and said that the situation was worse, and that she felt sure she and Carl would be splitting up. She just couldn't take it and Carl couldn't see what was going on and blamed it all on her.

In this case June was unable to relinquish the wish to form an instant close-knit family. Her need to be a "mother" appeared to be very strong and she found it impossible to take a less active role in the family. While there is ambiguity in the stepmother role, it seems often that the problem for stepmothers is less related to role ambiguity than to dislike for any role other than "mother." June's unrealistic expectations of herself, coupled with Celia's need to withdraw and Carl's lack of understanding of the feelings involved were producing an untenable situation.

Carmen

Friends of a mother/stepmother sometimes ask the question, "Is it harder to be a stepmother than it is to be a mother?" In most situations the answer is usually an emphatic "yes." The case of Carmen illustrates a situation in which a warm and loving mother found the role of stepmother extremely frustrating and unrewarding.

Carmen contacted a counselor when she became so upset that she cried out with frustration, "Earl, I'm at the end of my rope with Tim! I simply can't go on trying any more to relate to him. I give up." And Earl, Tim's father and Carmen's husband of three years, replied with sadness, "Poor Tim!"

Carmen had previously been married for 14 years and had a girl and two boys who were eight 11, and 12 at the time of Carmen's divorce. Two years after her divorce Carmen and Earl were married and Earl's 11-year-old son, Tim, came to live with them. Earl's nine-year-old daughter, Sally, continued to live with her mother, and visited with her father and stepmother on weekends and in the summer.

Carmen enjoyed being a mother and felt emotionally close to her children. She and her children had shared many activities and times of closeness both before and after the divorce although the three children had been somewhat distant from their father throughout their lives. At the time of Carmen's remarriage her children suddenly withdrew from her for awhile and sought more contact with their father and with friends and neighbors. Within a few months, however, they adjusted to having to share their mother with Earl and his two children, and they began to enjoy relating to the members of their new stepfamily. The stepfamily had moved into a home of their own shortly after the remarriage and this had eased the initial tension considerably because the children now had rooms of their own.

The situation between Earl's children and Carmen, however, was tense from the first and became increasingly antagonistic. Carmen cried and then became angry as she desribed her attempts to relate to her two stepchildren. When Sally came to visit she would closet herself with her brother Tim and both would refuse to play with their stepsiblings. When the group went on an outing together Carmen felt that her stepchildren wished she would vanish in a puff of smoke, and she felt upset and depressed. Earl tried to smooth the ruffled feelings but his efforts were ineffectual.

When Sally was not there, Tim had a good time playing with his stepbrothers and stepsister, but he was surly to Carmen and refused to do his share of the family chores.

Carmen and Earl spent many hours talking about ways to help Tim to become more a part of the stepfamily, and Carmen tried to talk to Tim about his feelings the way she talked to her natural children. Carmen also went out of her way to do special things for Tim, but the only result seemed to be that Tim's hostility increased rather than decreased. When Sally visited, the special occasions planned by Carmen went unacknowledged by either stepchild. If Earl suggested an activity, his children's response was one of joy and enthusiasm and Carmen felt left out, unappreciated and increasingly angry.

It seemed to Carmen that her stepchildren did everything they could to annoy her. Since Tim was living with her she felt that every day was filled with frustration and anger. She could not sleep at night because Tim would get up and bang his way into the bathroom; he would go to school leaving dirty clothes strewn all over the house; he forgot to feed the dog; and he would not listen whenever she attempted to talk to him. On the other hand, Carmen's three children continued as before to restrict their messiness to their own rooms, to do their chores with little prompting, and to express feelings of caring and appreciation to their mother.

Finally Carmen could stand it no longer, and when Earl refused to seek professional help she decided to do so herself. She had been moved by Earl's comment, "Poor Tim!" and she wanted to continue trying to relate to Tim since she considered that he received little affection from his natural mother. Carmen also knew how upset her husband felt about the way things were going, even though he believed that professional help would be useless.

As she talked to her counselor Carmen began to have an awareness of how hard she was trying to create a bond between her and her stepchildren similar to that which she enjoyed with her own children. She began to understand the loyalty issues faced by her stepchildren and she was able to back away from Sally and Tim and give up her attempts to push for a close tie with them.

Because of her good relationship with her natural children, Carmen continued to feel confident of her ability as a parent and, as her expectations of herself as a stepparent became more realistic, she relaxed considerably. The tenseness between Carmen and Earl decreased as she stopped "trying so hard," and Tim and Sally were slightly more agreable when Carmen was around. In fact, they would approach her more now that she was less demanding of their attention. Once in a while Earl would do things alone with his children and Carmen would plan activities with hers.

Earl and Carmen also arranged to spend an hour or two alone with one or more of their stepchildren, having a hamburger or going shopping. New bonds began to form and although a warm relationship did not develop, the emotional climate between Carmen and her stepchildren did become less tense.

Carmen had found that telling Earl about her frustration and hurt made him angry because he was unable to alter the situation, and he felt responsible and guilty and became upset because the presence of his children precipitated such turmoil. Having a counselor who was not involved and could listen and be understanding reduced Carmen's emotional volatility. The counselor's knowledge of stepfamily processes enabled Carmen to recognize the futility of her attempts to create "one big happy family." For a number of months she continued to rely on the counselor for help, and although she continued to wish for a warmer relationship with Sally and Tim, her increased understanding of stepfamily dynamics made it possible for her to accept less from her stepchildren than from her natural children. Letting go of her unrealistic expectations resulted in less tension between Earl and Carmen so that her emotional need for a close couple relationship was increasingly satisfied.

Carmen and Earl had recently joined an organization for stepfamilies and she had met a woman who had experienced much of the same frustration Carmen had felt. Her new friend had now been remarried for 15 years and reported to Carmen that when her stepchildren had grown to be adults and were independent they had begun to relate more warmly to all the parental adults in their lives. This information gave Carmen hope for a better relationship with her stepchildren in the future. Carmen was finally able to deal with her new stepfamily in a manner satisfactory to herself, and she discontinued her counseling sessions knowing that she could return if some future problem seemed unmanageable.

GROUPS FOR STEPMOTHERS

Following a research project carried out in 1977, Sardanis-Zimmerman formed a stepmother group. These women had volunteered to complete questionnaries in connection with the research, and following the clinical interviews they formed an ongoing group. Dr. Sardanis-Zimmerman provided the information that these women valued the opportunity to express their feelings without their husbands being present and rejected the idea of having their husbands join the group. Subjects discussed in the group included stepchildren, feelings of rejection, sexual difficulties and dependency needs.

From her work with these stepmothers, Sardanis-Zimmerman (1977) outlines three stages in the stepmother's assimilation into the stepfamily:

Phase I. Usually the feelings the stepmother has initially towards the children are positive. If she does not like the children, there may even be the defense of denial in operation due to her strong affection and desire to marry and live with her husband. This is the honeymoon stage. During this period everyone seems to put a best foot forward to make a good impression.

Phase II. In this second stage the stepmother begins to be aware of some negative feelings she has, usually towards one or all of her stepchildren. The situation is not working out as she planned and she feels trapped. If she expresses these negative feelings, what will happen? Her catastrophic expectations are: (a) If she was married before, she may experience once more the pain of divorce and failure; (b) if she has not been married before, she may fear divorce and failure and the waste of all her efforts in the marriage that is disintegrating; or (c) if she tells her husband how she really feels about "that kid/those kids," he will abandon her and, worse, choose and side with them.

Phase III. In Phase III some crisis occurs where the stepmother cannot hide her feelings any longer. This may come about as a result of a stepchild showing some symptom, necessitating the services of some professional (school counselor, doctor, or consultation with a teacher or minister).

If the stepmother takes a risk and states her feelings to her husband, and he accepts her, then there is opportunity for closer family unity and working out some of the interpersonal conflicts involved.

Often the stepmother attempts to please everyone in the family and does not get her own needs met. The more successful stepmothers do not look towards their children or even their husbands alone to meet all their needs. They usually have careers and other interests outside the family to enhance their self-esteem.

The major topics usually covered in group work or in individual work with stepmothers or wives of stepfathers are the following:

1. Problems in the area of expectations of instant love of and from stepchildren.
2. Tendency of stepmothers to rush in and come on too strong.
3. Handling rejection from stepchildren.
4. Difficulties with the wicked stepmother myth.
5. Unsuccessful attempts to keep everybody happy.
6. Inability to achieve close family unity.
7. Anger, jealousy, and competition for love and affection from spouse.
8. Anger at ex-spouses.
9. Guilt generated by all of the above.

Sardanis-Zimmerman outlines her guidelines for working with stepmothers in a group as follows:

The success of a stepmother group involves several stages. As stepmothers are usually afraid to reveal their negative feelings, it is important, initially, for the leader to provide a warm, supportive, non-judgmental atmosphere in order for trust to develop. Ideally, if the group leader is a stepmother herself, this allows the group to feel it is safe to share feelings which stepmothers have been repressing and are fearful of disclosing. Usually this fear stems from the stepmother bottling up her anger and resentments. As one stepmother expressed it, "If my husband really knew how I felt about his kids, our marriage would be over."

Initially, the stepmother tends to discuss "the main problem," which usually means the stepchild/stepchildren, the "ex," in-law interference, or lack of support from the husband. When each stepmother shares her own dilemma and the leader also confides to the group what her own situation is, a sense of cohesiveness begins to develop.

The first six months of the stepmother group tend to revolve around problem-solving, e.g., "What do you mean when you say you hate the kid (stepchild) and everything he does?" Suggestions are offered in the form of homework assignments. An example is a case where one stepmother tended to bend over backwards "to be nice." She was encouraged to let out "just a little anger" as an experiment. The following week she returned to the group excited. The usual chaotic dinner hour with her stepsons left her upset and frustrated. She reprimanded them for the first time and when they went out to play she began washing the dishes. Aware that she was still exasperated, she threw three dishes on the floor "and felt great."

For five stepmothers who attended a group formed in 1976, the weekly sessions seemed "something special." As one stepmother expressed it, "I had company drop in unexpectedly tonight. At 7 o'clock I said, "Excuse me, this is Thursday; I have something planned for tonight and I have to leave now.' I've been in other groups, but this one is different. It's just for *me* and I wouldn't miss it for anything."

Gradually in the second stage the focus moved closer to the stepmother herself—her background, how she met her husband, her expectations then, and what is missing in her life now. She is encouraged to "be greedy." What is usually missing is more time for herself, an evening out alone with her husband, time for old friends and time with her own child or children. Frequently stepmothers may be involved in individual therapy in addition to the group. Several women in the group mentioned above were in couple, family therapy, or combinations of these.

In the final stage, the group becomes a combination of a "working" group (discussing current problems) —yet leaning more towards being a social support group, with pot luck suppers at different members' homes.

The stepmother group can be compared to a woman's consciousness raising type of group that offers stepmothers an opportunity to 1. improve their self-esteem, 2. develop their capabilities and use their energies productively for themselves, rather than projecting many frustrations onto their stepchildren, 3. improve relationships with their partners, and 4. discover new ways to nurture and fulfill themselves.

Some of the ways the women in this group developed themselves were the following: One started singing lessons, another farmed out all five children (his and hers) and took off for two weeks with her husband for a holiday in Europe; another who was living with a man who had custody of his children, decided to marry him; another stepmother who had no children of her own became pregnant.

Although many of the stepparenting problems continued the stepmothers appeared more self-confident, able to handle crises and, generally, were not as threatened by their situation as they were in the beginning of the group sessions.

In many family difficulties, having both members of the couple work together with a therapist or counselor may increase the chance of success. However, in a number of cases, working with only one of the couple either individually or in a group can stop a downward spiral and shift the interpersonal relationships in a positive direction. Since the major stresses in many stepfamilies are an outgrowth of complicated interpersonal relationships, a shift in one individual requiring shifts in other family members can reduce the tensions and result in improved stepfamily functioning. Very often it will be the woman who will be the individual to seek help in coping with stepfamily problems.

6

Men in remarried relationships involving children

Men in stepfamily situations tend to have different expectations placed on them than have women. They are on the whole less involved with the raising of the children, which may be the reason there are no explicit stepfather myths to color the internal or external perception of stepfathers. There are many stories involving cruel stepfathers, but these are in adult literature, and do not appear in children's fairy tales.

The position of stepfathers with no children of their own is very different from the position of stepmothers with no children of their own. Statistically, women in this position have the most difficult time compared to other women in stepfamilies, while stepfathers with no children of their own have the least difficult time in stepfamily situations. They do not carry with them guilt at having left children of a previous marriage, and can therefore relate more clearly and easily to their stepchildren. They are inexperienced as parents and, while this may result in their having more difficulty with discipline and understanding of their stepchildren, the absence of ties to a former family appears to offset this disadvantage.

Fathers who are married to women who have no children do

not have to relate to stepchildren. However, these men ordinarily do not have their natural children living with them and as a result they often experience a great deal of guilt. They may try to be a "hero father" when their children visit, thus making the weekend visits a series of Disneyland adventures; often the wife feels excluded and angry. A remarried father wrote a clear statement of the difficulties that can arise in such stepfamily situations and the choices that he needed to make:

> I was married for 14 years, and as a result of this first marriage, I became the father of three children. When it became clear to me in the latter years of this first marriage that I was unhappy and that the marriage wasn't working, I spent several years wrestling with the emotional and financial issues surrounding separation and divorce. Accordingly, when my decision to separate was made I did so with full acceptance of the financial consequences and an emotional commitment to remain close to my children. The latter revolved around picking them up at their home for outings, as well as their spending weekends at my apartment. Much of this was certainly as a result of my own feelings of guilt. However, through the years my relations with, and love for, my children have grown significantly.
>
> Into all of this stepped my current wife who had never been married nor seriously dated a separated or divorced man. I hid nothing from her as far as my relations with my children or for that matter the long-term financial responsibilities that I have as to alimony and child support. We dated for a year and lived together for another year prior to our marriage.
>
> While all of these events were transpiring, I assumed that her awareness and apparent acceptance of the preceding would not result in material problems between us. That assumption proved incorrect for she apparently had not fully realized the impact that these commitments and priorities would have upon our relationship. It is important to note that I incorrectly assumed that she had relatively easily accepted a set of decisions and priorities that had personally taken me several years to evolve. Consequently, I was insensitive and not too supportive of her growing difficulties in dealing with these issues after we were married. . . . These factors contributed to her leaving for four months after about

18 months of marriage. I am very happy to report that we have since reconciled.

Through all of that, several things have crystallized in my own mind that I would like to share. That is, my wife and our relationship occupy a higher priority in my life than my children and my past life. Our joint emotional needs must be satisfied before those of all others. It hasn't been easy for me to sort all of that out and keep it straight. At times I feel as if I'm caught in a horrible cross fire between demands of my wife, my children, an ex-wife and my own personal requirements independent of everybody. I really don't expect any of the above to get any easier, although I am now better able to deal with these problems.

If fathers do have custody of their children because of the death of their wife or after divorce because of a court award, they often form a very tight bond with these children, thus making it difficult for their wives to break into the circle. Such fathers have difficulty disciplining the children or accepting help in this area from their wives. Generally it is the stepmother who is with the husband's children most of the time, and in some cases, as one child psychiatrist put it, "She isn't given even as much authority by the children's father as he'd give to a baby sitter." Typically, the stepmother wants acceptance and appreciation as she cares for the home and her stepchildren, but instead she may be faced with disobedience and hostility from her stepchildren. There are no trade-offs since she herself has no children to balance the stepfamily ledger. She and the stepchildren may begin to fight, the children's father is upset and becomes angry at his wife, and stepfamily tension grows rapidly. The wife feels let down by her husband as well as upset with her stepchildren. The wife feels that it is safer to be angry with the stepchildren so her anger is directed towards the children. The husband, on the other hand, is upset with his children's behavior as well as with his wife, but he directs all his anger at his wife. For each there has been a displacement of at least some of their anger. Unfortunately; the alliance between father and children frequently grows stronger and the coalition between the couple may disintegrate.

Men who are both fathers and stepfathers are involved in the most complex stepfamily structure of all. The usual pattern is for the husband's children to visit rather than live with their natural father, while the stepchildren live in his household. This father/stepfather has more familiarity with children than the man who has had no children, but frequently the stepchildren may be very different in age or a different sex from his natural children and he feels baffled by their behavior. In stepfamilies where the husband has no children, or no children from a previous marriage living with him, he is the outsider who must join a previously existing group. This can be a very difficult task for a stepfather and is the situation faced by the largest number of men in remarried relationships.

The role of the stepfather is a particularly ambiguous and ill-defined one, as he struggles to accomplish a series of tasks for which he has had no preparation. In a society in which the more obvious functions of the father are financial and educational, because there is still a natural father elsewhere, the stepfather is often left with only a partial financial obligation and a socialization or educational function. It has been said that stepfathers always face the question of "how much to be a parent." Other authors have questioned whether any stepfather can successfully assume a parent role, no matter how skillful his efforts (Fast and Cain, 1966, p. 488). Since social roles are learned, no step-relationship can be instantly defined or instantly successful. Simon (1964, p. 163) considers that in the case of divorce a man must overcome the stepfather prejudice that he doesn't count very much at all, that his role in the stepfamily is extremely amorphous.

In summary, the most common variation among the various permutations of stepfatherhood is that in which a man, whether previously married and a father or not, marries a woman with children. A stepfather who has had no children of his own appears to have an easier time because of minimal guilt about his previous relationships and no feelings that he has abandoned his children. On the other hand, a man with no experience as a parent has a certain handicap as he confronts the new experience of being a stepparent. The remarried father with stepchildren deals with the maximum complexity in stepfamily relationships. A father with custody of his children who marries a woman without children is not a stepfather himself, but needs to understand and help his wife to deal with her problems as a stepmother.

A variety of important general psychological tasks are faced by stepfathers:

> 1. Joining a functioning group and establishing a place for himself. (This is the reverse of the situation faced by the woman who marries a man who has custody of his children.)
> 2. Working out rules regarding family behavior.
> 3. Handling unrealistic expectations both on his part and on the part of the new family.

The new stepfather also confronts a number of specific problem areas requiring active coping efforts:

> 4. Dealing with feelings of guilt about his previous family, if he is a father.
> 5. Money.
> 6. Adoption, naming and inheritance questions with reference to his stepchildren.
> 7. Sexuality in the stepfamily.

JOINING A FUNCTIONING GROUP AND ESTABLISHING A PLACE

When groups are beginning to form there is space for shifts and for assimilation of new members. An "open group" with a shifting membership remains somewhat loose with expectations of constant fluctuation within the group. Provided that there are small continuous shifts, a group of this type retains space for new membership. Even in such groups, new members usually experience a certain hesitancy and discomfort initially, but shortly there is another new group member and the process repeats itself. Social clubs, fraternal groups, business offices, and church organizations are common examples of such groups.

A "closed group" bands together and remains intact as a group with an unchanging membership. In the beginning there is an amorphous structure with space for shifts of membership or role, but after awhile the group solidifies, a unit is formed, and there is little or no space for new members. If, for some reason, a new member joins a group of this type there is disruption and mixed feelings for all. The original group may be mourning the loss of a member, feeling anxious about the future now that the group is changing, or see the newcomer as an intruder. There is, in general, a sense of disequilibrium.

As for the new person trying to squeeze into the spot vacated by someone else, or orbiting around the periphery of the group because no space seems available, strong feelings of alienation and rejection may develop. In such cases, feelings of anger and frustration run through the group, behavior becomes increasingly strained and a vicious downward spiral is underway.

Many times stepfathers are in the position of trying to break into a unit of mother and children whose bonds predate the association between the adults. The longer this unit has existed, the more difficult it may be for the stepfather to be assimilated. As one single mother said, "When I was first divorced there was a missing slot in the family. But slowly the space was filled in and now the children and myself form a tight unit that would be hard to loosen to let another person in."

In most stepfamilies the mother and her children share a common history, background, and cultural values. The new stepfather has a different history and background, and his values may or may not vary considerably from those of his new stepfamily. As Satir (1972) says, "The chances of spouses doing at least some things different from one another are just about 100 percent, as neither was brought up in the same way" (p. 129). The first romantic hopes and feelings of love cause those concerned to brush aside the possibilities of difficulty in adjustment. They do not look carefully at the problems that might arise. In remarried families, even when the new couple is compatible in most respects, there is little consideration given to the fact that the children's backgrounds may be entirely different because there was another person involved in the child's growth and development. So children from two different family patterns may be joined together with resulting tension and conflict.

A few stepfathers are welcomed into the family group as saviors. The mother may have been lonely and may have had a difficult struggle with all the responsibilities of both parent roles. In many instances she may have been the breadwinner as well. The mother may be feeling overwhelmed by all her parental responsibilities, particularly those of discipline, and imagines that the new husband will help her with all of her problems—financial, personal, and parental. In some cases the children may also welcome a stepfather in the home, particularly when there has been careful preparation and a friendly relationship has been established. Sometimes, however, the reaction is an opposite one. The child resents the loss of the full-time attention of the mother, and the usurping of his or her position by someone who is regarded as an interloper. Children may react sullenly and defiantly to what they see as a takeover attempt. And the mother who thought she wanted help with discipline may find, when the stepfather tries to assert himself, that his attitudes are different and he punishes more harshly or for infractions which she would have overlooked. She may leap to the defense of her child, and the fuse has been ignited for a tense and difficult confrontation.

While the mother has been filling many roles, a divorced man has had little family life. As Owen Spann illustrates:

> I had lived the comparatively peaceful life of a bachelor for a year. Suddenly, I inherited: fighting for the bathroom, having no hot water to shave with, and being a phone-answering service for moppets. Believe me, all this can quickly dampen any newlywed's enthusiasm for what should be rightfully his peace (Spann and Spann, 1977, p. 8)!

A young unmarried man who had been living for three years with a woman with a young daughter sought help. He stated his dilemma, and the dilemma of many men, in this way:

> I moved into a ready-made family. If Shirley and I had just been married I'm sure we would have had children, or at least one child. But we had no chance to grow into it slowly. Before we decide to get married we've been living together for three years to see if it will work out.
> We're thinking of adding a room to our home so I have some privacy. I sit down to do something and eight-year-old

Joan is always there, or some kid is knocking on the door saying, "Can Joan play?" Saturday morning I'm used to sleeping, but now from seven o'clock on the cartoons are going on the TV and I can't sleep.

In thinking of adding I really have to evaluate if it's all worth it. Will the adjustment be too great. I've spent three years trying to adjust. I think I had the most adjustment to make because Shirley and Joan were already adjusted to each other. At first there was the question of my having some authority in the house. I had to come on easy and work into it. That's been all taken care of now. Joan is a good kid. It's not a problem of her being a bad kid.

Shirley and I have no trouble between us. We get along in a way I didn't know two people could. But I think a person should be happy more than 50 percent of the time. That's not enough. I'm wondering if we can work it out. It's not that I haven't been trying for three years—but is it ever going to get worked out? Whenever Shirley and I are alone and Joan's with her father and stepmother we have such a good time. We try to crowd everything into that short time together. I keep wishing it was that way all the time.

Fitting into the new family is difficult indeed. Often the step-father comes to feel like an intruder. A power bloc exists with the bond between the mother and her children. If the remarriage is to succeed, a new bloc must be formed between the couple, a bloc which is able to resist the attempts of the children to re-establish their old connections and undermine the new ones. As Bohannan (1977, p. 5) comments, Jessie Bernard pointed out as early as 1952 that there are three possible outcomes of the struggle: The stepfather may take control; the stepfather may be assimilated into the mother-headed family; or a new status quo may evolve from a process of change. In addition, Bohannan adds, the stepfather may be driven away. According to Bohannan and Erickson (1977):

> One of the most obvious difficulties comes from the "hidden agenda." This hidden agenda becomes serious when a woman or her children have expectations about what the stepfather will do, but they do not give any very clear picture of what those expectations are. The stepfather (who may, of

course, have a hidden a   ᵗʰᵉ picture
without knowing what   can he
divine it. He is soon   veryone
concerned (p. 7).

To some extent, the pr   the new
family is reflected in man   lasses and
books on the subject are often ...   are about
to undertake new roles. This gives prepaiaᵤ   ᴏme of the
problems, and the stepfather's expectations of instant success are
tempered by knowledge. However, Stern (1978) has commented
that at least one-and-a-half years seem to be necessary to integrate a
stepfather into a new family.

WORKING OUT RULES REGARDING FAMILY BEHAVIOR

Discipline frequently causes difficulties between natural parents
in intact families. This frequently occurs when one parent is inclined to be stricter and perhaps represents the "straight" values or
moral principles which the other parent may secretly support
while openly taking a view for more freedom and liberality. In a
remarriage, discipline is an area which frequently causes the first
real difficulties, leading to serious arguments from the start. While
consciously the mother says she wants help with discipline, "she
feels protective and does not want any interference in her relationship with her children" (Visher and Visher, 1978, p. 258).

Parents who have grown up with their children have had the
opportunity to work out their relationship and their family rules,
including enforcement styles, over a period of many years. When
there is a remarriage, the necessity of coming to an agreement is
immediate, and family chaos is often the result.

Bohannan and Erickson (1978) have commented:

> Undoubtedly, the touchiest point in founding a new house-
> hold is the way discipline is controlled by the two parents.
> The children, used to one mode of discipline, may have to
> make adjustments to another; the stepfather, feeling himself
> outnumbered, may withdraw completely from disciplinary
> action. . . . Fathers and stepfathers (both in natural families

and stepfamilies) reported that they were in charge in 37 percent of the families; the mother was responsible for discipline in 20 percent; and fathers and mothers both played a role in 43 percent (p. 59).

Children are often quoted as saying, "I don't have to do what he says. He's not my real father." Stepfathers just as frequently say, "I'm damned if I do and damned if I don't," or, "It bugs me when I tell them something and they go and ask their mother." Older children are particularly upset when a stepfather enters the family and begins to discipline them. The children feel that the autonomy they had gained in the single-parent family is being lost. While the mother may be willing to relinquish some of her autonomy after the remarriage, older children are usually not so inclined. Even younger children continually test the situation to see where the power lies.

Phyllis Noerager Stern (1978) has studied the vicissitudes of discipline in a stepfather family, that is, a remarriage in which the man marries a woman with children who are living with her. She has derived some interesting theoretical constructs to help explain what takes place. Stern sees the first task of the new stepfamily as one of achieving "integration." An integrated family is a group which has a set of norms or a "sentimental order," an attachment to the unit, status within the unit, and a clear idea of who is in the family and who is not. Because the new stepfather is an outsider, he must somehow break into the group. Stern believes that discipline is the key to the integration process, which is sometimes never achieved.

Beliefs about what is "normal" and "right" are deeply based in childhood experiences, and are usually emotionally charged, rather than rational. In first marriages parental differences in regards to what they believe to be "right" and "wrong" behavior get worked out gradually. In remarriages it is not possible for a couple to come to an instant agreement in such a complex area. A nuclear family can develop a set of commonly agreed upon values, but a stepfamily plunges in and starts to struggle almost immediately. While some mothers favor a gradual assumption of the role of co-manager by the stepfather, some stepfathers find the waiting untenable. They feel ."emasculated." Yet a sudden take-over of authority usually is very disturbing to the children.

As previously stated, a time period of one-and-a-half to two years is required for stepfather families to develop a "sentimental order" of their own. Most families are unprepared for such a long period of adjustment. They expect "instant love" and "trust" from all concerned, and stepfathers are hurt when their new step-children shun them. It is very frustrating to wait out the child's period of adjustment. The dilemma is that if the new stepfather attempts to become a co-manager and disciplinarian immediately, he is undermined by the mother, the child, or both; on the other hand, if he remains out of the management picture, he is isolated and an outsider. "The stepfather who moves slowly and attempts to make a friend of the child before moving to control him has a better chance of having his discipline integrated into the senti-mental order of the family" (Stern, 1978). It seems that the proc-ess of integration is likely to go more smoothly when the child is young. It may be more difficult when the child is older, has assumed a "man-of-the-house" or "mother's helper" role, and feels displaced.

Stern (1978) finds that the process of the stepfather becoming a friend to the stepchild is crucial to effective integration. A child who has a stepfather-friend is more willing to cooperate in the rules of the house, and to accept the discipline of the stepfather. A willingness to be disciplined is essential, and this willingness can only be based on mutual respect and friendship. Discipline based on nothing but fear of punishment will inevitably be de-feated or undermined by the child. Discipline is accepted because the person being disciplined wishes the approval of the person enforcing rules, and a positive relationship underlies the wish for approval.

One way for a stepfather to become a friend of the stepchild is to make it clear that he takes the child's side at times when he disagrees with the mother. For example, Susan wants to stay with her best friend overnight. Susan's mother says no, but Susan's stepfather points out to the mother and Susan that it is Friday night and Susan does not have to go to school the next day. Susan's mother considers the matter again and agrees that Susan may go with her friend. Since parents and children in stepfamilies often feel that parents discipline their children from love and that stepparents discipline their stepchildren from dislike, such an interchange indicates to both the mother and to the child that the stepfather is indeed fair to his stepchild. Several instances such as this can do a great deal to build a bond between a child and a stepfather, helping to integrate the stepfather into the family unit.

While a stepchild may resent discipline from a stepfather, at the same time the child may feel that lack of direction or discipline from the stepparent is proof of his lack of interest and caring. The stepchild's behavior may be a way of "testing" the stepparent. Misbehavior, as is well known, can be a plea for attention as a substitute for love, if the latter does not seem to be available in sufficient quantities. Working together as a couple on disciplinary problems can be difficult, but is the most productive approach with younger children. Originally, the parent will be the one to speak to the children, but very gradually this can shift to a couple responsibility so that the parent or the stepparent can deal with the children.

Not only is a gradual shift necessary for the child, but it is also necessary for the couple. Many times the mother is sending double messages to the stepfather. She wishes help with discipline, and at the same time feels the need to protect her children. In such instances the stepfather may respond with withdrawal; the mother then perceives this as lack of interest in her children, and feels let down and deserted by her husband. Gradual participation by the stepfather seems the best answer.

In stepfamilies where the children are older and the mother has been the head of the family for a considerable length of time, couples often work out a satisfactory system where the mother continues with her disciplinary function with the support of the stepfather. The stepfather is less integrated into the family with this system, but with older stepchildren the stepfamily unit is less likely to be a cohesive unit in any case.

HANDLING UNREALISTIC EXPECTATIONS

The expectations which a new stepfather has as he approaches remarriage are influenced by many factors. The usual situation is that he is blind to the complexity of the situation. There is a strong tendency to believe that somehow "love will conquer all" and that his new wife and he will be able to easily work out the problems of their new relationship.

One factor which influences the new marriage is the previous situation: Did the natural father die, divorce, or disappear? Was the previous father and child relationship happy? If the father-child relationship was a good one, a standard has been set which may be difficult for a stepfather to live up to. If the natural father has died, he may have become idealized, so that his human faults have been forgotten. If the father-child relationship was not a happy one, the new stepfather may inherit the children's expectations that the new relationship will not be a happy one either.

One stepfather, a mental health professional, felt sure that he could enter a second family easily because he could understand the feelings of his new stepson. The boy's father had died a few years earlier, and the new stepfather was certain that he could empathize with the boy. Even in his case, with an aware stepfather, the stepfamily situation did not go smoothly for some time. As the stepfather said, "My stepson felt I was pushing. I tried too hard. So I backed away and for about two years a state of neutrality existed, and now at last some friendliness between us is beginning to develop." As with stepmothers, stepfathers also need to hold back and take a slow, easy pace.

Very often, as tension develops in the stepfamily, the husband looks to his wife to improve the situation. He considers that she is the one responsible for the daily functioning of the family and therefore it is her mismanagement that is causing the upset. Frequently, the wife has the same expectations of herself and tries harder and harder to cope with and alter the situation. The harder she tries the worse things get, and the relationship between the couple usually suffers. The expectation that the wife is responsible for emotional relationships within the family is unrealistic, for no single person can unravel the complicated stepfamily situation. In fact, the wife, who is usually dealing with the major part of the interactions in the home, desperately needs the support of her husband.

Other expectations coming from the outside can impinge on the new relationship. For example, how do grandparents or other family members regard the new marriage? Some are supportive and accepting, but many are critical and undermining. Couples who marry expecting that relatives, colleagues, and friends will approve sometimes find that they face a wall of community and family rejection with which it is very difficult to deal. Some couples report that they are no longer on speaking terms with parents, and that their friends have pulled away or chosen to side with an ex-spouse. Cultural and religious institutions may also oppose the new relationship, so that the remarried couple finds an atmosphere loaded with rejection and disapproval.

The husband who has not anticipated all these problems and difficulties often finds himself ill-prepared to be tolerant and patient as attempts are made to work things out. It may seem to him as though his dream of another chance at happiness has come crashing down about him. He thought it would be simple and that love would find a way, and instead complexities and problems have reached overwhelming proportions. If he will work together with his wife to sort out unrealistic expectations of her, of himself, and of the children, the situation can slowly improve. As the community and stepfamilies themselves learn more about the dynamics of the situation, handling the complexity will be easier. Mental health professionals can be extremely helpful in clarifying the feelings of insecurity felt by all stepfamily members and thus bring about more reasonable stepfather expectations.

SPECIFIC PROBLEM AREAS

Dealing with Feelings of Guilt

One of the hardest problems which many stepfathers face is dealing with their guilt about leaving the children of their previous family to become the stepfather in a new family. One father

and stepfather recently described his feelings about leaving his
first family:

> There is a tremendous amount of guilt. It wasn't a decision
> that was made without a lot of feelings and concern about
> what would happen to the children at a vulnerable age. I
> think that maybe I was naive, but I had hoped that in some
> ways, though I felt I could never make up to my natural chil-
> dren for leaving, that I would be able to provide a substitute
> experience for them with me and with my new family that
> would at least partially compensate for the fact that I wasn't
> there in the old family. And the other thing I thought was
> that since in the old family I was terribly unhappy, it would
> mean a lot to the children to see that their father was happier
> and had a good relationship in the new family. This was the
> root of one of the reasons why I felt it was important to try
> to provide an ongoing second family relationship for my
> children. There are families where very frequently when
> divorce takes place the father just disappears. He makes no
> effort to keep in touch with the children of his former mar-
> riage because it's too painful (Visher and Visher, 1978,
> p. 259).

In many stepfamilies the father's children visit on weekends or
for vacations. If their relationship with their father is strained, his
guilt and feelings of rejection increase. Being with his children
may become so painful that he sees less and less of them.

For another father the guilt leads him to lavish time and money
on the children to the exclusion of his new wife and stepchildren
if he has any. He finds himself overcompensating, being the
"super-dad," trying to make up for all the days or months that he
has not been there when his children needed him. In a frenzy of
activity they go to Disneyland and Marine World on Saturday,
and to the beach and the aquarium on Sunday. After such a
weekend "Dad" climbs into bed exhausted to arise and go to
work on Monday. And next weekend it's a trip to the mountains
to go fishing and canoeing.

All the while the stepchildren see their stepfather during the
week over the dinner table before they go to do their homework,
and then on the weekends they disappear to see their natural

father, while the visiting children come and "live it up." In this way, many stepfathers have little opportunity to enjoy their stepchildren, and their wives feel rushed and deprived of leisure time with their husbands.

Many times a father in a stepfamily is sensitive to the distress of his wife, and since he is aware that it is the presence of his children that is making for stepfamily tension he begins to feel guilty that in his remarriage he has brought children to the relationship as "part of the package." His guilt may take many forms. He may withdraw from his children to smooth the situation; he may become angry at his wife, his stepchildren, or his ex-spouse; or he may start coming on "too strong" to his natural children in an attempt to have them "shape up and accept the situation."

For some fathers the guilt over leaving their natural children is made worse whenever they enjoy their stepchildren. They feel as though they are depriving their natural children of love and affection that are rightfully theirs, and they may then withdraw from their stepchildren. Very often anger and a feeling of helplessness compounds the feelings of guilt. This anger and helplessness come from the fact that the father does not have custody of his natural children and therefore has little control over their upbringing, or even over their contact with him. In an effort to insure continuing contacts with his children, many fathers find it difficult to say "no" to their ex-wives. They also find it difficult to say "no" to their natural children because they do not want to have the children return to their mother feeling angry and complaining to their mother about their father.

Such behavior can lead the new wife to feel that her husband cares more about the feelings of his ex-wife than he does about her feelings. She and her children see him allowing his natural children to "get away with murder" while he shouts at his stepchildren for "nothing at all." The wife becomes resentful and instead of receiving support from her husband he admonishes her to be more understanding. A downward spiral has begun.

Guilt is a heavy burden for stepfathers, and they are often unaware of the important effects it is having on them in their new relationships.

Money

Money, sometimes an important focus on difficulty in marriage, is especially important in the remarriage situation (Messinger, 1976). Divorce is an expensive proposition, and standards of living are frequently lowered in remarried families as the husband attempts to make the same income stretch even further to cover not only the new family and children, but also to assist with the financial problems of an ex-spouse and her children who are still living with her. Child support going out is often particularly irritating to members of a stepfamily in which there is no comparable child support coming in. Bitterness over money matters can be very strong.

One divorce attorney entitled a talk on financial considerations in divorce, "Too Much Is Not Enough." No one is satisfied. Traditionally, the ex-wife feels she is not receiving enough, while the ex-husband considers he is giving her too much. Remarriage often increases the dissatisfaction over financial arrangements.

Some stepfathers feel besieged by demands for monetary support to the point of feeling like "a walking checkbook." As Simon (1964) has said:

> . . . for the stepfather, money is not the simple language of responsibility, manliness, love and affection that it is for most husbands and fathers . . . he cannot finance his family on conventional terms; each act of giving becomes troublesome as well as generous, each parsimony challenges assorted family loyalty . . . he is damned if he does reach his hand into his pocket . . . and damned if he doesn't (p. 68).

And for the stepchildren, rivalries for love and affection erupt many times over money. One grown stepdaughter put it clearly:

> I think the subject of money is interesting because it is symbolic on the one hand and it ain't symbolic on the other hand. I've always been curious to know how much my stepbrother and stepsister have been financially supported and helped through college by Dad and Christy (her stepmother) so that then I can compare how much I've been helped.

Money is often a focus of serious difficulty between the father and his ex-spouse. No matter how much child support he is paying, his children always come to visit "dressed in rags." Bitterness can be very deep.

Many times money is used as the vehicle to express hostility toward an ex-spouse. "One young child broke a favorite toy. Although the cost of replacing the toy would have been nominal, his mother informed him that his father did not supply her with enough money to buy him a replacement. When next he visited his father and stepmother, the boy was withdrawn and angry and accused his father of depriving his mother of money that she needed" (Visher and Visher, 1978, p. 259).

At other times an ex-spouse may be confronted with extra and unanticipated expenses, such as the cost of orthodontia. She may approach her ex-husband to see if he will pay for it. Perhaps this father's guilt is still causing him difficulty. He has little extra money, but he does not want to appear to be disinterested in the welfare of his children, so he agrees to pay for the orthodontia, but at the cost of depriving his new family of money they had saved for a vacation. Now the man may be caught between a temporarily satisfied ex-wife and a hurt and furious new wife.

As the children grow older, contrasts between the life-style and standard of living of the two families may become apparent. The ex-spouse may have decided, for example, to work only part-time with the result that her income is low even though she is receiving alimony and child support. Resentments arise and the children ask questions about why the father's new family can afford certain vacations or items which seem like luxuries to the family of his ex-spouse.

Another source of tension over money arises in stepfamilies in which a mother marries a man with no children, or with children not living with them. Many times such women feel guilty that their husbands must support stepchildren. Even when the mother is receiving support for the children, she often continues to feel guilty that her husband must contribute financially to the raising of her children. In one form or another she says, "It's not fair.

My husband married four people—me and my three children—not just me."

When children grow to adulthood money problems do not evaporate. There are complications in such issues as inheritance, wills, family heirlooms, and the like. One set of grandparents may be wealthy, but refuse to recognize stepchildren and leave them out of their wills. Feelings about "blood relations" run deep. Even when the natural father has disappeared, a stepfather often does not feel that his stepchildren are really his own, and he is reluctant to have them inherit his assets. Family antiques and heirlooms are sources of dissension, as questions arise such as, "Shouldn't Grandmother B's things stay in the B family?"

Messinger (1976) comments that respondents in her study of remarried families frequently reported difficulties in financial arrangements:

> Many remarried men were reluctant to speak freely about their financial assets and remarried women were often secretive about monies they may have brought into the marriage . . . Having had one marital dissolution some women confided that they felt it necessary to keep some money aside in the eventuality of yet another divorce. Reflecting a similar uncertainty about the new marriage, some men appeared reluctant to revise their wills, insurance, and property assets. The impression conveyed was that the financial area was a poorly resolved and sensitive one for many, reflecting hesitation in making a commitment to the new marriage.

This hesitation leads to feelings of insecurity and distrust between the couple, and financial arguments can become commonplace.

Some stepfamilies have established a marital contract in which the wife and the husband have agreed to a complete separation of assets and expenses. This can work relatively well in some stepfamilies where both partners have similar and adequate incomes, but in other instances not combining incomes leads to fragmentation of the stepfamily. If the couple is not married, separation of income and assets is common, but at times also results in financial conflicts and tensions.

The major stress under the contract arrangement comes in step-families in which both the wife's children and the husband's children live under one roof. Frequently the husband has more money than his wife. With separate assets and strict agreements the wife and her children are not able to join the husband and his children on special vacations; the husband's children can dress better than the wife's children, and they can have toys, or horses, or cars that the wife's children cannot afford. When this is the case, the feelings can go right off the top of the scale.

Adoption, Naming and Inheritance

Stepfathers frequently decide to adopt their stepchildren as a demonstration of their affection and commitment. One-third of all adoptions in the United States are of stepchildren by their step-fathers. When the natural father is still living, many authors advocate a cautious approach to this decision. The severing of a tie to a blood parent can be a difficult experience for a child. If the natural father is still living, he must approve the decision (Egleson and Egleson, 1961).

Spock (1962) points out that it is basic human nature for a child to want to feel loyal to his own parent and think of him, whatever and wherever he is. The age and wishes of the children should effect an adoption decision. Adoption does not in and of itself diminish problems since names do not create a sense of belonging to a family; relationships do that.

When adoption has taken place, the legal relationship of the child to the stepfather has been settled. The child takes the step-father's name, and there is no longer confusion at school about the child with one name and the parents with another. Now the step-parent is recognized legally and can sign medical release forms, driver's license forms for minor children, etc., and inheritance questions are solved once and for all.

Bernard (1956) states:

> Although adoption involves powerful legal sanctions, its impact on the assimilation process is probably primarily symbolic . . . It is doubtful if the kind of man who is willing to

adopt his wife's children would be any less conscientious in his behavior toward children without the legal sanction of adoption. His "fathership" is not improved by formalization of the relationship. It is the symbolic aspect of the adoption that is important (p. 22).

As previously discussed, some stepfathers are not eager to assume legal and financial responsibility for their stepchildren:

> One stepfather with a distinguished family name complained, "How do other stepparents feel about a strange child taking their names? He just uses my name. He wants it. He won't change his other name legally, and there are all sorts of embarrassments with passports and things. But my family name, well, I suppose I'm ridiculous, but it's an old New England name and I resent him using it!" This man did not object to the fact that the boy, who had lived with him since infancy, called him Daddy (Maddox, 1975, p. 7).

Maddox outlines the pros and cons of adopting stepchildren:

> . . . Adoption is permanent, and it gives the stepchild status and rights indistinguishable from any other child of the marriage. For many stepfamilies it spells emotional security. The stepparent need not fear losing the child, and the child's natural anxiety about the stepparent withdrawing affection will be allayed and he will have less need to be jealous of the new babies born to the marriage. It ends the business of the incest taboos in the stepfamily. . . .
> The arguments against are also powerful. They center on the fact that adoption not only creates a new family link, it destroys one. Adoption by stepparent implies that a natural parent has been deprived of his parental rights, and not always voluntarily. There are a number of states with statutes providing that the consent of a parent to adoption is not necessary if he has been deprived of custody in a divorce. Yet losing custody is far less drastic than losing parental rights . . . (p. 169).

One situation in which adoption might seem to have definite indications is one in which a parental relationship of long-standing exists between a stepparent and a stepchild. In order to avoid having custody of the child awarded to the other natural parent, in the event of the death of the custodial parent, when it might not be in the best interests of the child, adoption would seem to be something that might be seriously considered.

No general rule can be established about adoption and changes in the legal relationship of the stepchild and the stepparent. If the relationships within the stepfamily are tense and unrewarding, adoption is not a cure for this unhappiness. And adoption workers point out that the manner in which the custodial parents view the biologic parents of an adopted child has an importance for the welfare of the child that is similar to stepfamily relationships. In both adoptions and in stepfamilies, the good adjustment of the child is positively correlated with the degree of acceptance that the custodial parents have of the child's natural parents. There are many factors of a highly individual character which must be weighed in each instance, and a final decision on adoption may need to be made with professional assistance.

Sexuality in the Stepfamily

The need to deal with sexuality within a stepfamily unit can be a greater source of tension than in a nuclear family. Young children suddenly living together may develop strong affectional and even sexual feelings for one another which are often concealed by fighting and discord. Teenagers who have not grown up together suddenly find themselves in close living quarters, and with the emerging sexuality of these years sexual attraction and stimulation are much more likely than between teenagers who have lived together since childhood.

Stepfathers may find stepdaughters attracted to them and behaving in seductive ways, and these feelings are sometimes returned, particularly when things are not going well in the marital relationship. Repressed impulses are perhaps less rigidly controlled because of a weakened "incest taboo" which applies to blood relationships. The novel *Lolita* describes the attraction of one stepfather for his adolescent stepdaughter.

It is difficult to obtain accurate data on the frequency of sexual relationships between stepfathers and stepdaughters as compared to natural fathers and daughters. In a clinic specializing in the treatment of incestual relationships, 50 percent of the client families include stepfathers and stepdaughters. This would appear to reflect an increased rate of sexual relationships between stepfathers and stepdaughters since much less than 50 percent of families are stepfather families. However, the fact that stepfamilies are less cohesive than intact families may result in more sexual acts between step-relations being reported.

It is clear that sexuality plays a more prominent part in stepfamilies than nuclear families because of the joining together of groups of individuals, many of whom are pubescent or sexually mature children. In addition, there are newlyweds in the home. "For me that house was far more sexual than the one I had been used to before the divorce," said one young woman in regards to her mother's remarriage. "In the first house nobody ever touched each other at all. For the first 15 years of my life my parents sat at the opposite sides of the room and that was always true. And then all of a sudden this new household where parents were touching each other all the time . . . I didn't know what to make of that kind of environment."

The more open sexuality between the newly married couple is stimulating to the children, in contrast to children in an intact family, who are not so aware of the times when their parents are affectionate with each other.

In her study of stepfamilies, Gerda Schulman (1972) found that many mothers were jealous of the relationship between their daughters and the girls' stepfathers. She found that stepfathers often became overcritical of their stepdaughters for fear that their wives would misinterpret their interest in their stepdaughters. In other instances Schulman felt that the stepfathers withdrew because they feared that they might not be able to control their sexual impulses towards their stepdaughters.

Therapists and counselors are more than familiar with Oedipus and Phaedra themes in the analytic literature. These unconscious elements have a heightened effect in the stepfamily, as the son confronts another man taking his place with his mother, and a daughter competes for the attention of the substitute-father. However, despite the need to deal with stronger sexual feelings, having a stepfather in the home can be beneficial to the children since sons can identify with an effective male model, and daughters can learn about masculinity and maturity from an important adult male figure.

7

Working with

men in

stepfamilies

It seems as though women go into therapy and men go into court. This tendency may result from two major influences:

1. The emphasis in America that has been placed on men to be action-and achievement-oriented. In contrast, women have been expected to be relationship-oriented. Only recently have these models begun to shift.

2. For the most part, following a divorce men do not have custody of their children or do not have physical custody of their children even if "joint custody" has been stipulated. Being at least partially cut off from their children has left countless fathers feeling helpless and out of control of their relationships with their children. Many fathers withdraw and even disappear in response to the pain this causes them. Others battle with their ex-wives and seek legal action in an attempt to establish or regain a relationship with their children. For many men these attempts do not alleviate the feelings of helplessness, and their anger increases rather than diminishes. One such man expressed himself by saying, "The court system has taken away any feeling of power that I have. I feel helpless."

Remarriages does not eliminate custody or visitation problems.

For many men in stepfamilies custody battles begin after their remarriage because at that time many fathers feel that they are once again in a position to offer a home to their children. In other cases custody issues at the time of a father's remarriage arise from a different source: the mother's fear of the loss of custody of her children to the father now that he has remarried. If both parents have shared custody (joint custody) the mother may now attempt to obtain sole custody of the children to prevent them from moving away from her into their father's new home. The fact that another adult female has entered the picture can at times throw a previously relaxed custody arrangement into disarray. The need to "share" children introduces an emotional dimension not encountered in nuclear families.

Visitation agreements also can change after a remarriage. In some instances fathers wish to see their children more often when they have a wife with whom to share the care of the children when they visit.

The emotional relationship between parent and child is a very basic relationship, and a disruption in this relationship stirs many deep and powerful feelings. The feelings of hurt and anger, and the sense of loss and failure which can accompany the dissolution of a marriage relationship often produce a difficult climate for working out visitation and custody issues. Many of these feelings remain or are reactivated when an ex-spouse remarries, so that clashes over visitation and custody arrangements are common.

If agreement cannot be reached in these areas fathers often seek the help of an attorney. Some attorneys and courts are beginning to realize the deep emotional conflicts underlying custody and visitation issues, and as a result there is an increasing liaison between attorneys and mental health professionals. This is a step in a needed direction, and it is to be hoped that, as sophistication grows in the area of custody and visitation issues, parents will receive more help in working out satisfactory solutions. Many of the problems for men in stepfamilies are related to difficulties arising from the disruption of their relationship with their children, and from difficulties surrounding their attempts to become a functional part of the newly formed stepfamily unit.

WORKING WITH INDIVIDUAL FATHERS/STEPFATHERS

When the initial therapeutic contact is made by a man, he tends to call because of the stepmother's reactions to his children or to himself. One frequent complaint from a husband is that his wife is upset because she feels left out when his children visit. As has been mentioned, "weekend fathers" often feel guilty about the short amount of time they have with their children and they may exclude their wives emotionally, if not otherwise, when their children are with them. One wife talked of her feelings this way:

> Whenever his kids come Sam drops everything else and rushes off to take them sailing. They sail all weekend and the kids love it. Sailing's not my thing and there isn't room for me in the boat anyway. I work all week too and I'd like to go out with Sam for dinner and a movie once in a while Saturday night. But it doesn't happen because by then he's too tired after sailing all day. My kids are gone on the weekends so there I am alone at home cleaning up the place. Sam's kids have him all to themselves and they lap it up. I'm glad Sam wants to be with his boys but I'm getting lonely and I feel mad and left out. Sam says I'm being selfish because he and I see each other all week and he only sees his boys on the weekends.

Another frequent presenting complaint has to do with the wife's upset over the care of the husband's children when they are with their mother. Bill's call to a counselor illustrates such a situation as he says that he has been remarried for five months and his wife is very upset over his ex-wife's care of the children. His three children live with him and his new family and his son and stepson share a room. Colette (Bill's wife) is extremely concerned because her son is unhappy at sharing a bedroom with his stepbrother because this 12-year-old stepbrother is smoking pot. Bill's ex-wife allows her son to smoke pot and even supplies him with it. Bill is feeling extremely upset and caught in the middle between the two women.

When Bill came for an appointment with the counselor, he elaborated on his dilemma. He did not approve of his son's smoking pot, but he also did not agree with Colette that his son should not be allowed to visit with his ex-wife, since his ex-wife was the child's mother and therefore had a right to see all of her children. Bill agreed to talk with his ex-wife about the situation and he felt certain they could come to some agreement about the matter because he had maintained a good relationship with her in the past. It soon became clear, however, that cooperation between Bill and his ex-wife had declined now that he was remarried to Colette. Bill had difficulty acknowledging the shift and was at a loss to think of what he might do if changes could not so easily be worked out. When the counselor suggested that he and Colette might come together for an appointment, Bill stated that Colette did not consider the matter her problem and that she would not come. In response to the further suggestion that Bill himself might find it helpful to have an outside person with whom to talk, Bill could see no reason to come by himself. His reason for coming once was to determine who was right and who was wrong: Was it right for his son to visit with his ex-wife or was it wrong? Since the counselor had not settled this issue and was thinking in terms of exploration, communication, and consideration of various alternatives, Bill saw no need to pursue the matter further. Although the pattern is changing, many men still appear to consider that family dynamics are the woman's responsibility, and see little value in pursuing family issues individually.

In Bill's case, for example, it might have been helpful to the stepfamily if he had been willing to examine his alternatives in dealing with his wife and with his ex-wife. Bill was withdrawing and becoming more passive as he felt more pressure being put on him by Colette. His withdrawal was aggravating to Colette and their relationship was deteriorating. As he withdrew, she became more upset, which caused Bill to withdraw even more. With help Bill might have been able to gain a sense of more control and become more active, dealing with his ex-wife effectively, thus improving his and Colette's relationship.

As has been previously discussed, men who are stepfathers often have difficulties in breaking into an already formed group of mother and children. Their wives sometimes are willing to seek help from an outside person to aid in the integration process, but it is not a need which men acknowledge easily. Whereas mothers or stepmothers often feel individually responsible for stress within their stepfamilies, fathers and stepfathers do not usually appear to feel the same individual responsibility.

Men with custody of their children living in single-parent households often do seek professional help as they take increased parental responsibility for their children.

With the shift in American society in the direction of equal sharing of parental and homemaking tasks between both partners, more men are sharing the responsibility for the smooth running of intact families and of stepfamilies. This may result in more men seeking professional help even when their wives are reluctant to participate.

Although men may not seek individual therapeutic help they explore many specific issues when they come with their wives or their families for counseling or therapy:

1. The feeling of having failed as a father in a first marriage can lead to a man's being more committed to being a stepfather. He may take more interest in his stepchildren and be more supportive of them than he was of his children in his previous family. And with the feeling of being less responsible for what kind of individuals his stepchildren turn out to be, a stepfather may be more relaxed and accepting of his stepchildren's behavior than of his biological children's behavior. If he is living with his stepchildren this acceptance can be very meaningful to the stepchildren in terms of their growth and development. In contrast, for some stepfathers their reaction to a sense of failure as a parent in a first marriage is to try to make the stepfamily "turn out right." In this case the stepfather's pressure on the stepchildren can make for problems, and he needs therapeutic help to gain an awareness of what he is attempting to do.

2. The stepfather may not have experienced the traumas, the illnesses and the "terrible two's," and as a result he may be more objective than the mother about her children, and thus provide a needed balance if the couple can work together on raising the

children. If the children are younger this can happen to a greater extent than if the children are older. With older children who are more independent there is less stepfamily cohesiveness and less adult-child interaction.

3. Sometimes stepfathers who have not had sons before, or daughters before, are happy to have a stepson or a stepdaughter. As long as they do not have unrealistic expectations of children, and do not attempt to import a style they felt worked for their first family, the relationships may be rewarding to all concerned. In stepfamilies where there is a warm relationship between a stepfather and a stepchild, the relationship with his natural children may be effected. His natural children may see him for weekends and vacations and may resent his attention to his stepchildren. Balancing the many relationships is a complicated task.

4. Discipline problems are often major upsets in stepfamilies. For men who have experienced little control in their growing years, and perhaps in their first marriage as well, the anxiety caused by ambiguity and the need for control can push them into attempting to exert control soon after they become stepfathers. Often they are harsh disciplinarians and the stepfamily becomes fragmented as the stepchildren rebel and the wife/mother feels torn between her children and her husband.

Mike is an example of a father/stepfather who experienced extreme distress after his remarriage. Mike's father had died when he was young and he had lived with his grandparents for several years until he was older and more independent, after which time his mother was in a financial position to have him come to live with her. Mike left home and became self-supporting at an early age. He worked for a small company and within a few years, at the age of 22, he formed a small company of his own. Soon after that he married and had two children. Mike and his first wife had a poor relationship and they divorced after six years of marriage.

Mike had experienced several losses of parents and grandparents at a young age, and as a result he had withdrawn from close interpersonal relationships. He also had felt "out of control" in his growing years and it became important to him to be in control. No doubt because of this need he had chosen a work situation that he could control—one in which he was in the position of authority.

After being divorced for four years Mike married a woman slightly older than himself who had two children. His new wife was more nurturing and less demanding of Mike's attention than was his first wife. She also needed help managing her children, who were 10 and 12. Mike considered that the children were undisciplined and he immediately stepped in and attempted to be a firm disciplinarian. When the children visited with their father they were allowed "to do as they pleased," and when they were with him and their mother Mike saw his wife as being unable to set limits. Mike had lost contact with his natural children because there were problems working out definite visitation agreements with his ex-wife. The uncertainty of scheduling visits with his children was "driving him crazy," so Mike stopped seeing his natural children and concentrated on providing rules and regulations for his stepchildren.

Within six months the stepfamily was disintegrating. Mike's wife was depressed and feeling hopeless, the children were rebellious and failing in school, and Mike was furious at everyone. Mike fought constantly with his stepchildren and with his wife, and the harder he tried to control the situation the worse it got. Finally Mike agreed to accompany his wife for counseling but this attempt was short-lived. Mike believed the only solution to the problem lay in his wife's "standing up to the children," and setting very strict limits. She agreed that she did need to be more firm, but she could not accept the strictness of his standards. As far as Mike was concerned, he needed to change nothing, and he soon terminated both the counseling and the marriage.

Because of his early history Mike had difficulty in situations he could not control. His first wife wanted more from him than he felt comfortable in giving, and after the divorce the ambiguity in the situation with his children resulted in his moving away from his natural children. Mike remarried a woman who was more like his mother and did not expect to receive the emotional support and sharing his first wife had required. However, Mike's stepfamily situation was even more out of control than was his first marriage and Mike failed at his attempts to get it under control. Unrealistic expectations and lack of understanding of the reactions in newly formed stepfamilies prevented Mike from having any clear awareness of the difficulties. There was another parent outside of the household whom he could not control; he could not get his wife to set limits; and his stepchildren had no desire to please him or obey his orders. Stepfamily structure combined with individual dynamics, so that the control that Mike had anticipated bringing to the stepfamily did not materialize, and within six months the marriage became intolerable to him.

Tom, in contrast, was able to utilize therapy to put his expectations of himself and of his children and stepchildren into perspective. Although Tom was the person to make the initial contact with a therapist, he did not wish to be seen alone. His wife of six months was more than willing to come with him. The five children were not seen. After two months of weekly meetings the remarried family was making good progress towards integration.

When the couple came for the first appointment both agreed on the problem: The three boys and two girls were making their lives miserable. They felt the children were out of control and Tom and his wife, Alicia, were discouraged and feeling that the remarriage was more than either one of them could handle.

Alicia's two children, a boy and a girl, lived with her and Tom while Tom's three children lived with their mother and were with Tom and Alicia for weekends and for some vacation periods. Tom's daughter and one son were close in age to his stepchildren while his younger son was only six, four years younger than the youngest of the other four children.

Until recently Tom's three children had come on the weekends without many complaints, but now his children had been refusing to be with their father and stepmother. Previously when they had come the four older children had enjoyed playing games together, but the younger child had raised a fuss all weekend and had been hit and yelled at by the older children. The weekends had become chaotic.

During the week, the situation with Alicia's two children was somewhat more peaceful, except that whenever Tom would ask his stepchildren to do something the two children would refuse to obey. If he insisted on anything, his stepson would become very angry and had even kicked Tom during one violent exchange.

Alicia wanted to be helpful but both adults felt that Tom and his stepchildren needed to work the situation out between themselves. Alicia was also disturbed by the anger that her children had begun showing towards her. Alicia and Tom could still work together most of the time, but the tension had begun to put a strain on their relationship and Tom's children were beginning to act in ways that caused heated arguments between Alicia and Tom. A major source of conflict revolved around the fact that Tom's three children would whine until Tom granted their requests even though he knew he was giving permission for something that violated house rules.

Tom was the new person trying to find a place in an ongoing family system, and his children were also concerned with their status in the new family. Alicia's children resented having to share their home and their mother and had no emotional commitment to Tom so that they did not care whether they acted in a way that would please him. In the therapeutic sessions the opportunity Tom and Alicia had to ventilate their feelings, together with knowledge gained from readings and direct suggestions from the psychiatrist, brought about many positive changes within a few weeks:

1. Tom recognized that he needed to build a relationship between himself and his two stepchildren before the children would be willing to accept discipline from him. Until this relationship existed, Alicia needed to be the one to work with her children on limit-setting. She and Tom could work together at times when the situation involved Tom, and slowly Tom would be able to act independently in this regard. To accomplish this, Tom began to play games occasionally with his stepchildren, and have them accompany him when he went on errands. There would be an ice

cream cone for each, or some similar treat from time to time. In this way a bond between them began to develop.

2. Tom was feeling guilty about being a "weekend" father and this made it difficult for him to stick with the household rules when his children pushed for him to bend the limits. Tom also felt helpless about having any lasting influence on his children. As a result he became somewhat withdrawn and passive when the children were with him.

Tom reacted positively to the concept that his children did "live" with him part of each week. He bought a special dresser for each of them so they had toys and clothes and a spot of their own in his home. Tom also accepted that he could indeed be an influence in his children's lives when they were with him, and he became active rather than passive in his contacts with them.

3. The couple recognized that Tom's youngest son was disruptive because he felt left out and had no one his age with whom to play. When it would work out, a young friend was invited to spend the weekend so this youngest child would have a playmate. Tom also made a point of playing catch with the six-year-old and encouraging neighborhood children his son's age to join the game. This helped the little boy find friends in the neighborhood in which his father and stepmother lived. It also left the older children alone so that they could play their more grown-up games without interference from a younger child. The fighting between the children diminished greatly.

4. With the tension reduced, Tom and Alicia were relating more smoothly, and Tom was feeling much more adequate as a father and stepfather. Alicia was more relaxed with her children and they were settling down. Tom's expectations of his children and stepchildren were more realistic, and as his guilt decreased Tom had less difficulty setting limits for his children. Once again, Tom's children were willing to come for the weekends, and the stepfamily planned family outings from time to time that they all enjoyed.

WORKING WITH MEN IN GROUPS

There are an increasing number of consciousness-raising groups for men but groups for men that are focused on family difficulties seem to be a rarity, if indeed they do exist.

While groups for stepmothers have been reported (Sardanis-Zimmerman, 1978), groups for stepfathers only have not been reported. In the literature there is one paper concerned with a group for stepfathers and their wives (Mowatt, 1972).

In Mowatt's group, three couples were chosen who had children exhibiting problem behavior who could not be seen in individual treatment at the time. Although the variety in stepfamily structure was great, "group treatment from the first moments provided these couples with an accepting peer group and identification models. In the first session they expressed surprise that such nice parents could have such difficult children! . . . The common bonds of remarriage and stepparenthood seemed to accelerate the growth of solidarity, which usually appears more gradually in parents' groups" (Mowatt, 1972, pp. 328-329). Mowatt's paper gives a good description of what took place during the six-month period of weekly meetings. The three couples exhibited similar dynamics, and all three families were helped by the group experience of the couples.

The wives had viewed their husbands as "saviours" for their families, and when their husbands began disciplining their children, the wives became upset and considered the discipline to be too strict. Attempting to work together on discipline problems created many tensions, and very often the couples used the ex-spouses as targets in their own interpersonal disagreements.

Rivalry between stepfathers and their stepsons was discussed, as were sexual problems, means of giving affection to stepchildren, and the pitfalls to avoid in dealing with the children. However, by far the most important theme was discipline and the enforcement of rules within the stepfamily.

CHANGING ROLES FOR MEN

Parents often become acutely aware of their relationships with their children when a divorce has taken place. Many fathers are now willing to accept their nurturing qualities, and are beginning to take a more active role in family relationships. An article by Daniel D. Molinoff (1977) describes the changes in custody arrangements that occur as an increasing number of fathers are seeking custody of their children following a divorce. Molinoff reports that "most fathers maintain that they do not seek sole custody out of vindictiveness or as a ploy to reduce alimony. Rather they stress a coming to terms with their own nurturing instincts.

"As they accept the fact that today's women are fighting for equality, the men demand equality in their fight for custody liberation. . . . Husbands are arguing that since children are not being reared exclusively by mothers and are surviving the experience, the mother is not indispensable to a child's development."

Increasing attention is being given to the influence that fathers have on the growth and development of their children. The importance to a child of keeping a relationship with both parents after a divorce is being documented (Nolan, 1977; Kelly and Wallerstein, 1976) . Now that men as well as women are putting a high priority on their parenting and stepparenting roles, mental health professionals may find an increasing number of men seeking help in developing these skills and understanding the emotional complexities of interpersonal relationships within their family or stepfamily. Transition periods bring conflicts as old roles disappear in the evolution of the new roles. One-third of all American children under 18 are now living with only one biological parent. In the past, custody issues were clear: Except in cases where she was declared "unfit" the children remained with the mother. Since this area of custody is changing so rapidly, divorcing parents are now facing the difficult and often conflictual task of making conscious decisions in regards to the care of their children.

As the new role definitions for both men and women become culturally and personally acceptable, the children stand to gain if they experience a continuing relationship with both divorced parents. Remarriage then can represent the gain of another adult without the corresponding loss of a previous parental relationship.

During these years of transition in parental roles, it seems likely that an increasing number of men as well as women will be seeking therapeutic assistance as a result of these changes.

8

Recoupling—

stepfamily couples

In a first marriage the couple is moving together into a totally different pattern from their previous living situations. They are exploring together their ways of relating as married individuals and as "nest builders." Roles become defined slowly, and the character of the home evolves gradually. Wedding gifts often reflect joint requests of the couple. A new sofa is purchased after considerable deliberation. And dreams of careers and family become refined as jobs are found suitable or not; pets and pregnancy pave the way to added family responsibility. A library becomes a nursery, a baby is born and a new individual unfolds from day to day. Answers are sought as problems arise.

In stepfamilies, the forming of a viable satisfying new couple unit is frequently a very difficult task. Prior to remarriages, the dreams have turned to nightmares, or at least have become unpleasant. The trappings of the former life-style, however, continue. Family style and values have usually become familiar and continue through single parenting and into remarriage. If the values of the two adults are similar, the "merger" can be relatively smooth. The usual merger, though, is between two individual or groups who have gradually acquired certain tastes, needs, and relationships that are quite different from each other. An antique grandfather clock bumps the low ceiling as it stands awkwardly beside a modern plastic and aluminum chair. A standard VW and a Chrysler Imperial park together in the garage with great discomfort. Discussions between stepfamily members become as one couple put it, "continuous group therapy with each group being acutely aware of the interpersonal interactions of the other group."

Being the overseers of these mergers becomes a monumental task, the difficulties of which have not been anticipated by the couple. One woman put it clearly in talking about the break-up of her second marriage: "My husband and I were stoned on each other and we thought everything would be okay with the children. But we soon learned that being stoned on each other wasn't enough. I tried for five years. He was a very nice man, but we just couldn't make it." Another woman reports: "We went for counseling but the counselor kept putting himself into our situation and we couldn't live up to his expectations. So things got worse and we divorced. The counselor couldn't understand our stepfamily problems."

Obviously, the difficulties in stepfamily relationships for men and women that were outlined earlier overlap and are intertwined with the couple interactions to be discussed in this chapter. A woman's expectations of herself, her insecurity in the unfamiliar role, and her anxiety, competitiveness, and anger, together with the man's guilt, sense of inadequacy in his new role, competitiveness and feelings of pressure, make for many troubled relationships between remarried couples where there are children from a previous marriage. These emotions, together with other pressures, make for problems in recoupling.

In a recent study of family functioning, Jerry Lewis and colleagues (1976, p. 210), report that one very important dimension in psychologically healthy families is the cohesiveness of the couple in the family. If the relationship between the spouses is strong and withstands attempts by the children to split or weaken the alliance, the family unit is able to cope successfully. In stepfamilies there are more strains than in most intact families, and as a result the alliance or coalition between the couple seems particularly important and also more difficult to achieve and maintain. While there can be similar pressures for intact families, the number of stepfamilies feeling such pressures, as well the negative quality of the pressures, can be magnified many times.

EXTERNAL PRESSURES ON THE COUPLE

Moving into the Partner's Neighborhood

One type of problem which frequently interferes with efforts to establish a strong bond between the remarried couple occurs when wives or husbands move from other locations into the area in which their spouses have been living. The most frequent pattern is for wives to move. These wives are outsiders and may get compared unfavorably to former wives by their husband's friends, relatives and business associates.

It is even harder if a wife moves into the same house in which her husband has lived previously. Friends and in-laws often seem like enemies, and the couple may feel torn apart and unable to deal together with these outside people in their lives. Such a situation was faced by Yvonne and Dick when Yvonne moved into the home where Dick, his wife, and their three children had been living prior to his wife's death.

> *Dick*: Yvonne and I started out being demonstrative and affectionate with one another, but it wasn't enough. We tried to stay together, to back each other up, but we didn't do a very good job of it. I understood Yvonne was having trouble but I didn't know what to do about it. I wanted to say to my friends, "Here's my new wife. We're different than the other couple (Dick and his first wife) even though we live in the same house." But it just didn't work out. We expected it to. At least I did.

> *Yvonne*: I did too. I thought it was just going to be fine . . . I had no idea . . . I was just a new bride and I thought people would be happy the children had someone to care for them.

> *Dick*: People were nice when Yvonne was first introduced, but then later on the newness and the curiosity wore off,

and no one came around. I didn't know what to do about it. I just thought time would cure it . . . and then the first year came and went . . .

Yvonne: And then it went into the second year and I could see that it wasn't going to change and I said, "Let's get out of here."

Another wife remembered the early years of her second marriage:

Another thing that made it hard for me was that I moved into Don's territory and I never had a feeling of being accepted. The only place I felt secure was within my own home. When I walked in the front door I was secure. When I got outside my front door I felt very insecure. I can remember that once in a grocery store, after we'd been married for a few years, I met somebody that I'd known before. She came up and was nice to me, and I absolutely broke down and cried. Her friendliness was so unexpected I started to cry, I just simply had to leave the store.

Although a remarriage does not seem sudden to the couple, to former friends and neighbors it often appears as a sudden change. Sudden changes stir anxiety in many individuals and at times produces a rejection of the couple or of the new person coming into the area. Other factors, such as friendship with the ex-spouse, negative feelings about divorce and remarriage, identification with the stepchildren, or discomfort at seeing others divorce and remarry when one's own marriage is unsatisfying, also can lead to negative community pressures on the remarried couple.

Negative Responses from In-Laws

Many couples talk of problems with one or both sets of parents.

Mary: "Since my remarriage neither one of my parents will have anything to do with me or with their grandchildren. They've disinherited us all completely. John's parents keep some contact with their grandchildren but only through his ex-wife. Instead of sending birthday or Christmas presents to his kids at our house, even though his kids live with us, they send gifts to their grandchildren at John's ex-wife's house. And they help her with money all the time too.

John's parents only seem to phone him to complain about his not doing enough for the kids or for his ex-wife.

Ralph: My mother disowned me when I got divorced. She didn't contact me in any way for three to four years. She told my ex-wife not to let me see my children in the hopes I'd stay married, and when I remarried a woman with children, she wrote my ex-wife that this woman was marrying me to get my money and have someone to look after her children. It was a bad beginning to our marriage.

Alice: My new in-laws won't have anything to do with me or my children. They give presents to their own grandchildren, but don't even give a card to their stepgrandchildren. And they don't even give Dick and me a joint gift at Christmas. They always get a sweater or something just for Dick. If they come to see us they don't even look at me or talk to me. They just chatter away as though my children and I don't exist. And Dick just basks in their attention and I get so hurt and angry at them, at him, at everybody.

On the other hand, in a number of stepfamilies it is the in-laws, the grandparents/stepgrandparents, who can relate well with all the children in the stepfamily and create a feeling of unity between the couple.

Unfortunately, responses of in-laws similar to those quoted occur frequently and may result in friction between the couple. For example, the favored spouse does not notice his or her parents' rejection of the other spouse, fears anger from parents if an issue is made, and attempts to have the rejected individual "try harder to get along" or "not be so sensitive" to the coldness or neglect of the new in-laws. In some situations, of course, rejection by in-laws, particularly if it is by both sets of parents, binds the couple together in their struggle against a common threat.

As Simon (1964) comments, grandparents often step in after a divorce and take care of the children, and relate once again to the parents, their children, as they did before that parent's marriage. Therefore, the grandparents often feel displaced and displeased with a remarriage, and are hostile towards the new person in this remarriage.

Characteristics of Community Institutions

It was pointed out in the introductory chapter that schools, Boy Scouts, churches, and most community organizations are not yet structured to deal easily with stepfamilies. The intact or nuclear family has been well served by these institutions in the past and in the present, but the time lag in recognizing and validating this new family structure leads to problems for the remarried couple. One major difficulty occurs when a stepparent is confused about his or her role, the community is confused about the stepparents' role, and this double confusion tends to isolate the stepparent from the rest of the stepfamily, thus driving a wedge between the couple.

One common assumption is that unless the adult's surname is the same as the child's surname, the adult has little concern about the successes, failures, or disasters affecting that child. While it is true that some stepparents have little to do with their stepchildren, most stepparents care about the welfare of their stepchildren. This is true even when the stepparent has strong conflictual feelings towards the stepchild.

When the school recognizes only the two natural parents of a child, if a stepparent exists, this lack of recognition reduces the stepfamily couple alliance. The stepparent often feels tentative about participating in the school in the first place, and lack of inclusion reinforces this tendency and increased withdrawal may follow. This withdrawal can increase the natural parent's school involvement, as well as contributing to tension between the couple.

The role of the stepparent varies depending on the particular stepfamily constellation, and it seems wise for schools, churches, etc., to be aware of the need to create opportunities for stepparents to participate as they feel comfortable. Stepparents need to know that they are acknowledged and are welcome. Both the school and the members of the stepfamily can benefit from this.

Recently a stepmother spoke enthusiastically about her local police department. She had called the department to report a stolen bicycle. After giving the child's name, description of the bicycle, etc., the officer asked very matter-of-factly, "Is your name the same as your son's?" In this case the name *was* the same, but this woman's joy in the conscious recognition by the police that individuals in a family do not necessarily have the same surname indicates the discomfort stepfamilies may have with the existence of mismatched last names.

Legal Considerations

Donald Lunde, a professor in the areas of both law and the family at Stanford University, expresses the opinion of many stepfamily couples when he says that family law is very antiquated as it refers to stepfamily situations. Custody and visitation rights are terms regularly used in reference to prisoners in jail rather than to parents and children (Ricci, 1976). As Ricci says, "The use of these words promotes the position that one parent has all the authority, responsibility and rights, while the 'visitor' parent has to meekly obey all the rules of procedure in order to be allowed access to the institution."

New custody and parenting arrangements have been proposed (Woolley, 1975), but as yet most laws are unchanged despite the changes in family patterns.

The fact that stepparents have no legal rights regarding their stepchildren can create many problems if there is a death or divorce in a stepfamily. A 38-year-old woman, Marie, was recently admitted to the hospital because of severe depression. Twelve years ago Marie had married a man whose wife had died shortly after the birth of their daughter. The baby was nine months old when Marie and her husband were married, and Marie raised the little girl until the child was ten years of age.

Marie and her husband divorced at this point, and despite Marie's pleas, the little girl remained with her father. Marie had no claim to the child because she was not the natural mother.

For the two years since the divorce Marie has been attempting to get custody of her stepdaughter. She has talked to attorneys and even to her congressman. They all tell her she has no chance of getting custody of the girl. Only occasionally does Marie's ex-husband allow her to visit with the little girl and every time she sees a little girl her stepdaughter's age Marie becomes depressed; this time she became so depressed that she needed to be hospitalized. Marie's depression is increasing as her anger and sense of helplessness grows. There is nothing she can do to fight for the child she raised.

Of course, the court might not award the custody of the child to Marie if, indeed, it were legally possible for her to have the matter referred to the court. However, legal visitation rights might be worked out in such a situation, and Marie would have the satisfaction of knowing that she had the right to visit with and to be heard with regard to future plans for the young girl.

Even when the situation is less basic, remarried couples are unequal in many important areas. In many locations, parents without custody cannot sign for medical procedures or for a driver's license for his or her child. A stepparent can never sign, even when the stepchild is living with him or her. This means, as frequently happens, that a child may be hurt and the stepparent is helpless because there is no legality to the relationship. When asked, hospitals reply that in case of "life or death" procedures a doctor is able to sign if the stepparent and not the parent brings the child to the hospital.

One stepmother told of rushing her stepdaughter to a hospital when the little girl hurt herself to be told that she could not sign the medical release for the needed treatment because she was not a legal guardian. "It's almost as though we don't exist," was the stepmother's comment, "and I feel that way sometimes." If the stepmother had had a power of attorney for the child, or if the custodial parent or parents had signed a form authorizing the stepmother to represent the parent, then she would have been able to complete the form.

Attorneys have commented that obtaining legal documents authorizing a stepparent to sign for medical or dental procedures may be more complicated than it sounds, because anger on the part of a custodial parent at times is expressed by a refusal to sign the form. Stepparents with minor children need to be aware of the necessity for such an authorization.

Another illustration concerns the conciliation court. Stepparents frequently go uncounted in matters before the conciliation court, even though they are a very live part of the child's world. One 12-year-old girl, Laurie, who lived with her mother and stepfather and visited with her father every weekend, began to grow restless with this arrangement and wanted to have more leisure time with her peers. Her mother tried to arrange this with the father, but he refused. Laurie tried to arrange it with her father but he refused. So, eventually, Laurie, her mother, her father, and her stepfather went to meet with the conciliation court to iron out the matter. For three hours the court counselor met with Laurie, her mother, and her father, while her stepfather, with whom she lived, was required to wait alone in the lobby.

Family law, like other societal institutions, has difficulty shifting quickly enough to meet the needs of altered family patterns. This means that for stepfamilies there are times when the law rather than personal choice may be a factor in the dilution of a stepparent couple relationship, or a stepparent-stepchild relationship.

INTERNAL PRESSURES ON THE COUPLE

Differences in Life-Style

A major barrier to interpersonal harmony is the difficulty individuals have in tolerating and accepting feelings, needs, opinions, and ways of doing things that are different from their own. Incompatibility between people makes for trouble in first marriages, and in subsequent relationships the differences that need to be worked out are magnified considerably because of the complexity of the family structure and the fact that the parental and marital pattern of each of the couple has developed and solidified before the present relationship.

When there has been a divorce, obviously the first relationship has not been mutually satisfying to the couple, but even so certain styles of adult behavior have been developed, and distinct living styles have emerged. Successfully joining together parents from two very different systems requires considerable tolerance and flexibility on the part of the individuals involved. Even seemingly unimportant characteristics become unbearable irritants because they occur over and over and over. As one parent said, "The trouble with life is it's daily." Other parents and stepparents have commented:

"My children were raised not to swear, and my stepchildren are allowed to swear all the time."

"We always said grace before meals and those little heathens think grace is a woman's name."

"I had grown up with my girls from the time they were born until they were eight and ten, and then suddenly I have to relate to a 14-year-old boy. I'm bewildered. I know nothing about 14-year-old boys and I don't know what to expect next. I'd like to be a good example for him, but I don't know what he wants."

"I'm used to living in a big sprawly place. My husband lived in a city apartment. We did get our own home, but it's tiny and crowded and sometimes I feel like I'm going to scream. It doesn't bother him, but having everyone under foot drives me crazy."

"My wife thinks it's right to let the children take care of their own homework, and I've been used to seeing it was done before the kids could watch TV. This is a constant battle between us."

Working out these different and long-standing patterns is more than many remarried couples are able to do. They become enmeshed in constant quarrels about the right and wrong of the various alternatives, and have difficulty disengaging enough emotionally from their own value system or needs to work out new patterns together. Helping these couples to recognize that there is not a "right" way or a "wrong" way, but many ways, can do much to defuse the tensions in stepfamilies. The fact that the patterns have solidified over a number of years and have suddenly become questioned may lead to daily conflict, contributing immeasurably to the degree of anxiety and tension experienced by the couple, as well as by the children in the stepfamily.

Previous Bonds Existing to This Relationship

One of the unique characteristics of stepfamilies is that there have been bonds between parents and children before the present relationship between the two adults existed. This stepfamily characteristic is one that makes for many problems.

In first marriages the couple has time alone at the beginning of the relationship to form a bond between the two of them with no children intruding upon their privacy. There is a honeymoon period even if no honeymoon is scheduled. Then, as children are born, each one is assimilated into the family structure, and each parent's bond to the child is of equal time duration. In remarriage relationships it is difficult not to feel jealous as many cues remind the spouse that the partner's relationship with his or her children predates the present couple relationship, often by a considerable number of years. This generates a sense of exclusion. The couple's relationship has had little time to mature and become secure, so the previous family relationships which predate the remarriage relationship appear solid and therefore threatening. For a long time many couples consider, and often rightly so, that "if push came to shove" the spouse would choose his or her children over the adult partner. This breeds insecurity, which makes it difficult to achieve couple unity.

A father/stepfather outlined the situation clearly when he said,

> "Basically we are newlyweds faced with the problems of adjusting to each other. But on top of that we have to help all our children adjust to us, our marriage, and each other. It's hard enough for two people to adjust to living together, but when two families try it . . . ," his voice faded as he shook his head in bewilderment (Canton, 1977).

Because of a long association with natural children, "You're used to your own children's misbehavior patterns," said one father/stepfather. As a result there is friction between the couple as they view the children's behavior very, very differently.

Because the stepparent has not changed the stepchild's diapers, walked the floor during those first nights, watched each faltering step and heard each new word as the child grew older, the steprelationship begins with no gut level feeling about the stepchild similar to the feeling of the natural parent. As mentioned before, expectations that an adult with little previous contact with a child will feel the same way towards a child as an adult with a bond of long emotional significance is unrealistic and can create problems between the couple so deep that the couple bond may never be able to develop.

Another way in which the preexisting parent-child bonds affect the new couple relationship is in creating in many remarried parents strong feelings that they are being disloyal to and betraying their children if they form a primary bond with their new spouse. Children do experience loss when a remarried parent makes this commitment, but in the long run the needs of the children, as well as of the adults, are met because the stepfamily functions more effectively and the children have a model of a good couple relationship to influence their choice of a partner in the future.

The following letter and answer appeared recently in "Dear Abby," and illustrates in still another context how bonds predating the marriage cause tension and insecurity:

> *Dear Abby*: A year ago I married Ted. His wife (Maxine) died and left him with two children, ages six and eight. This is my first marriage.
>
> I say that after Maxine died, Ted is no longer related to Maxine's relatives. Ted says Maxine's parents will always be his in-laws.
>
> Well, I have parents, too, so where does that leave them? A person can only have one set of in-laws at a time, and *my* parents should be regarded as grandparents, too, and they aren't. The titles of "Grandma" and "Grandpa" go to Maxine's parents. My parents are called "Papa Pete" and "Mama Mary." Do you think this is fair? And what can I do about it? (Signed) *In-Law Trouble*
>
> *Dear Trouble*: Even though technically Ted is no longer the son-in-law of Maxine's parents, I advise you not to be so technical.
>
> There is a strong bond between Ted's former in-laws and their grandchildren, so if you're wise, you won't tamper with those bonds because they were established before you came into the picture. Grandparents are grandparents forever.

Relationships with Ex-spouses

The relationship with ex-spouses is a major area of difficulty for many remarried couples. If there has been a previous marriage in which there were no children, contact with the ex-spouse is usually dropped soon after the divorce. If, however, there have been children, there is most frequently a continuation of some type of relationship between the parents of those children. Fighting with each other about relationships with ex-spouses is an unfortunate occupation for many remarried couples. A common scenario may go something like this:

Just before the newly married couple, Louise and Ralph, turn off the lights for the night, the phone rings. Ralph's ex-wife is calling to talk to him about the trouble his children have been having in school. Ralph feels guilty that he left his children behind when he divorced, and so he wishes to let his ex-wife know that he is very interested in his children. Ralph also does not want to ask his ex-wife to call at another time, because he fears she may become angry and not let his children come for their next weekend visit with him and Louise.

So Ralph talks for 30 minutes to his ex-wife, while Louise lies beside him in bed, growing more and more upset. At first she says to herself, "Of course it is important for Ralph to know what is happening with his children. I have nothing to be jealous about— Ralph is married to me and he keeps telling me how he and his first wife couldn't get along. He loves me very much I know. But why does he talk so long? And he sounds so interested and sympathetic."

Finally Louise gets up in a sudden burst of anger, of which Ralph is aware. Anxiety crowds out his feelings of guilt—he feels caught somehow between two women. Uneasily Ralph draws the telephone conversation to a close and sputters at Louise for not being understanding. Ralph and Louise each feel let down by the other, unloved and unappreciated. They had anticipated this evening would be enveloped in closeness; instead it has degenerated to bickering about Ralph and his relationship with his ex-wife.

or

Lisa and Andy have been married for a year and the tension between them is building up. They never have any time alone because her children visit their father every weekend while his children usually visit Lisa and Andy on the weekends. There's little time alone and also no time that they can go to Disneyland or on a vacation all together. Andy would like to relate more with his stepchildren in a relaxed setting, but Lisa feels bound by the divorce agreement that had been made four years earlier, so that she is unwilling to ask her ex-husband for an occasional change in the every weekend visitation schedule.

Lisa's ex-husband spends each weekend being the "hero father" to his children as he lavishes attention and fun-filled hours on them. Andy feels more and more in the background with his stepchildren who see him only when he comes home in the evenings tired from his day of work. There is homework to be done, and no time for really special events and easy relationships. Andy asks, "Lisa, ask your ex-husband to let us have the children for a weekend once a month, or for a two-week vacation once a year." Lisa feels uneasy, caught between the two men. Andy's feelings of competitiveness with Lisa's ex-husband increase as she appears to be more concerned about her ex-husband's feelings than about his feelings. And they argue more and more about her relationship with her ex-husband.

Relationships between ex-spouses have an important effect on the new couple relationship and on the well-being of the children. These relationships, however, can seem confusing. On the one hand, it has been found that a cooperative working relationship between ex-spouses enables the children to relate freely to each natural parent and to stepparents. On the other hand, a continued relationship between ex-spouses can prevent a close alliance between the new couple, and can prevent the assimilation of a stepparent into the stepfamily.

Careful investigation of these interactions may clarify many of the issues, but psychological knowledge and clinical impressions suggest the following dynamics.

After the death of a spouse or a divorce there is a period of adjustment which for most individuals includes the need to deal with loss and separation. After a divorce many ex-spouses are unable to separate emotionally because they still wish and hope for affirmation and validation from the other person. Personal acceptance has not been a part of many marriages where divorce has taken place, and therefore to hope for such affirmation after the hurt and pain of a divorce is usually unrealistic. The feeling often seems to be "I just wish he or she would recognize I'm not a mean and bad person." But anger and non-acceptance continue, holding the couple together as they keep trying to pull apart. If an individual is not able to let go of the need for validation from an ex-spouse, then an emotional separation or a "psychological" divorce is not usually achieved, and hostility may continue.

During this post divorce period cooperation between the ex-spouses is helpful to the children. At times, however, easy cooperation signifies considerable continuing emotional involvement between the ex-spouses rather than simply mutual respect and recognition of concern with the welfare of the children by the two biological parents.

During the stage of single parenting such overdetermined cooperation may work well. However, if a remarriage takes place and an unrecognized emotional involvement remains between ex-spouses, the new couple relationship is often strained and the lack of emotional separation from the previous spouse then introduces problems.

When adolescents and young adults achieve individuation and separation from their parents, they can then have an independent, cooperative, and satisfying relationship with their parents, at the same time that they have new primary interpersonal relationships. In such families, positive feelings towards the parents can be acknowledged but do not act as a bond that dilutes the new relationships.

Similarly, such cooperation can take place between ex-spouses where emotional separation has been achieved, without the contact being a threat to the new primary couple relationship. Even when the former spouse has died, there is the same need for a psychological separation before a new primary bonding can take place.

Many ex-spouses are not able to achieve emotional independence from one another, and they find that the only way to eliminate unproductive arguments is to have a minimum of contact. In other cases, after a remarriage, continued contact of a "cooperative" nature may also be unproductive because the interactions prevent a new couple and stepfamily alliance from forming.

Therapeutic assistance in working out these separations is the task at hand with many remarried couples who are experiencing stepfamily difficulties. In such stepfamilies the stepparent is usually unhappy about the relationship between the partner and the partner's ex-spouse. The stepparent may be feeling alienated from the spouse and the stepchildren, and be angry at one or all of them. Therapists and counselors report working out the old relationships with the new couple, just as many old relationships with parents are worked out in present therapeutic relationships rather than with the patients or clients and their family of origin. Unsatisfactory, cut-off relationships between ex-spouses at times become re-opened as a result of therapeutic work with the new couple, or the unsatisfactory communication or lack of communication with ex-spouses becomes more objective and non-destructive of present relationships.

When he was investigating divorce and remarriage, Paul Bohannan (1971, p. 128-129) was struck by the number of "divorce chains" he encountered as a result of a "chain of relationships" formed among spouses and their ex-spouses." Bohannan says, "It is as if the ex-husband-ex-wife relationship were almost as strong as genetic relationships in the formation of such groups."

It is unlikely that therapists and counselors will see many stepfamilies where "pseudokinship groups are formed on the basis of links between the new spouses of ex-spouses" (Bohannan, 1971, p. 129). As Bohannan states, this is not the usual pattern.

Financial Difficulties

Research studies have indicated that higher socioeconomic status is related to better stepfamily functioning (Bowerman and Irish, 1962; Bernard, 1956; Langner and Michael, 1963). It has been postulated (Simon, 1964, p. 234) that these differences have to do with role expectations, with remarried individuals in lower socioeconomic groups looking for a parental replacement, which makes difficulty for the stepchildren. An additional factor may be the simple fact that with more money there is one less source of tension for the adults.

At the beginning of a series of group discussions, one stepmother, Helen, with no children of her own, outlined her and her husband's greatest problem in the following manner:

> Joe has two children who live in Florida with their mother. He pays high child support, even more than he has to according to the court, and I am going to school and working part-time to help meet our expenses. The thing that's not okay with us is the money. I really resent the child support because we have very little money. Joe's ex-wife has a full-time job now—and we keep saving our money to send for those kids so they can come out to visit for three weeks in the summer, or so we can go back to visit with them. And that costs a lot of money. We've been married two years now and we haven't been on a vacation ourselves—and now I'm feeling two years of resentment all of a sudden. I thought of all that money going to bring the children out and entertain them, and we haven't had any vacation for the two of us in the two years we've been married. I suddenly thought I want to enjoy our money too.

It became clear that Joe was feeling extremely guilty about "leaving" his children when he was divorced, and whatever his ex-wife asked for he gave her so that he would not jeopardize seeing his children. He panicked at the thought that his ex-wife might threaten him by refusing to put his children on the airplane to come and visit with him. Even with his guilt, if Joe and Helen had had more income Joe's need to give so generously to his ex-wife and his children would have affected his and Helen's life-style to a lesser degree, and their relationship might not have been so strained. Because this couple had very little money, contributing as much as he did to his ex-wife and children left Joe and Helen with a very meager income. They were working long hours throughout the year and never taking any vacation for themselves, and the couple relationship was disintegrating rapidly.

In contrast, Ethel and Charles talked of the ease with which they were able to weather the joining of two families because of the fact that they had a high income. As they looked back on the early years they realized that their freedom to relate to each other as a couple had not been lost when they married. There was live-in help to take the burden of household chores and child care, and the whole family could do many fun things together. Ethel and Charles made a point of going out to dinner alone every week, and of having a weekend to themselves in some relaxing spot every four to six weeks. They saw their financial situation as being of paramount importance in their ability to nourish their own relationship, and they shook their heads as they thought of the difficulties remarried couples have when they have few financial resources.

Discipline Problems

Problems with discipline are common in all types of families. In a study of 66 stepparents and spouses who came for stepparent group counseling, McClenahan (1978) found discipline ranked as the number one area of difficulty. Stern's (1978) study of discipline in 30 "stepfather" families concluded by saying that if stepfathers attempted to discipline before establishing a bond of friendship with their stepchildren, the stepfathers might never be able to form close bonds with the family unit.

Stepfamily couples often find it helpful to recognize that many of their problems with discipline are problems encountered by natural parents in nuclear families. They also find it useful to be aware of the particular risks in stepfamilies—stepchildren will refuse to accept any discipline if they have no relationship with the adult involved in the disciplining. Basically, discipline works only when the person receiving the discipline cares about the reactions of and the relationship with the person doing the disciplining.

In intact families parents can work out their differences in methods of discipline slowly as the child grows. In remarriages the couple is faced with instant decisions. One grown stepson stated it clearly:

In stepfamilies I think it's harder than in first families 'cause you are just married and the kids are already there. There are decisions to make and you haven't felt it out with your spouse necessarily, so you really don't know the feeling of the other person. When Roger and Alice [new parents in a first marriage] had their twins they were starting from scratch, and they made decisions on the way up without the twins ever knowing about it, 'cause the kids didn't have feelings about the decisions at that young age. . . . So stepparents made their decisions on how they are going to raise their kids when the kids are thrust on them at an adult age, or whatever age. Those kids are asking for something immediate that the parents have never discussed together.

Divisiveness of Stepchildren

In nuclear families children learn to play one parent against the other, and become skilled at doing so if it appears to work to their advantage. Let a threat to the existence of the family occur, however, and these same children usually will do all in their power to keep their parents together. In stepfamilies the situation is different.

With the complexities and the disorganization in stepfamilies it is very easy for the children to "divide and conquer." And if a breakup of the couple seems imminent, many children rejoice since they have retained a fantasy, even after remarriage, that their two natural parents will be reunited. A separation of the remarried couple is seen as paving the way for a reunion of the natural parents. "During the early years of my second marriage I remember thinking I was either being a little paranoid or my stepson was trying to break up my marriage. Many years later he admitted he had been trying to break us up. He had plans A, B, and C all aimed at making me give up and leave," said a stepmother who had weathered the storm successfully.

If the couple can recognize and accept the existence of these strong feelings and unite to deal with the children, then the desire of the children to split the couple will not succeed. Therapists and counselors can be extremely helpful in clarifying these issues and supporting the couple's attempts to maintain a satisfying and cohesive adult bond.

SUCCESSFUL RECOUPLING

Even in the midst of the stress and turmoil of stepfamily interactions many adults speak of these years being the happiest years
of their lives. There appear to be several reasons for this reaction.

For the couple to succeed in a stepfamily there needs to be a
great deal of communication. Communication will not be low
key and about the weather; many of the interactions will be
heated and painful.

If the couple resists the temptation to criticize and withdraw,
emotional sharing can produce a relationship of closeness because
of the constant need to deal with meaningful and urgent situations. There is an awareness of the relationship which does not
sink into unconsciousness so that it is taken for granted. The relationship requires constant attention, and if it develops amid the
vicissitudes of stepparenting, the bonds are very strong and deeply
felt. For many couples, group discussions, counseling or therapy
can provide assistance in this difficult and essential task.

The next chapter will deal with specific ways in which to provide therapeutic help to couples, so that they may be able to realize
their wish for a good and meaningful relationship. Realization of
this dream will benefit not only the couple, but also their children
and their children's children.

9

Working with

stepfamily couples

WORKING WITH INDIVIDUAL COUPLES

Although most of the programs for stepparents and their partners are oriented towards a group setting, individual couples are being seen by counselors and therapists. Since the number of remarried parents is increasing rapidly, the number of such couples seeking help is also growing. Unfortunately, in most instances, by the time the couple comes for professional assistance they are feeling rather desperate. As stepfamilies become a more accepted segment of American society, and knowledge about the particular hazards in stepfamilies becomes widely recognized, then couples in stepfamilies will undoubtedly feel more free to seek help before the sky is falling in.

Some couples seek professional help before the marriage. Couples with a strong commitment to each other who wish to understand the problem areas and learn ways to reduce the tensions gain a great deal from these premarital therapeutic contacts. Couples who are ambivalent about the marriage or who are blinded by unrealistic expectations tend to drop the professional contact before resolving the issues.

A middle-aged couple about to join two sets of children illustrates one such pattern. As they talked with a counselor about situations in which the children were rude and uncooperative, or other times when the couple fought over who was going to discipline whom, more and more problem areas began emerging. The couple abruptly broke off contact with the counselor and decided to marry immediately. The inability to tolerate and work out the inevitable stresses suggests that living with these frictions will be extremely painful if not impossible for such couples.

Another couple came for help because they feared for the emotional health of the children if they married. Erica had an eight-year-old son, and John had six-year-old twin boys, and as Erica said, "When we have the families together it is very tense, but when we're alone it is fine."

Both agreed that it was Erica's son, Denny, who caused the problem. Erica had always had difficulty setting limits for Denny, and when he was with John's two children Denny became particularly boisterous and irritable. If they were at John's house Erica could think of no way to discipline Denny other than nagging, because, after all, it was John's house and they were just visitors. John preferred to have Erica and Denny come to his house because he worked longer hours than did Erica, and he had two children and Erica only had to bring one child with her.

John felt that his children did not like Denny, and he was clear that he considered Denny a "spoiled brat." As John viewed it, "Denny isn't losing anything if Erica and I get married, but my children are. They will have to put up with Denny. I don't know if it will work out for my children if Erica and I get married."

Erica was even more conflicted. "We wouldn't be happy with a divided family. We keep putting off getting married because of this situation with Denny, and we're not getting any younger. This makes me angry at Denny! To think that a child could prevent us from getting married! I like my job but if we get married I could give it up and spend time with the children at home, so maybe it would go better."

Several problems are highlighted by Erica and John:

1. Couples tend to focus on one particular child as causing the difficulties, and to consider the parent of that child to be the person responsible for changing the situation. Joint planning and co-operation between the couple are usually required to shift the dynamics.

2. Neither adult recognized that all three children would "lose" something by the marriage, namely, an exclusive relationship with the natural parent. (Both ex-spouses were out of the area and had little or no contact with their children.) It is likely that some of the tension when they were all together stemmed from competitiveness of the boys for their parent's attention, and not simply from Denny's misbehavior.

3. Erica and Denny considered themselves "intruders" in John's house. Territorial conflicts are common in stepfamilies and appear to be very evident in this situation. If Erica and John changed their pattern to a more alternating one in which the families got together sometimes at John's house and sometimes at Erica's house, tension might be reduced.

4. After a remarriage, when a woman leaves a job she has liked to become a full-time "homemaker," it often compounds rather than simplifies the situation. The relationship between step-mother and stepchildren may be strained and the stepmother may be unhappy at home, having given up the emotional supports that she had on her job. Her resentment may grow and the home situation will deteriorate rapidly. Erica was proposing giving up her job as a partial solution to the problem. For the reasons just outlined, such a move on Erica's part could increase rather than decrease the level of stepfamily stress.

If the remarriage has already taken place when couples appear, they are usually fighting with each other, and one is accusing the spouse of being totally responsible for the havoc in the stepfamily. The stepmother is unloving and mean to the stepchildren, the father is oblivious to the terrible behavior of his children, or the stepfather is a cruel and harsh disciplinarian who is driving the mother's children away to their natural father's home. Even with all the resentment and hostile behavior, over and over again couples will say that they still relate well to each other except where the relationship to the children is concerned. Many times this appears to be true, and the therapist or counselor needs to reserve judgment on the marriage relationship. In many instances, the problems between the couple are secondary, with the complex parent/stepparent-child/stepchild relationships being the primary source of the stress. As Richard Fisch (1977) states, "Stepfamily difficulties spill over into the couple relationship, rather than the reverse."

At times a spouse will attempt to persuade the professional that the marriage is, indeed, the problem. Sometimes this is an attempt to put the focus on the marriage partner and not on a particular parent-child interaction. For example, in a stepfamily in which two sets of three children lived with the couple, the husband wished to pinpoint the wife's emotionally volatile nature and strict house rules as responsible for disturbing their relationship, focusing only secondarily on the entire family. In working with the couple it became clear to the counselor that the husband did not wish to look at his daughter's disruptive behavior, nor at the unhealthy symbiotic relationship between the two of them which was making it impossible for the stepmother to become integrated into the family. Of course, in this case, the problems grew from deep personal factors coupled with stepfamily complexity. In stepfamilies where intrapsychic factors as well as situation factors are very important, much therapeutic help is required to alleviate the tension. However, many remarried couples, individuals who have functioned effectively throughout their lives, find the stresses overpowering when they become part of a stepfamily couple. Many excellent parents become insecure, unhappy stepparents. Often in such cases minimal contact with a therapist or counselor can help a remarried couple form a relatively secure partnership, enabling them to deal with the complex problems that occur.

In the book *Helping Parents Help Their Children* (Arnold, 1978), there is a very helpful chapter by Fast and Chethik reviewing the therapeutic work done with one stepfamily couple and concluding with a summary of major guidance implications for stepparent couples.

Now that the courts are becoming aware of a myriad of problems surrounding custody and visitation arrangements, many more attorneys are recommending counseling to their clients. After divorce, children may become pawns as the parents continue to fight using custody and visitation as a vehicle to express their hurt and anger. After remarriage the fight may continue, or a new battle may start as remarried parents seek changes in the legal arrangements with ex-spouses. Often the introduction of a new spouse triggers many feelings of insecurity in the natural parent of the same sex, and the pulling on the children escalates.

Attorneys are working with therapists and counselors and, where they exist, conciliation courts are referring divorced and remarried couples to court-appointed mental health professionals to attempt to work out custody and visitation issues with all the concerned adults. Recently, such a court-related therapist commented on his success in working with ex-spouses and the husband's second wife. The three adults met with the therapist with the very explicit focus being the welfare of the child, who was living with her father and stepmother. The ex-spouses slowly began to be able to talk with each other after several years of no communication. By re-establishing minimal contact between all of the adults, the therapist hoped that the constant custody and visitation battles could be prevented.

Often joint meetings are not in relation to custody or visitation battles, but simply to pave the way for as smooth a transition as possible for a child who is moving from one household into the household of the other parent. Such a therapeutic approach involving all the adults may become an explosive situation, but some professionals are attempting to work this way, at times with a favorable outcome. In other cases, stepparents report that in custody change evaluation and counseling they are not considered as playing a very important part in the child's adjustment. In actuality, the existence of a stepparent usually complicates the emotional responses of the child and of the adults, so that including the stepparent is often crucial to an effective resolution of the difficulties.

GROUP WORK WITH STEPFAMILY COUPLES

As interest in working with stepfamilies has begun to develop, group programs are emerging in various communities. One major thrust is towards workshops and groups for stepparents and their partners. Most of the couples who participate in these programs are married, though a small percentage are couples living together or planning to be married. Lillian Messinger (1976) proposed that an educational program in preparation for remarriage would reduce or remove some of the hurdles faced by stepfamilies. It seems doubtful that all difficulties could be removed, but couples attending such programs before their remarriage, or soon after remarriage, do report a reduction in the severity of their stepfamily problems.

In a paper entitled "Preparation for Remarriage Following Divorce: Group Techniques" (1978, p. 272), Messinger and associates summarize their work with four groups of couples as follows: "The feelings and experiences expressed met with reassurance and with sympathetic and empathic responses that relieved the sense of personal aloneness and inadequacy in coping with problems."

Discussion Groups

Stepfamily Foundation of California, Inc. is training professionals to lead "Stepparent Survival Courses," four-week discussion groups for stepparents and their partners. Evaluations by the participants are being analyzed, but systematic results are not yet available. Comments by participants include the following: It was helpful. . . .

> "to get insights into how parent-child relationships work."
> "to learn what is 'normal' behavior in this (stepfamily) circumstance."
> "to get a better understanding of relevant problems and issues."
> "to get a perspective in our situation."
> "to recognize that values and individual differences are magnified in stepfamilies."

"to learn how and why various family members feel threatened and insecure in a new stepfamily situation."
"to have an opportunity to share with others in similar situations."

Stepparents and their partners are appreciative of the help that is being offered by such groups. This approach seems to meet the needs of many couples in remarried families who are having considerable difficulty coping with their stepfamily problems. For some couples such groups are the first step towards more intensive ongoing individual or group therapy experiences.

It is important for these types of "courses" to make a clear distinction between the need for "education" and the need for "therapy."

McClenahan (1978) studied certain characteristics of 66 persons who attended four-week discussion courses in San Jose, California. These individuals included 28 married couples, two couples who lived together, and five married individuals whose spouses did not attend the classes. In this group 42 percent had been remarried less than one year, with the average length of remarriage for the entire group being 21 months. Stepfamily problems usually are manifested almost immediately after the new marriage.

The average age of men was 40, while the average age of women was 34. McClenahan notes, "The husbands' first marriages lasted 12.4 years while their wives' first marriages lasted 11.5 years. The pattern of those couples who were on their second marriage shows that the men were first married in the early twenties (mean age 22), divorced in their mid-thirties, and remarried in their late thirties. The wives in this sample married in their late teens (mean age 19), divorced around age 30, with remarriage coming in their early thirties." These figures correspond to those found in the groups of stepfamilies studied by Messinger (1976).

For couples on a third or fourth marriage, it was found that the first marriages for the women had lasted almost twice as long as the first marriages for the men. The remarriages of the men lasted for a shorter period of time than the remarriages of the women with multiple marriages. In other words, there appears to be a tendency for women to stay in their marriages for a considerably longer period of time than men. The couples belonged to middle to upper-middle income groups.

One finding was that 45 percent of the men who attended these discussions had custody of children from their previous marriages. In 13 percent of the families this had been the result of death of the natural mother, while in the remaining 32 percent of the families the father had been granted custody by the court at the time of the divorce or subsequently. Since the percentage of fathers having custody of their children is less than 10 percent nationwide, the 45 percent figure in this sample indicates that a disproportionately large number of remarried couples where the men have custody of their children sought help. In many of these stepfamilies, two sets of children had been joined together under one roof; this, as has been pointed out earlier, is a particularly difficult combination. Fathers with custody of their children may feel an added responsibility in their parental role and are therefore willing to participate in family-oriented discussions. In stepfamilies in which the natural mother has died, the stepchildren often have greater difficulty accepting a stepmother, another possible factor contributing to the participation of a larger proportion of couples where the father has custody of his children. More research is needed to further clarify these issues.

In McClenahan's group (1978), participants listed the most troublesome stepfamily areas as being, in order of importance: 1. disciplining stepchildren and being rejected by stepchildren; 2. relationship with ex-spouses, and, of equal importance, communication between the new couple; and 3. general nonspecific difficulties in adjusting to stepchildren. In responding to a questionnaire, McClenahan's group (1978) considered the realization "that we're not alone, that others have the same problems" as the single most important result of attending the classes. Sharing feelings and relating to other individuals in similar family situations were also considered important. Less important was discussion of specific problems. Although the groups had varied in size from six to 14 persons, satisfaction with the group experience was high for all groups.

A particular advantage of such a group setting is the objectivity that can be achieved. In one session a father and stepfather suddenly exclaimed, "If our ex-spouses and their mates were here talking together they'd probably be sounding just like us!"

Messinger (1976) found similar responses from interviews with 70 remarried couples. She also compared the major difficulties reported in first marriages and in the remarriages.

> In their first marriages, they gave the usual responses, ranking a global factor, 'partner's immaturity' highest, sexual difficulties second, followed by personal lack of marriage readiness, in-law interferences, and then a number of factors such as differences in values and in social interests. But problems around child-rearing, financial problems, and cultural differences ranked quite low. By contrast, in their remarriage the biggest source of difficulties reported were with children, followed closely by financial problems. Other frequently mentioned problems were relatives, differences in social value systems, sharing of tasks, and so on. But these along with sexual difficulties were rarely seen as important compared to children and finances (p. 196).

Discussions in these groups usually deal with the following major topics:

Mourning the loss of the dream of a nuclear family.
Acceptance of stepfamily structure and roles.
Relationship with ex-spouses.
Relationship with in-laws and ex-in-laws.
Problems around differing needs and sets of values.
Expectations of "instant love."
Dealing with anger and guilt.
Jealousy and competition for love and affection.
Rejection and insecurity.
Cruel stepmother myth.
Need to compensate the children for their past upset.
Visiting stepchildren.
Adolescent stepchildren.
Rivalry between children.

Discipline.
Sexuality in stepfamilies.
Financial arrangements.
Forming good couple unity.

The usual pattern for stepparent discussion groups is four-to-six two-hour sessions, at weekly intervals. From that base, some couples continue with some other form of help, including self-help groups, while many couples seek no further assistance.

One group, consisting of five remarried couples with a remarried professional couple as leaders, is typical of discussion groups of stepparents and their partners. In the first session each person started by outlining his/her problems as he/she saw them.

Cleo and Carl

Cleo: We have very different priorities in our family. My children are studious, Carl's children are not. Our priorities are all different.

Carl: There's a lot of hostility between my son and daughter who live with us, and most of it is my daughter's fault. My two children and Cleo's two children get along just fine, but my two fight like cats and dogs.

Jill and Jeff

Jill: We've been living together for two-and-a-half years and we just got married four months ago. Jeff's 11-year-old son came to live with us then. He's a neat kid but I've had a lot of difficulty having him come. I've never had any children, and now I feel I'm competing with my stepson for his father's time and affection.

Jeff: I don't understand this. I'm very happy having my son living with us. I have a completely different perspective on it. I'm interested in the cruel stepmother myth because Jill is sweet and nice and patient, but I think she has a lot of feelings about being a stepmother that she isn't talking about.

Gerri and George

Gerri: I can understand what Jill is saying because I have two of George's children living with me and my three children, and I feel just like Jill says. I get upset and then I am the cruel stepmother.

One day George's ex-wife just left the children and their things on our doorstep and now I have to take care of them. I go right up the wall when I see any behavior in one of my stepchildren that resembles their mother's behavior. We have problems with George's ex-wife.

My stepchildren feel there is favoritism. George and I are different in our feelings about how the children should be raised. . . . But other than that we're fine! (All laugh.)

George: Yep. I have my problems dealing with my stepchildren because they have a hero father. He has them not just every weekend, but every weekend, every holiday, during vacations, and sometimes even during the week. I can't compete. I can't compete with that at all.

The other extreme is that my wife [meaning his ex-wife] seldom sees my kids. A few hours maybe two to three times every six months. Now it's more consistent and now my kids are saying they'd rather not go.

Gerri sees what's wrong with my kids and I think the thing that bothers me the most is that most of the time she's right.

Flo and Floyd

Flo: Our problem is the outside influence. Floyd has two girls in their twenties, and one is home now. Then I have an older boy who lives with his father, and I have a son nine, and Floyd has a son 11. My ex-husband is an outside influence on us, and other people also stick their noses into problems that are none of their business.

Floyd: My problem is with my son and stepson. My stepson feels that I'm unfair to him if I ever try to discipline him.

Sue and Sam

Sue: I have a very disturbed stepson. We've had all kinds of visitation problems. We've kept going to court trying to get some visitation. I've not had children and now we've just adopted a little boy of our own. My stepson is 14 and he can't make any decisions for himself, so we've been trying to see him and his sister separately. He can't even say what he wants for breakfast. It's really pitiful. His sister leads him around by the nose.

He's seeing a psychologist now, and we've been working with him too and we hope it's going to work better.

(*Sam:*   was not present. He listened to the tape recording of the session and attended the remaining three sessions.)

The first session gave the couples an opportunity to talk briefly about their family constellation and their differences in feelings. The problems touched upon many crucial issues for stepfamilies:

Differences in priorities.
Hostility between children.
Competition for love and affection.
Inability to understand partner's responses.
Problems with ex-spouses.
Competition between the natural father and the stepfather.
Discipline problems.

During the second session many important interactions and exchanges of emotions took place. Sam, who was present for the first time, expressed the feelings of many remarried fathers:

I feel so out of it because I've been so ignorant about lawsuits and everything. Not being able to phone my children for a year, or see them . . . I think about things like this every day.

Now I've been trying to figure out how to communicate with my ex-wife. I've been to court so much and I have a thing against lawyers. I have so much anger and I feel so helpless. I may be feeling sorry for myself. I have trouble sorting it out.

Then I realized I have to take a stand and I have to say, "Hey, I want to see you. I'm going to see you." For so long I wouldn't take the risk of making a stand because I feared I wouldn't see my son for three months. It was just agony. If I did something my ex-wife didn't like she wouldn't let me see the children.

My son has been going to a psychologist and the psychologist was able to help in court and get visitation changed so that it is now automatic. So in the last year I feel I'm beginning to live.

In this session several people spoke about how helpful it was to get some perspective on their own situation, and to find others who had similar feelings.

There was considerable discussion about the unrealistic notion of instant love of stepparents for stepchildren, or of stepchildren for stepparents. Feelings of competition for love were expressed as an issue for all the families. Jill was resentful of Jeff's relationship with his son, feeling that they excluded her and that Jeff seemed to ask his son permission for him and Jill to do something without him. Jeff recognized certain conflicts in that area and said to the group, "I don't know where kids are and how to establish a relationship. I listen and hear people here having a strong sense of what the parent does and how the kid responds. I don't have that sense."

Parenting issues were raised and comparisons made between stepfamilies and intact families. In all families, children are messy and disobedient at times. However, in stepfamilies, stepparents at times have difficulty saying, "I'm not your parent, but this is the way it's going to be done in this house."

Gerri and George talked a great deal about the lack of relationship between George and his stepchildren because the stepchildren were not around when he was home. George felt he could not compete with their "super-dad," and he also considered Gerri and her children missed a lot by not having leisure time together. The group suggested they try to work out a slightly different visitation schedule with the children's father.

Other areas of discussion were the following:

> The difficulties for children and adults alike in finding their places in a new family and community.
> The need to try to cram everything into a weekend visit, when some of the children visit rather than live with the parent.
> The difference it made to move into a new home rather than living in a home formerly occupied by one spouse and his or her children.
> Much discomfort over introductions of stepchildren. Are they called "stepchildren"? Do you say whose child it is? Do you include both the first and last names?

The problems of integrating two sets of family traditions, and the lack of control over the upbringing of the children who visit.

The masking of positive feelings towards stepchildren by resentments that are not expressed, since the positive feelings get buried beneath the resentments.

Different feelings towards stepchildren and adopted children because in the latter situation "we both actively sought this child."

The major themes of the session were the recognition of patterns that come up repeatedly in stepfamilies, the fact that these situations cause certain emotional reactions, that familiarity with these patterns reduces the difficulty in dealing with them, and that families need to work out their own family solutions together if possible.

Discipline was the main topic of the third session. While discipline can be a difficult task of parenting, in stepfamilies there are many complications. Floyd talked at some length about his withdrawal from disciplining his stepson because the boy's father would make trouble for them over any disciplinary action. Since the boy knew this, if his mother or stepfather disciplined him, he would call his father and exaggerate the situation. Once his father had reacted by sending the police to the house to protect his "abused son."

A situation had arisen during the week in which the boy had been punished by being told he could not visit his father for four weeks. At this point George erupted, "If my ex had ever disciplined the kids that way when my kids lived with her I'd have been in court the next day!" It turned out that the boy's father *was* taking Flo and Floyd to court over the matter, and there was considerable discussion about not disciplining in any way that involves the rights of the non-custodial parent.

Differences in discipline were seen as dependent upon stepchildren versus natural children, when, in fact, sometimes the differences turned out to be merely differences in the two adult approaches—differences which had always existed. Even so, parents tended to deal more lightly with their own children. It did not work for stepparents to discipline before they had developed a good relationship with their stepchildren.

This discussion led to ways in which adults could do special things with different children, or groups of children, to form new bonds and maintain old ones. It came out that the rivalry that had always existed between Carl's son and daughter had been recently augmented when his 18-year-old son had came to live with him and Cleo. Carl's 17-year-old daughter had been living there for a year and she probably had felt displaced when her brother moved in. Carl felt encouraged that he might be able to improve his daughter's relationship with her brother by having a few special times with her alone, as well as with his son alone. Hopefully, this would help restore his daughter's feeling of being special to her father—a feeling she had probably lost when her brother suddenly joined the family group.

Jeff was not able to attend this session and the group sent him a strong message via the tapes of the session to think of ways in which his son could become familiar with his new school and new neighborhood, so that the boy would feel more at home and comfortable when his father and Jill did some things together without him. Jill had been able to identify with her stepson's feelings of being excluded and had had a very good talk with her stepson about his feelings of being left out. Jill had been very pleased that he had come to her with this problem, and was sorry she couldn't promise him he'd always be included. She realized—and was supported by the group in this—that she and her husband needed time alone to build their own couple relationship.

Again, trouble communicating with ex-spouses was an issue, with two of the five couples turning to the courts to settle problems, while the third had had a court appearance at the instigation of the ex-husband. The group discussed ways to communicate with ex-spouses. In most instances it does not work to have the children carry messages, and become go-betweens who frequently feel caught in the middle between their natural parents. Some ex-spouses can talk over the telephone; others use written communication. In other situations the mother and stepmother or father and stepfather can relate satisfactorily in regards to the children even when the ex-spouses are unable to talk to each other without an explosion. Examples were contributed by several group members of successful planning efforts with an ex-spouse by their stressing to the ex-spouse that both of them were interested in the welfare of the children.

The difficult relationship between stepmothers and stepdaughters received comment, as Cleo told of being bewildered as a young stepchild herself when she perceived the intense jealousy her stepmother felt about her relationship with her father, "But now, as a stepmother myself, I can certainly understand it."

When the group met together for the fourth and last session there were many feelings and concerns left dangling. Jeff was still away on business and his wife Jill talked about ways in which she understood her husband and her stepson's feelings much better. They had decided to include a friend for Jeff's son when they went on excursions so that there would be two boys to play together, thus breaking up the difficult threesome.

Cleo and Carl seemed more relaxed and shared their views that natural children expected more from parents and less from stepparents, and so differences in giving at Christmas and other times was less of a problem.

Gerri and George talked of some difficulties they were having as a couple, and the group spoke of the need for the couple to be a unit and not undermine each other. The children had been playing one adult off against the other by going first to one and then to the other if they did not like the answer given by the first adult. The couple was urged to talk to the children *together* so that even when they were not in agreement the couple would be working as a unit on finding a solution.

Flo and Floyd continued to talk of trouble working with Flo's ex-husband, and how the continued anger between them apparently stood in the way of any smooth working relationship.

Considerable change was reported by Sue and Sam, who were dealing in an increasingly direct manner with his two children, not worrying as before over what the consequences might be in terms of "retaliation" by the children's mother. Indeed, Gerri and George also had asked for and were going to have Gerri's children for a weekend with them every month. Fear of the responses of the ex-spouses had begun to diminish, and no longer did they consider it an absolute must for them to keep things smooth at all costs.

One change in all but Flo and Floyd's stepfamily appeared to be much more frequent conversation between adults and children. At times these were serious conversations that were producing increasingly warm relationships among the stepfamily members.

The leaders presented a list of "tips"* on stepfamily functioning which had previously been given verbally to the group, as well as suggestions derived from the group discussions with the five couples. The group discussed the list briefly and asked for copies to refer to now that they would not be meeting together. They thanked the leaders and talked of meeting together on their own to continue to share with one another.

Therapy Groups for Couples

Long-term therapy groups for stepfamily couples seem few in comparison to the number of time-limited discussion groups. Availability of therapy groups is important for the couples where intrapsychic problems are causing couple difficulties which are exacerbated by complex stepfamily relationships. Acquainting couples with the added complexities of their family structure can supply a background for exploration of their specific difficulties, and for this reason a number of couples find it helpful to attend a discussion course or workshop before seeking therapy.

In a therapy group, background information will emerge when appropriate rather than being given at the beginning. In this way couple interactions and feelings become the focus of attention rather than more didactic material and intellectual suggestions for change.

In some instances a selection process places similar couples together. A report on a group of stepfathers and their wives led by Mowatt (1972) was included in the chapter on working with stepfathers. Usually the number of couples seeking such help is not

---

* The "tips" are included in the list appearing as guidelines in Appendix A.

large enough to select a group according to similar basic family patterns.

The inner feelings and conflicts experienced by stepmothers, stepfathers, and their partners have been described in preceding chapters. These feelings will frequently emerge in therapy groups for stepfamily couples and will be dealt with as in other therapy groups, the particular method and style reflecting the approach of the leader or leaders of the group.

If the leader of a discussion group is not a stepparent, the group usually spends some time at the beginning evaluating the leader's understanding of stepfamilies. Since these groups are somewhat didactic in nature, knowledge of the problems can be demonstrated by the leader so that trust often develops quickly. In therapy groups, it usually takes several sessions for the participants to build up trust in non-stepparent leaders. Leadership understanding and discussion of this concern are most helpful. Obviously knowledge and understanding of the feelings will come through in such a group if the leader is sensitive and is familiar with the information available about stepfamily interactions. Groups of parents are not always led by a person with children, a couples group by a married leader, or a stepparent group by a stepparent.

Support Groups

Ongoing support groups are proving to be helpful for stepparents and their partners. These groups are often held every other week rather than the traditional once-a-week meeting.

Frequently couples coming into such groups have participated in a workshop or a discussion course prior to the ongoing group. If the majority of the group has attended discussion courses, there is a fairly lengthy transition period from the group course format to a group therapy format that focuses on discussion of feelings and on interchanges and group process.

One leader reported that it took nearly six months for her group to level with each other. After a number of couple changes within the group, a stable core group developed, and the evening that two individuals were finally able to deal with their hostility towards one another, "the group became a group."

Some couples in ongoing support groups want problem-solving groups, not therapy groups. Discussion of stepfamily situations occurs for a period of time, and then, if the group continues, a therapeutic orientation develops. Stepfamily problems per se recede into the background and marital interaction and parenting problems move into the foreground.

Drop-in Discussion Groups

Drop-in discussion groups are less stable than ongoing support groups, and often are held only once a month. These groups usually are come-as-you-feel-the-need groups. They are being led by facilitators who have group leadership training, or by counselors and therapists particularly interested in working with stepparents and their partners.

These groups, because of their fluctuating membership, remain on a supportive, problem-solving level. Many times the mere ventilation of feelings is helpful to the participants, even if no solutions seem apparent. Leaders help with productive movement in the group session and work to insure a supportive and friendly group atmosphere. Since the emotional climate in stepfamilies is very often highly charged, havng a group in which to discharge feelings is helpful. Knowing that others in the group will be able to identify with and understand the basic stepfamily traumas makes for quick bonding between members. This means that such groups, even though they are made up of a more transient membership, provide considerable help for a number of distressed stepfamilies.

Self-help Groups

Self-help groups are slowly developing. In their book *Stepparenting* (1977), Jean and Veryl Rosenbaum include a section on self-help groups. While many couples prefer group experiences with professional leadership, other couples because of financial considerations or personal preference will choose to form or join self-help groups. At times self-help groups are formed by a group of couples who know each other through their participation in a workshop or discussion course.

The enthusiasm of self-help group participants is illustrated by the comments of members of one such group:

> The amount of money this group has saved us in lawyer's fees and in doctor's fees is phenomenal! We have the opportunity to talk things out and then they seem so unimportant that we don't have to seek other help.
>
> Our children have become the greatest boosters for our group and talk about wanting a group too. They can't get over the way their parents have changed.

Workshops for Couples

All-day workshops for stepfamily couples are making an appearance, and very often they are offered through colleges, junior colleges, or clinics. A few schools are beginning to include such workshops in their service to the families in their district.

Workshops provide a good introduction to the situations faced in stepfamilies, and the evaluation sheets filled out by the participants indicate that they consider the time profitably spent. Since the couple needs to work together, both adults are strongly urged to attend even though one may not be a stepparent. Interactions between parent and stepparent can be even more difficult than between a couple where both are parent/stepparent.

Usually the workshops are led by professionals who themselves are in stepfamily situations. This factor of identification makes an immediate bond between the leader, or leaders, and the participants. If the leaders are a stepparent couple the participants appreciate learning that "the leaders" have had and may still be having certain stepfamily difficulties, but they do report confusion and discouragement if the leaders convey the impression that they are still floundering and cannot provide useful tips or guidelines.

A number of couples prefer workshops because their anonymity can be preserved if they wish. For some couples this is very important. Since workshops provide a wide variety of stepfamily situations, they seem to offer a helpful climate as participants recognize many similarities between their difficulties and the problems others are having. After one workshop, for example, two women with children, living together as a couple, said with considerable feeling, "Today has been most reassuring. We're not so different after all."

The most helpful format appears to be a short didactic presentation of a list of agenda topics prepared by the leaders and then added to by suggestions from the group. Group discussion of each topic area is encouraged. When the group is small there is time for more discussion, while in a large group the didactic material predominates.

Knowledge of research on stepfamily situations and outcomes is welcomed by the group. The guidelines listed in Appendix A, as well as the reference list of books written for the general public (Appendix B) are also appreciated.

It is obvious that a long discussion of many topics is impossible in one day. While there is much overlap between the topics, having a written list tends to satisfy participants who are more comfortable with structure than with group discussion. If some topics are less important to the group, or are neglected because of the shortness of the time, at least having the list is an acknowledgement of the existence of these problem areas.

Breaking an all-day workshop into two separate sections on different days can work more effectively in many cases. After two-and-half-to-three hours, people's attention span and physical comfort deteriorate rapidly. Hopefully, the chairs and ventilation will be reasonably comfortable, and no antagonistic remarried ex-spouses will appear for the same workshop!

Individuals who attend groups or workshops without their partners often comment on their need to share the experience with their spouse. In many instances the couple does attend a future workshop or group together. Joint participation usually nourishes and enhances the couple relationship.

10

Children in

stepfamilies

While some adults in stepfamilies are not stepparents, virtually all children in stepfamilies at the time of remarriage are stepchildren. As for the feelings of these stepchildren, Anne Simon (1964) states it very simply when she says that the feelings of stepchildren are the emotions of all children—exposed. In intact families children may love one parent more than the other, or shift their loyalty from time to time. Children often have difficulty coming to terms with their love and hate, their "bad" mother and their "good" mother image. Children manipulate and play one parent off against the other when they find the opportunity to do so. Children scramble for love and affection, and fight with their siblings. Children struggle to form an identity of their own, taking from parents and peers. And children withdraw when emotionally hurt, and suffer acutely when rejected.

So it is in stepfamilies too, but here it is as though one is looking at the process through a microscope. Love and hate are magnified. Rivalry and competition for attention are magnified. Insecurity and the search for identity are magnified.

Remarriage for the adults is a gain of an important adult relationship. For the children remarriage frequently represents a loss of a close parent-child relationship. The child must now share the parent with one or more new individuals. For these reasons the reactions of adults and children at the time of remarriage may be very different. In essence, the scene is set for a serious and at times heartbreaking drama.

DEALING WITH LOSS

A study has been reported involving a sample of 41 disturbed stepchildren brought to the Institute for Juvenile Research in Chicago. In 50 percent of the cases the onset of symptoms in stepchildren was at the time of the parents' remarriage, with less than 10 percent occurring at the time of the divorce or death of the parent, during the interim period, or at some point after the remarriage (White, 1943). One reason for this statistic, no doubt, lies in the sense of loss experienced by children when their parents remarry.

In looking at the process of divorce and transition to the remarriage, one is aware of the almost universal feeling of loss and grief experienced by the children. In a high percentage of families, as the first marriage begins to disintegrate one parent may seek emotional support from the children. Shortly prior to the anticipated separation one mother spoke to her two teenage daughters about her loneliness and lack of closeness with their father. In reply one girl said, "But what are you going to do? We'll be grown soon and then you won't have us to talk to." In many families parent-child bonding becomes even stronger at the time of the actual divorce; at other times the parent-child roles become reversed.

When the divorce takes place, even if the marriage has been miserable, the parent is experiencing the loss of a dream, and the children are confronted with a parental loss that they have not chosen. Even when the loss is due to death of the parent, the children usually feel rejected and abandoned. So in either case, the children go through the familiar stages of grieving—denial, guilt, anger, and despair. They may draw even closer to the parent with whom they are living and who is also experiencing loss so that, as Goldstein et al. (1973) state, "parent and child will enter into an exceptionally close and overdetermined relationship."

If remarriage occurs in a short space of time after the death or divorce, it is likely that the mourning and grief are not yet over for the children, and as a result the children are not prepared to accept new adults into their lives. If the new partner is presented as a replacement for the lost parent, the resentment and grief are particularly acute. The children see their parent's remarriage as a betrayal of the former spouse if that spouse has died, or even when the remarriage follows a divorce. A further loss of both parents is anticipated by the children.

If there is a long period between the death or divorce and remarriage, the special bond between parent and child has been in existence for a greater period of time. Often the child has shared the custodial parent's bedroom; a younger child may even sleep in the same bed with the parent. Remarriage disturbs the closeness of this relationship, and the child again experiences a loss.

During the courtship period the children are often not included. This is the time in which the parent is euphoric with the hope of a new and satisfying couple relationship, while the child may feel increasingly abandoned. When the wedding day dawns, the parent is happy in the addition of another parental adult to the child's world while the child, in contrast, often experiences total loss of the parent to the new spouse. No wonder the Chicago Institute pinpointed the onset of problems for 50 percent of the stepchildren as being at the time of their parent's remarriage! To many children they are not gaining another parent, but, rather, they are being totally abandoned by a distant parent, or losing their only remaining parent.

Even children who are anticipating the addition of a parent very often experience loss instead. In retrospect a grown stepdaughter recalled, "I had been looking forward to having another parent to relate to. I was an only child. My mother and father were divorced when I was nine, and my mother remarried when I was 13. But when they got married I was more lonely than ever. I can understand it now, but then I was devastated because every night after dinner my mother and her new husband would go upstairs to their bedroom and lock the door. And there I'd be downstairs all by myself." Even in stepfamilies where there are more children, there is frequently the same feeling of loss rather than gain.

At times the loss is related to perceived (and certainly many times real) changes in the personality of the parent. A stepdaughter said to her father during a discussion many years after the remarriage:

Dad, you expressed that you had a desire to show yourself as being more happy in your new situation (remarriage). You said you wanted to show us you hadn't really left us and that you wanted us in the new situation. My perception of what happened was that you really went away. I mean completely. . . . Your personality as I knew it was gone, and the man I knew as you was completely submerged into your relationship with Christy (his new wife). There was no way of knowing you as an individual person anymore, so essentially you were completely gone. No longer did I feel as though I had a father at all because I didn't know you anymore.

The feelings of the adults and the feelings of the children may be more discrepant around the time of remarriage than at any other time during the divorce-remarriage process. Because of this discrepancy, the adults are usually unable to fathom the children's emotions and consequent behavior. If a therapist or counselor can serve to bridge this gap and create for the adult some awareness of the children's experience, much pain can be avoided for both the children and the adults in the newly formed stepfamily.

DIVIDED LOYALTIES

A mother hangs up the receiver of the phone and explodes in anger at her ex-husband. Her 12-year-old son is within earshot and hears his mother's anger. The boy becomes upset and his mother explains to him carefully that she is not angry at him, she is simply mad at what his father had said to her during the telephone conversation. Her son, however, is not cheered, and his mother cannot understand his moodiness. An older child may have stated the underlying feelings of this boy when she commented to her counselor.

> I want to say that I think one reason why saying negative things about an ex-spouse to the children is unfair is because the children are very vulnerable cause they are half and half. When you say negative things about their parent, you're saying negative things about aspects of them (the children) also, cause they are half that parent. So if Don (stepfather) and Mom said negative things about Dad, I feel I'm part of Dad to some extent, and then they're saying negative things about me.

The fact that a child is a part of two parents underlies the strong feelings of being split apart which most children feel at the time of a divorce. Most children feel the need to choose sides, and since it would seemingly court certain disaster to side with other than the custodial parent, children customarily choose to move towards the parent with whom they live. In most cases, then, this means that after a divorce children are concerned about their mother as they attempt to meet her needs and protect her from emotional pain. At the same time, there is a need for a relationship with the other parent, and the child is torn by the pull of conflicting emotions.

When one or both of the parents remarry the conflict for the child may become even greater. A single mother who was in therapy for personal reasons not directly related to her relationship with her seven-year-old daughter talked of a disturbing change in her daughter's behavior. Julie, who had been only two at the time of the divorce, had visited her father regularly since that time with no outward signs of tension. In fact, as far as Julie's mother could see, Julie had never shown any upset in regard to her parent's divorce. Then suddenly Julie began asking if her mother was going to get married, and if she would see her father anymore if her mother remarried. Julie also was being "naughty" when she visited her father, a dramatic change which was upsetting the father.

The precipitant of the change became clear. Julie's father was to be remarried, and Julie's insecurity as to what this meant in terms of her relationship with both her parents was resulting in behavior which her parents found unacceptable and unexplainable. When the loyalty issues were clarified to the mother, she was able to assure her daughter that her father would always be her father, no matter whether he or both parents remarried. Julie continued to visit with her father as before, and after this discussion her insecurity quickly disappeared.

One high school senior insisted that only his mother and his father could attend his graduation. This meant, according to the son, his mother was to attend the ceremony with her ex-husband and not with her new husband. If she was unwilling to do this, then this young man was adamant that his mother was not to be present at all. The loyalty issues were made very clear, and decisions had to be made. In this particular case, the mother chose not to acquiesce to her son's demand, and for a number of years afterwards their relationship remained strained. The son's deep loyalty conflicts had produced a situation with no satisfactory solution.

After the death of a parent the children cling to the memory of that parent. Many times the children and also the remaining parent begin to idealize the dead parent, and any new close relationships the remaining parent forms are seen by the children as examples of disloyalty to the dead spouse. In cases of remarriage of widows and widowers the loyalty issues for children can be even more difficult than after a divorce, because in the case of a death the other parent is not simply living elsewhere, presumably enjoying a new life-style.

Important also is some degree of comfort between natural parents and stepparents, and to a lesser extent between the different sets of grandparents. Unfortunately, amicable relationships of this nature are difficult for many—and impossible for some. With the steep increase in the number of divorces and remarriages, mental health professionals are working more and more with all the caretaking adults in stepfamilies in attempts to settle basic custody and visitation issues, and more cordial relationships between these important adults are being reported.

Since any remarriage with children involves at least a partial separation of children from a parent, divided loyalties cannot be eliminated. Loyalty issues are minimized, however, when the relationship between the natural parents remains cordial or at least civil. If natural parents can be civil to each other or, better yet, friendly and comfortable, the children have much less need to choose sides. When ex-spouses are friendly, the children do not experience the trauma of going back and forth between two armed camps.

Isolina Ricci (1978) writes,

> There appears to be considerable agreement among professionals that when children are involved, the most successful or least traumatic divorce is one where the children retain a continuous and healthy relationship with both parents after the separation. Now some evidence is emerging to support this intuitive premise (Nolan, 1977). It appears that children with cooperative parents were characterized by a qualitatively different and overall satisfactory adjustment compared to those children whose parents were less cooperative. Research by Kelly and Wallerstein (1976) and Hetherington, Cox and Cox (1976) provides the basis for most discussion regarding the impact of divorce on children's social and cognitive development. Both researchers found that children who fare the best following a divorce are those who are free to develop "full" relationships with both parents.

The most detrimental situation for the children is when they become pawns in the struggle between their natural parents as they vent their hostility towards each other. The natural parents may fight over visitation, child support, money for therapy, private school tuition, and on and on—withholding nurturance of many kinds from the children as the struggles drag through the courts. No matter what the outcome, in such battles it is the children, with their attachment to each parent, who are the victims.

In the majority of stepfamilies there is moderate discomfort between the adults in the two households, and as a result the children have difficulty dealing with their wish to be loyal to both of their parents.

The issue of the adults' feelings about ex-spouses is a confusing area. Many adults are aware of the children's loyalty to the other parent, and of the children's need for a good relationship with that other parent. Because of their sensitivity they attempt to hide their feelings, which can create a covert rather than overt situation with which the children must deal. In her book *Stepchild in the Family*, Anne Simon considers that a certain candor by the adults is necessary, and she points out the conflict when she says:

> Intellectually the parent gets the message: his emotion must be swallowed in colossal repression and along with it his very real and crucial opinion; better the parental stomach be ulcerated than the psyche of the child. . . . Whether all parents can follow these instructions is a question mark to the pragmatist; whether they should is a moral inquiry rarely raised. The protective injunction is so firmly established in divorce mores that to challenge it is almost heresy (1964, p. 109).

If parents are dishonest about their feelings, it can create conflicts for the children and for the other adults. For example, a mother verbalizes to her children that she is most anxious for them to visit with their father and stepmother, while behaviorally she sends a very different message. If the visits do not go well, a stepfamily discussion of what may be preventing greater harmony bogs down because of the need to deny certain feelings.

On the other hand, feelings can be acknowledged and expressed in a destructive manner if the parent is insensitive and hostile. Children can deal with some degree of openness, but are adversely affected when they are faced with continuous hostility. An adult stepchild talked about the parental dilemma:

> I think there obviously are some negative feelings about the other spouse, or there wouldn't have been a divorce. . . . I think it's very different to know there are negative feelings about my father, than to have somebody walk around day in and day out and say, "Boy, when Craig (her father) did that, boy, he certainly was a pig and that was awful." That kind of a constant repetiveness would make it much more difficult for me to love him.

I think it's important not to discuss some of the things about an ex-spouse, particularly if there are younger children. Kids can be mean enough themselves, and parents don't need to give them ammunition that comes from an adult's perspective. I also think there can be an awful lot of feelings under the surface, but unless somebody comes out and says something point blank, the feelings are under the surface and can only be guessed at. In many cases I think that's very valuable.

The message seems to be that parents and stepparents need to acknowledge their feelings, both positive and negative, but details and elaboration of negative feelings about the other adults in the children's lives are not necessary or helpful to the children.

WHERE DO I BELONG?

Mental health professionals find that children's areas of concern keep reappearing and reappearing as though they have never been dealt with. Over and over again a mother may need to reiterate that she and her husband are getting a divorce, and she may need to explain to the children over and over again the general reasons for the dissolution of the marriage.

In the mourning process, after this acute period of denial, there usually come guilt and anger, followed by despair or depression. Individuals have different rates of moving from one stage to another. Many times counselors and therapists can be helpful in assisting both adults and children with this mourning process so that satisfactory reorganization can then take place.

Whether or not stable reorganization has occurred prior to a remarriage, at the time of the remarriage a totally new reorganization needs to occur. Remarriage is the last phase of the disintegration-single parenting-remarriage process and it also is the beginning of a new phase in the lives of the stepfamilies members. The difficulties for the adults in integrating themselves into a group with previous alliances have been mentioned earlier. For the children a major question becomes "where do I belong?"

For the majority of children their world has been turned upside down. The familiar "givens" are no longer present. An oldest child may no longer be the oldest child or a youngest child the youngest child. An only child may suddenly have two or three siblings; mother or father now needs to give time and attention to three or four children rather than to one child.

Eight-year-old Janet remained with her mother after the divorce. When her mother remarried Janet lived with her mother and stepfather, but things did not go well in the new family. Janet did not see her father very often because he lived in a different city, but after Janet's father remarried she came to live with her father and stepmother. Janet's father and stepmother were very pleased to have Janet join their family, and Janet herself was excited with the prospect of renewing a close relationship with her father. However, the woman Janet's father had married also had a little girl about Janet's age who lived with them. The displacement felt by Janet, as well as the anxiety and insecurity she felt at not knowing just where she was going to fit into the family structure, left her bewildered and depressed. Fortunately, the family sought professional help soon after the formation of this new family group.

For older children the displacement and confusion can be even greater. Imagine a teenage boy who has been the "man of the house" for several years suddenly being asked to relinquish this status to a strange (or even not so strange) male. No longer does the adolescent have the responsibility for cleaning the car, washing the windows, or carrying the heavy loads for his mother. Perhaps he complained bitterly about the tasks at the time, but he did have a recognized status in the home which is now eliminated.

Or take the situation of a 16-year-old girl whose mother had died and who had been doing the housework and cooking for her father and younger brother for several years. Her father is planning to be remarried to a woman with strong motivation to be a super wife and mother, who is rearranging the kitchen and talking about "her" kitchen and all the delicacies she is going to prepare for the poor motherless family. The stepmother-to-be is full of the very best of intentions, but the daughter who has been running the household feels upstaged, replaced, and crowded into a very small corner. Where is there going to be a place for her? How can she return to being a child again under the tutelage of an adult when she herself has been the almost-adult female in the household?

If the adults can be helped to see the fears of the children in regards to the family reorganization, attention can be paid to the needs of all the individuals. The concerns can be expressed, the feelings accepted, and a clearer delineation of new roles can be achieved.

MEMBERSHIP IN TWO HOUSEHOLDS

The diversity provided by having a membership in two households can eventually give children in remarried families additional role models and a wider variety of experiences from which to learn and grow. Many children, however, do not perceive the back-and-forth trek from one household to another in a positive light. They feel helpless and out of control; they seem to be faced with constant change which feels like complete "culture shock."

The sets of rules in the two homes may be quite different, and unless the children have some help in recognizing that there are many different acceptable patterns of living rather than a "right" and a "wrong" way, they may constantly battle at least one pattern. In doing this they cut themselves off from one parent as well as from a richness of experience that is available to them.

Many times the children's upset at going back and forth between two homes is a result of the recognition on the children's part that one parent is threatened if they enjoy the other environment. The more nurturance provided in the "other" home, the greater may be the children's conflict. If the children spend less time in one household, it is usually that home that is the threat, since the parent with whom they really "live" is the one whose love and approval are of primary importance and can be threatened.

This conflict is directly related to loyalty issues that have been previously discussed. In a recent paper, Messinger, Walker and Freeman (1978) give an example of what can happen:

A mother reported that her daughter was so upset when she came back from a visit with her father and his wife, that the mother was terminating the visits. On further questioning from the group, this woman admitted that child and father had a loving relationship and that the child's upset might be a result of her loyalty conflict. She wanted to be with her father and she liked his wife, but felt guilty about this because she sensed her mother's disapproval and resentment of this relationship (p. 268).

UNREASONABLE EXPECTATIONS

Just as the myth of "instant love" brings unhappiness for the stepparent in a remarried family, the expectation that a child will instantly love a stepparent also brings unhappiness to the child.

Children may know that it takes time for trust and caring to develop, so when stepparents rush in with words of love, they may draw back and become distrustful. Indeed, the lack of trust may generalize to many other areas.

Often a child has experienced several losses—a parent by death or divorce, and grandparents who cared for the child during the time of the single-parent family. Two familiar patterns may result from these losses: The child becomes withdrawn and builds a protective wall to insure a distance from any new caretaking adult, or the child demands nurturance from a new adult to make up for the hurts of the past. When withdrawal is the pattern, any expectation of affection towards a stepparent is met with hostility on the child's part. The stepparent is bewildered and feels rejected, and very often the relationship spirals downward. If the stepchild demands love, this also complicates the picture and may result in frustration and disappointment since no new "parent" can make up for the hurts of the past.

The age of the stepchildren also is a factor in determining the stepparent-stepchild relationship. As Anne Simon (1964) put it:

The older the children, the more difficult the situation. A baby can be cuddled into security, a small child entertained without violent emotion, but as adolescence approaches with the need to achieve personal identity, evidence of a stepparent-rival is unsettling (p. 117).

On the whole, stepsiblings relate to each other more warmly and more easily than do stepparents and stepchildren. One reason for this may lie in the fact that the expectations for these relationships are more realistic. Parents recognize that children fight and, as one stepdaughter, said, "I really liked my stepsister. I could relate to her because I *wanted* to, not because I *had* to."

FANTASIES OF NATURAL PARENTS' REUNITING

Even after the remarriage of both parents, children often cling to the fantasy that their natural parents will be reunited. They consciously or unconsciously attempt to split up the new couple as the first step in making the fantasy come true. Children's stories and movies sometimes support the fantasy that the child can be the agent responsible for re-establishing the nuclear family.

Wallerstein and Kelly's study of divorce (1978) indicates that parents frequently do not talk with their children about the divorce. In such families the children's fantasies about their parents coming together again can be particular strong.

In working with families after a divorce it is clear that the parents will need to deal many times with the same questions. Children's questions come again and again and need to be accepted and discussed even though the parent recognizes that the question has been asked a number of times before. It is as though the children keep hopping that the original family will materialize again, and they need recurring feedback that a new family pattern is being established.

The tenacity of this fantasy is illustrated by a newspaper story reporting the comment of a grown woman when her parents remarried each other. The parents had been divorced when the woman was young, both parents had remarried other people, and now both were single again and had remarried in their seventies. Their daughter, now in her fifties commented: "I always knew they'd get together again!"

Many children look for signs that their parents will reunite, interpreting friendly gestures even after the parent's remarriage as signals of reconciliation. They often write stories and recall dreams in which their natural parents come together and they all live together "happily ever after."

In some stepfamilies the fantasy becomes reality as the natural parents do reunite. This may come about because the natural parent, burdened by guilt, cannot withstand the wishes, depression or anger of the children. The stepfamily then disintegrates and the natural parents re-establish their intimate relationship. Usually this reconciliation attempt fails, and the children are once again faced with the loss of a natural parent. This time, however, the children are more certain of their power and may become tyrannical as they wield this power in the household, believing that the limits will bend and they will again have their wishes fulfilled.

When this difficult situation becomes unmanageable, professional help is often sought. Obviously, there is a need for the establishment of a workable balance of power so that adults and children can accept the limitations as well as the freedoms in their lives. Clear and unequivocal parental messages, both verbal and behavioral, repeated many times, are often necessary to introduce the reality of the situation. To have wishes and fantasies is common and understandable—but children must be helped to know what is fantasy and what is reality.

GUILT OVER CAUSING THE DIVORCE

Closely related to the fantasy of reuniting the parents is many children's deep feeling of guilt that they have caused the divorce of their natural parents. In second marriages some children carry an even greater load of guilt and worry that their behavior will cause a second divorce. Since it is often the relationship between adults and children in a second marriage that causes observable strain, the children's feelings of guilt may have a realistic base. Guilt breeds resentment and anger and itself precipitates much of the behavior which the adults find difficult to tolerate or handle.

Latency age children, six-to-12 years of age, are particularly apt to think in these terms. Children at this age are struggling to gain mastery of their environment, and to cling to the belief that they caused their parent's divorce does impart some sense of mastery. To give up that belief may reduce the guilt, but it also is a clear recognition of the child's helplessness to control the environment. It is easier to believe "if only I had been different my parents would have stayed together," than to accept the inevitability of the situation no matter what the behavior had been.

ADOLESCENT STEPCHILDREN

Adolescence, a time of emerging sexuality and individuation, is chaotic in many nuclear families. The young person is separating from the nuclear family and establishing roles apart from the family. Separating from two stepfamily households can be more difficult than separating from one, and confusion over role models can lead to added tension for an adolescent.

If there is an adolescent stepchild at the time of a remarriage, the status this individual enjoyed in the single-parent family may be partially usurped by the new stepparent. As one 16-year-old said, "I can't go back to being a child again."

Often the new stepfamily is attempting to establish a sense of family cohesiveness, and the adolescent is asked to be a participating member of that family at the stage of personal development that requires the loosening of emotional ties with the family. This produces a collision course which can only be averted if the adults in the teenager's life will allow the young person considerable personal space and distance from the family.

At this stage of development, many children faced with divorce and remarriage of their parents withdraw from both their parents, and quickly seek sustaining relationships with peers. If this is accepted by the adults, teenagers relax and begin to appreciate having more than two adult role models as they determine what adult characteristics feel personally useful and comfortable.

Sexuality in stepfamilies is more of an issue than in intact families. Young children suddenly thrown together and living in the same house may be attracted to each other. Many times they deal with these feelings by fighting with the object of their affection. Teenagers suddenly relating under the same roof have even more difficulty with their sexual feelings. Stepchildren's attraction to stepparents can lead to withdrawal and hostility to mask the feelings and to help control the unacceptable impulses.

A young man looking back at his experience of becoming a stepson in his early teens states the sexual conflict clearly:

> I was always thinking about girls and I was always thinking about sex. And one of my fantasy objects was my stepsister. This was particularly tough because I felt both attracted to women and afraid of women, and there she was in various states of undress. Whether she actually was or not I really don't remember. I was attracted to her and I was curious about her both as an individual and as a symbol. She was too close to ignore. I couldn't distance from her in that house.
>
> Another one of my objects was my stepmother. And that was even worse! It was even more threatening to me because I was attracted to her sexually and I went out to her emotionally too. There was a lot there in my head. Really my fear about my sexual feelings about my stepmother kept me from expressing some of my positive emotions towards her.

Teenagers are aware of the sexual relationship between the newly married couple and this is disturbing to them. In intact families adolescents tend to think of their parents as asexual beings, while in remarriages the adolescents are forced to recognize sexuality as a part of the adult relationship. Although no systematic study has been reported, clinical observation suggests that the greatest conflict is that of teenage girls as they are faced with their mother's sexuality.

CHILDREN OF THE NEW COUPLE

There has been little study of the effect on a stepfamily of the birth of children to the remarried couple. Duberman (1973) has reported that the birth of a baby makes for a better relationship between the stepsiblings in the family. Since all children in a stepfamily are equally related to a new half-brother or half-sister, the birth may act as a link between the stepsiblings.

Clinical impressions are mixed. When one of the spouses has not previously had children, the birth of a child suddenly produces a new strong set of positive feelings for many such adults. There is then a difference in emotional response to this child and to a stepchild, which may produce sudden tension in the stepfamily. Where both adults are parents/stepparents from the beginning of the stepfamily, differences in emotional responses to natural and stepchildren have been present from the first, and the children have shared a parent with other children from the first. In such stepfamilies a birth will bring shifts within the stepfamily unit but the changes appear to be less disruptive.

Children in stepfamilies often express the fear that there will be new babies born to the couple who will totally disrupt their relationships to the adults. They may say, for example, "The baby would have direct blood ties and would be more valuable in this family because it would be related equally to both parents." Children in all families tend to fear a loss of position in the family when a new child is born. As in other types of families, reassurance and acknowledgement of the children's fears do much to relieve the apprehension and pave the way for more positive responses.

Many motivations lead to a decision to have a child. The need to assure spousal commitment, demonstrate family solidarity, or satisfy cultural expectations are reasons for conception that often lead to future difficulties. Unfortunately, the first two motivations can be particularly strong in stepfamilies. One other source of future stepfamily problems is the desire to produce a new family that will compete with and hopefully surpass the family of the spouse's former marriage. Where a child is born to support the foregoing needs it is less likely that the birth will enhance the functioning of the stepfamily. On the other hand, children born from the loving commitment of the couple can produce positive gains for the children as well as for the adults in the stepfamily. As with many other stepfamily areas, longtitudinal as well as cross-sectional research is needed to clarify these issues.

ADULT STEPCHILDREN

Although counselors and therapists may seldom see adults who are seeking help around stepfamily issues it seems important to point out that age does not necessarily eliminate the strong feelings. One woman stated the conflicts clearly:

> Here I am a 35-year-old woman who has been married and divorced. Then a few years ago my mother died and a couple of years later my father remarried and when I walked into his house for the first time after they were married I had the strangest feelings. Everything was changed. The furniture was different and things didn't look the way they had before. I found it very upsetting.
>
> I felt like an unbaked cookie. When things started to heat up I started to rise. My stepmother feels insecure with me because her children have had real problems, so she keeps wanting to feel that I, one of her stepchildren, am also not perfect. This makes her feel better about herself since she sees her children as a reflection of herself. So everything I do or want is somehow wrong.
>
> As for me, I was very close to my mother and my father didn't give her as much of his time as he could have. Then my mother died and my father changed and it's awfully hard to see another woman getting what I always wanted my mother to get. I identify with my mother and so this makes me very resentful.
>
> Also, my mother dies and my father remarries and I get nothing but a chest of drawers. My mother worked for half of their money and now I have no trust that I will ever get any of it. It's really not the money that's the most important. It's the things with emotional significance. My mother was an interior decorator who created the beauty in our house. My father would have been satisfied to live in a sterile little place. Then after he got remarried, his new wife didn't like the furniture and other things, and she gave a lot of things away without asking me if I'd like any of them. That really made for a go-around. If she just could have checked with me first to see if I wanted the things. I would have even paid for them.
>
> My stepmother tends to resent my relationship with my father, and I have a hard time feeling that my father isn't rejecting my mother, and part of me, when he's at the beck and call of my stepmother. So the stepmother-stepdaughter relationship is most difficult. And the family traditions are all changed. I'm sentimental and when we don't keep them somewhat the same, it says that what we did before was the

wrong way. As I said before, here I am, married and divorced myself, and I'm an adult and I can't help it, this remarriage bit is hell.

Statistics from the Department of Health, Education, and Welfare (*Vital Statistics*, 1974) indicate that by 1974, 315,000 divorces were granted in one year to individuals over 45 years of age. This means that many adults become "stepchildren" after the remarriages of parents following divorce or death of a parent. As illustrated by the young woman quoted, the feelings and reactions of these adult stepchildren are often the same or very similar to those of younger children. In addition, there is frequently much concern with wills and inheritance when a parent has died, and an increased sense of guilt when there is a divorce and the "children" are told or believe that their parents stayed together in unhappy marriages "for them."

A recent article tells of the experience of counselors meeting with adults whose parents have recently divorced. These professionals report that "adult offspring affected by these divorces claim to be no less shattered by the divorce than they would have been as children." Corroborating this are the words of one woman who feels that she has finally accepted the divorce and remarriage of parents, which occurred when she was grown and married herself. "It would have been so much better if we had tried to understand each other's viewpoint. Instead, we all fought like adolescents for what we wanted. It was hard on my children too. Those Christmas dinners with only one grandparent! To say nothing of the dilemma of having to choose between inviting my father or mother. It's still difficult, *especially now that my father has remarried*. But we are all trying—my parents, my brothers, my own family. We've buried our anger—and that's a beginning (*Parade Magazine*, 1978, p. 7. Italics added).

Shattering of the nuclear family bonds is upsetting to individuals irrespective of age, and the formation of new attachments by the parents stirs many conflicting feelings in the "children" of any age.

11

Working with
stepchildren

Adults in stepfamilies have chosen this pattern of life. Children in stepfamilies are in stepfamilies through no choice of their own. The adults have many difficult situations and sets of feelings with which to cope, and they continue to do so when the overall pattern of their lives brings them personal satisfaction. The children face equally difficult situations and sets of feelings, which they must continue to try to handle even if there is no corresponding personal satisfaction. Many adults recognize this difference and express deep concern over subjecting their children to lives of turmoil and unhappiness because of their own search for happiness. Stepfamily couples might be more comfortable if they realized that to date the research findings are encouraging as researchers look at the long-range effects of divorce and remarriage on children. A number of child therapists also express an optimistic view as they comment that under even moderately satisfactory conditions, children in stepfamilies may have advantages not enjoyed by children in nuclear families.

Dr. Walton Kirk of Walnut Creek, California, writes the following in response to questions about the prognosis and therapeutic focus for stepchildren:

My own view is that stepchildren, if handled even moderately well, have at least an equal if not better emotional base than children in intact families. I refer particularly to stepchildren, which assumes a two-parent family rather than a single-parent family. The exposure to profound change and even fair resolution of the anxiety involved is, I believe, an experience in loss and grief and disruption which provides a child with conscious exposure to the increasingly obvious existential nature of our culture. At least it fits with my existential-interactional theoretical position.

A few interesting aspects came up when I reviewed ten fairly current cases with stepchildren involved. I think these aspects will probably hold up if a larger more reliable sample was taken from my practice.

The majority of stepchildren I see are within the age range of 12 to 15 (at least 75%); 80% are male, 100% present school problems of varying degrees, and all of the children are within the range of high average to superior intelligence.

A finding that even surprised me is that 80% presented a picture of passive-aggressive personality or passive-resistive behavior. The parental refrain is "he won't do anything we tell him to—nothing we try seems to help—he just won't do anything in school."

I find the children concerned about which set of parents (custodial or non-custodial) is telling the truth or is "right," even in families where there is a minimum of conscious or unconscious parental manipulation of the children. I find this has more to do with the child's ability to tolerate ambiguity than it has to do with conflict between the two sets of parents. There is almost always some anxiety reduction in the child when he comes to understand there may be two points of view and that both points of view may be valid; the child is learning to deal with relative rather than absolute values.

Children find relief as soon as the stepparents become more certain in their own relationship with each other and in the way they deal with the children (so what else is new?). I have consistently found that where there is a fair amount of conflict between the stepparents, the child is better able to handle these differences and resolve ways of handling the differences between the stepparents than are the parents themselves. Therefore, unlike many therapists, I rather frequently see children in therapy with only a minimal amount of consultation with the parents. When the child understands the parents' conflict and can handle his own anxieties, it assists in focusing the interaction where it should be, i.e., between the parents rather than involving the child. I have seen this happen so consistently that I frequently see a child in therapy for a period of time before working intensely with the parents.

The main intrapersonal psychodynamic is helping the child deal with his anger and grief. These two feelings are present without exception. I find children derive some therapeutic benefit from the simple recognition that there is a problem. I never cease to be amazed at the child's willingness to acknowledge problems and deal with them if one is open about it. Even the most passively hostile child (non-talker) will still verbalize acknowledgment of a problem and a desire to deal with it. Providing a child with no pressure and the inviolate respect of therapy being his own time is essential in the initial phase of therapy.

Many therapists and counselors agree with Kirk's approach and meet with stepchildren on an individual basis. The basic problems of children have been discussed in the previous chapter under the following headings:

Dealing with loss.
Divided loyalties.
Where do I belong?
Membership in two households.
Unreasonable expectations.
Fantasies of natural parents reuniting.
Guilt over causing the divorce.
Adolescent stepchildren (problems with identity and
    sexuality).

Naturally, the ways in which the therapist or counselor works with a child depends to a large extent on the age of the child and the training and theoretical background of the therapist or counselor. Richard Gardner's book *Psychotherapy with Children of Divorce* (1976) is a valuable resource book for therapists and counselors. Although there is only a small section devoted to remarriage, the book deals at length with the feelings of abandonment, guilt, anger and grief which most children experience before and after the formation of a stepfamily.

PRESCHOOL CHILDREN

Grief over the loss of the parent who died or partially disappeared because of a divorce occurs for all children, with the possible exception of those who are young infants at the time of the loss. Young children have little differentiation from the caretaking parent, and if close contact with this parent is maintained through the first 18 to 24 months of life, infants experience little disruption. Sudden loss of both parents can result in the anaclytic depression noted by Spitz, and needs to be avoided if at all possible. Addition of a stepparent during these months may cause little trauma so long as the continuity of care by the nurturing parent is constant.

Incomplete mourning of loss is a basic problem for children in remarried families. Usually the parents go through the stages of denial—guilt and anger—depression—and then reorganization more quickly than do the children. In most cases, the mourning period is shorter for the adults who were conscious of wishing to end the previous marriage.

As far as the child is concerned, suddenly there is another "parent." Preschoolers are still developmentally attempting to differentiate themselves from their parents, and they engage in much "magical thinking." When angry at a parent they may wish that parent to go away, and when, indeed, that parent does go away, a young child may tie the event and the angry wish together. Consequently, confusion, guilt, and a wish to have both of their parents together may be seen in preschool children in stepfamilies.

After a death or divorce, young children frequently regress in their behavior and become very needy in terms of attention and affection (Wallerstein and Kelly, 1976). If there is a sustaining relationship through this period, children are usually able to react positively, and after a remarriage, if there is an absence of adult turmoil, the preschool-age child can often accept a new parental figure.

For the preschooler, divorce and remarriage often are confused, and both are associated with loss. New adults may mean a change to a new home and new playmates, with a loss of familiar faces and places. Wallerstein and Kelly (1976) consider that working with the adults produces more positive change for this age child than seeing the child alone. It is probable that in most situations where there are preschool children, whether they involve divorce, death, or remarriage, working with the adults will be the most effective way to promote growth and change. Only the most acutely disturbed young children usually need to be seen by therapists.

If the natural parents are able to maintain a civil relationship, it is important for the young child to have contact with both parents. Some child therapists feel that for a preschool child to deal with two warring parents is more than a child of this age can handle, and that in such cases it is better for the young child not to see the non-custodial parent or to see the non-custodial parent very infrequently. This is a question that needs objective study; at the present time research data are not available.

If a preschool child is seen in therapy the usual toys and play therapy techniques are employed. One therapist uses pillows to cover himself and demonstrate to the preschoolers that he has disappeared and can appear again if they seek to remove the pillows to find him. This therapist feels that the children's joy in their ability to actively regain a relationship with him helps to instill a sense of mastery over their relationships with both of their parents.

Preschool children who have experienced family disintegration and reorganization need the opportunity to express feelings and to have a sustained relationship with a supportive individual. The therapist or counselor can provide this relationship, thus enabling the child to regain a sense of trust in adult relationships, thus encouraging the young child to form interpersonal ties with parents and with stepparents.

Fortunately, most young children are able to respond quickly to a warm and caring stepparent if there is little animosity between the parental adults. Since the maintenance of a working relationship between the involved adults is crucial for young children, the usual therapeutic approach is to work with the adults. At times biological parents may be seen by the therapist or counselor, or the biologic parents and stepparents may be seen. The focus of the therapy is on ways in which the adults can work together for the good of the child. Attention to the relationships between the adults is customarily not a part of the sessions when ex-spouses are involved together in therapeutic meetings.

STEPCHILDREN SIX-TO-TWELVE YEARS OLD (LATENCY AGE CHILDREN)

Children of this age express their feelings relatively easily so that, as a group, they tend to be the easiest to reach therapeutically. Cognitively they are beginning to differentiate themselves from their parents and to deal in relative rather than absolute terms.

Anger at their loss and general feelings of helplessness often have become uncontrollable, and hostility towards others may get these stepchildren into trouble. For some it is dangerous to express anger to their parents because then "Dad may really, really, leave (reject) me." So the anger is directed towards teachers and peers. Acceptance of these feelings by a counselor or therapist, and the opportunity for release through a punching bag, boxing with a pillow, hammering, etc., leads to mastery and control of the feelings, and a progression to the next stage. Depression may come next, followed, in due course, by a readiness to attempt reorganization.

An important task of the mental health professional is to help the children realize that they can have extra parental figures rather than needing to give up parents if they accept stepparents. Children of this age have usually had many experiences with babysitters, and they know that babysitters are different. Utilizing this experiential example, latency age children can begin to grasp the idea that they do not have to give up a father or a mother if they accept a stepfather or a stepmother. Instead, as with babysitters, they can have more than two parental figures in their lives, men and women who are different and whom they can at least like, or even love. Very often the therapist or counselor takes the role of a father or mother figure in between the mother and stepmother, or father and stepfather, so that the transition is gradual in the child's acceptance of more than the two natural parents. In this way grieving over a loss may be replaced by acceptance of new nurturing.

Some children of this age have experienced several losses through death or multiple divorce, and they may withdraw and be unable to relate to others. As with severely disturbed younger children, these children need a reliable relationship with a counselor or therapist to regain trust so that they may slowly move forward again and test the reliability of individuals inside and outside the family setting.

There is a shift from early to late latency in children's ability to separate psychologically from their parents. Magical thinking slowly disappears, but a sense of guilt at causing the disintegration of the parents' marriage frequently remains. Instead of the divorce being the result of spoken or unspoken wishes, latency age children may see bad behavior on their part as the cause of the parental break-up. Even with therapeutic help, it is difficult for many children to relinquish the feelings of control that this belief gives them. After a remarriage six-to-12-year-olds may still continue to believe that their behavior can separate or reunite their natural parents.

Often children respond with "too good" behavior, or they find that misbehavior earns them parental attention. In some cases remarried parents have even returned to ex-spouses in response to a child's demanding behavior. The usual outcome of such a reunion is a second separation of the natural parents. The stepfamily may then be reunited, or a single-parent family results. The child is devastated and maintains that the custodial parent is completely untrustworthy. Since the misbehavior worked once, and since the feelings of rage are so strong, the usual reaction of the child is to become a complete tyrant in the new household. In such cases the adults frequently need help in establishing and maintaining reasonable limits, and individual and family therapy may be needed.

As well as grieving for parental loss, as six-to-12-year-olds differentiate themselves from their parents they experience many feelings of low self-esteem and self-doubt. The most extreme rejection comes when a parent has "abandoned" the spouse and children. Very often, the children consider that there is something wrong with them that caused their parent to completely disappear. To combat such painful feelings, these children often cling tenaciously to an idealized fantasy of the absent parent and to the belief that the parent will one day come back. When a parent has disappeared, the therapist or counselor has the task of helping the child come to terms with the fact that the parent is no longer available, and that the disappearance was due to a parental problem and not due to the child's being bad or unloveable. Even after the death of a parent many children of this age consider that they have been abandoned because of their own inadequacies.

Mental health professionals often raise the question of adoption by stepparents, usually by stepfathers, when a parent has disappeared after a divorce or remarriage. Adoption is a psychologically complicated issue which needs considerable scientific inquiry before any clear guidelines can be established. The child's sense of unloveableness and low self-esteem that accompany total withdrawal by a parent need to be recognized. Many non-custodial parents cut off contact with their children after a remarriage because they believe it to be best for the children. It appears, however, that even minimal contact allows the children to feel that they are valued by their absent parent. As one grown stepchild anguished, "Even if my father had been stopped from seeing me by my mother and stepfather, just knowing he had tried to see me would let me believe that he really did love me. But I don't think he did love me because he moved away and never wrote, or telephoned, or came to visit."

A counselor or therapist can be very helpful in assisting a child to accept a parental disappearance, so that dreaming about and clinging to the past can give way to acceptance of a new parental figure and appreciation for the positive elements which exist in the present reality. Similar feelings are present after a death or parental divorce, and may become even more acute after the remarriage of a parent.

The case of eight-year-old Jim illustrates the way in which a therapist or counselor can help a child through this difficult readjustment: Four months after his mother's remarriage, Jim began telling his third grade classmates that his stepfather, Roger, was mean and cruel and that he, Jim, was planning to run away and live with his natural father. At home there had been mounting tension between Jim and Roger. Jim accepted no discipline or direction from Roger and was generally openly defiant. Jim had recently begun to whine and cling to his mother, Sheila, and was complaining of severe headaches at bedtime. Roger was losing patience. Sheila felt helpless. At first she responded with tolerance, then anger, and now guilt.

The initial sessions with Jim in the playroom clarified issues which were characteristic of a problem with adjustment to a stepparent situation. Interpretation of Jim's play revealed confusion regarding the role of a stepfather. Concerns about loyalty were evident, as was a sense of loss regarding any possibility of reconciliation between Jim's natural parents. Jim responded to interpretation of these conflicts as well as to repeated explanations and reassurances.

During the period following her separation from Jim's father, Sheila had turned to her relationship with Jim for emotional support. This not uncommon occurrence was now impeding Jim's adjustment to the new marital situation. Jim had derived gratification from his special role in his mother's life; it had diffused some of Jim's distress over his father's absence. Now Jim felt displaced and betrayed. In addition, Sheila had been rather lenient with Jim. Roger's tendency toward strictness was interpreted by Jim as ill-will. Jim needed assistance from his therapist and his parents in order to relinquish his former role with Sheila and return to being the child in the family. It would take time for Jim to grasp that he would ultimately be more gratified by accepting Roger as a stepfather than by opposing Roger. Accepting his stepfather would set the stage for Jim's continued psychological growth within his new family.

In addition to the direct work with Jim, interventions were made in his behalf with his mother and stepfather, who had been participating in a stepparent group. Jim's feelings and behavior were interpreted to his parents, management issues as well as possible changes that could be made at home, were discussed. The basic groundwork was laid for the difficult task of becoming a cohesive family unit.

Latency age boys often identify with their fathers and often worry about them when they are depressed and living alone. These boys retain a fierce loyalty to their fathers and want their fathers to remarry, expressing pleasure that, "Dad has found a new girlfriend." They are less happy when their mothers remarry because then they have a rival for their mother's affection. Girls of this age who remain living with their mothers seem to show less disturbance after divorce. They are more closely identified with their mothers and do not react as do the boys to their father's distress. As with the boys, latency age girls feel added loss at the time of a remarriage, often becoming rivals with a stepmother for their father's affection, or at times with their mother for the stepfather's affection.

One concern that school-age stepchildren have is what to tell their friends about their family. They may feel there is something terribly wrong about being a stepchild, and a difference in last names can be very embarrassing to them. Even though one-third of the children in many classrooms are stepchildren, individual stepchildren continue to feel different and alienated. Restoring a sense of perspective and self-confidence to such children can be a realistic goal of counseling or therapy. Since their cognitive abilities are developing, children this age can begin to understand intellectually the social and emotional situation.

While children may have felt angry after a death or divorce, following a parental remarriage there is a necessity to adjust to new adults, new children, new rules. The original anger may become even greater as they share their bedroom with visiting stepsiblings, share their mother's attention, change the way they dress to conform to new requirements, or give up special TV programs because of competing preferences. A myriad of changes

are taking place. How could their parents split up and then require even greater sacrifices? And then in their second household
there is another set of rules. Often the children become stubborn
and uncooperative, passive-aggresive and provocative in their behavior. When therapists and counselors are able to convey the
idea that there are many ways of doing things, all equally valid,
and that provocative behavior brings added unpleasantness to the
child, some of the stress can disappear. In stepfamilies in which
the adult expectations of the children are unrealistic, help for
the children can reduce some tension, but it is likely that the
couples will also need to explore their values and negotiate differences between them that are producing stepfamily chaos.
There has been no opportunity for stepfamily individuals to grow
slowly into a workable family pattern.

To illustrate: A mother with two teenage girls has been married for a year to a man with an eight-year-old boy and a seven-
year-old girl. The husband's two children visit every other weekend. Since there are only two bedrooms in the apartment, the
seven-year-old girl sleeps on a cot in the older girls' room while
the eight-year-old boy sleeps on the couch in the living room.
The tension in the stepfamily on these weekends is extreme. The
older girls, who want to spend the weekend with their friends
resent the intrusion of the young girl. However, if they do go
out in the evening they must arrange things before they leave so
that they will not wake the young children when they return. In
addition, on weekends when the couple has a social engagement,
one of the teenagers is expected to stay at home to babysit the
younger children.

The visiting children have no friends in the neighborhood and
so they are "underfoot" except when they go somewhere with
their father and stepmother. There is a distant and somewhat
suspicious relationship between the teenagers and their new stepfather and these girls have no desire to make friends with his
children. The younger children become whiny and demanding
the minute they walk in the door. This family came to the attention of mental health workers when the seven-year-old was
brought to a mental health clinic the day she bit her stepsister

following an episode in which the older girl had slapped the younger child when she found that the seven-year-old had tampered with her cosmetics.

While the seven-year-old needed support and understanding, family negotiation soon became the focus of attention. Practical issues such as living arrangements can be much more important in stepfamilies than in intact families where shifts occur as the result of gradual changes. The following changes were instituted:

1. An arrangement whereby the teenagers continued to have their room to themselves, even when the younger children were visiting.
2. A plan for the adults to arrange some outside activities to help integrate the visiting children into the neighborhood.
3. Payment to the teenager who did any babysitting, and the hiring of an outside babysitter if both teenagers had plans to do things with their friends.
4. A drawer for each visiting child to keep clothes and special toys.
5. Personal belongings of each person considered private property with promises that they would not be touched by others at any time without permission.

Interpersonal relationships and many entwined, complicated sets of emotions were then explored, but the initial dealing with major practical considerations immediately diffused an explosive situation and made further changes possible.

A major concern of children after a remarriage of their parents is the answer to the question of where they belong. Every weekend they "go from Jupiter to Mars." Their thought is, "If only I can get my natural parents back together again then I'll have a place again."

In one clinic utilizing children's groups as a method of treatment, many of the children in the groups are stepchildren who are feeling displaced. The leader of this group has found that when these children suddenly find that they have "a place" in the group, they feel better about the other things in their lives, and they begin dealing more effectively with their family situations. Groups for stepchildren would be helpful, though it does not seem necessary to restrict the groups to children with similar family structures. It seems important, however, to restrict groups agewise since developmental changes are so rapid through childhood and adolescence. Usual age groups are:

Age 6-9 (latency)
Age 10-13 (late latency and early adolescence)
Age 14-16 (middle adolescence)
Age 17-19 (late adolescence)

While younger children have little difficulty accepting such groups, many teenagers are reluctant to participate. To form a group for teenagers takes considerable work on the part of the leaders, but once the group is established the persuasiveness of the present group members enables teenagers who are willing to "try" the group to stay and benefit from the group experience.

Dr. Robert Herman, a child psychiatrist, summed up his work with latency-age stepchildren in this way:

> There is nearly always incomplete mourning of the divorce. About the time the parents come out of this the children have not progressed that far. The children are still trying to get along with one parent and then all of a sudden there is another "parent." Parents can't understand why children can't accept this new person. In fact it makes it twice as hard for the child if the stepparent is nice because the child feels disloyal to the natural parent if he or she loves the stepparent.
>
> A little girl came in because she was suicidal. She was angry at her father for leaving. She had had a place with her mother—then her mother remarried and the little girl lost her place there. She was very sad and went to live with her father and stepmother, but she felt again without a place since there were other children in the family. She can't tell her Dad how she feels because then he'd get very angry. She needed to have a relationship with me (therapist) so that she could feel better about herself and begin to accept her new place in the new family.
>
> When ex-spouses fight over who can provide the most and who can be the best parent the children try to figure out how to live in those two worlds. "How can I give up my

mother or my father?" The therapist needs to get across the concept that they don't have to give up either. The child can have a third or fourth parental adult.

I try to have the child talk to the parent with whom they live. Some children have been able to tell their parents that they are still grieving for the other parent. The ability to do this varies with the intelligence of the child, how verbal the child is, and what the parent is like.

Many younger kids have a tremendous loss of self-esteem. For example, a boy who loses his Dad. He has to figure out why his Dad doesn't come to see him. Is it because he's not worth very much? "I'm not very valuable if my Dad doesn't want to see me. If I'm worth a lot I could get my parents back together again. If I'd been more powerful I could have stopped this and gotten my parents back together again."

With low self-esteem these children tend to make teachers dislike them and so the low self-esteem is perpetuated. They get into a negative system. You can always get someone to hate you; you can't always get someone to love you—so they settle for that.

Because of the loss there is a fear to get close again, so the children develop a wall and don't want to get close to the stepparent because the loss of the parent hurt so much the first time. It's a theme of loss, of having a place and losing it, and of being expected to accept a new person as a parent.

In therapy if you can get children to like themselves, then they can start working into the new family. Many children come to terms with their stepparents after they have worked through their grief reaction. Then they can accept that they have another parental figure in their lives.

In some stepfamilies the children may have been having difficulty prior to the death or divorce. In such instances, the added stress may then become too much for the child to handle. Usually therapeutic contact will need to be less focused in such situations. Jenny's counselor comments on this aspect as she talks of her work with Jenny:

Mr. James called requesting help for his daughter Jenny who was having difficulty adjusting to her new stepmother. Jenny, who was seven, was having outbursts of anger and temper tantrums in which she banged her head, all in re-

sponse to the seemingly slightest stress. When the stepmother's family visited the James' home, Jenny called them
intruders and locked herself in her room. Jenny's school
work was suffering and she was defined as a behavior problem in the classroom.

A careful history revealed certain stresses commonly associated with a reconstituted family. However, there were significant problems which were not in reaction to the current
home situation, but which were a reflection of the child's
internal conflicts.

An evaluation of Jenny in the playroom showed her to be
a very angry and highly anxious child who had just barely
received "good enough" care during her early years. Mr.
James described her as difficult, but manageable up until the
present time. It seemed that the current stresses in the home
required coping skills that Jenny was not yet capable of and
called forth more clearly some of Jenny's developmental
problems.

It was important that stepparent issues be separated from
problems which were of an internal nature. Certain changes
could definitely be made at home to facilitate adjustment
and lessen some of the stresses on all the family members.
However, ongoing therapy was clearly indicated for Jenny,
with some level of participation by her father and stepmother. While adjustment to the stepparent family would be
an issue for Jenny, it would not be the main focus of her
therapeutic work.

ADOLESCENT STEPCHILDREN

Therapy or counseling with adolescents is often very difficult.
This is particularly true with adolescents who suddenly or not
so suddenly become stepchildren. They tend to deal with their
feelings of loss by withdrawing from both their parents, and by
taking an "I don't care" attitude. But they do care, and they need
help in working through their feelings.

Because adolescents have developed to the point where they
have become differentiated from their parents and are cognitively
mature enough to observe what is going on around them psychologically, they can figure out that their parents and stepparents
are themselves feeling insecure in their new roles.

Very often because of their anger and their intense feelings that the father has been betrayed by the mother, adolescent boys who are living with their mother displace their anger at their mother on to their stepfather. "He is not really in the family. I had two parents, then I had one, and now he's taking her away."

Research indicates that the most difficult step-relationship is that between stepmothers and stepdaughters (Duberman, 1973). Duberman also finds that older stepmothers have more difficulties than younger stepmothers. The difficulties may be related to the age of the stepdaughter as much as to the age of the stepmothers since older stepmothers will tend to have older stepdaughters. Research is needed to clarify these complex interpersonal relationships, but it seems possible that teenage daughters identify strongly with their mothers and resent any woman who replaces their mother in her ex-husband's affection. Teenage daughters also exhibit much competitiveness with their stepmothers for the father/husband's affection.

Sexuality is an area of great difficulty for teenagers in single-parent homes and in stepfamilies. Adolescent girls are upset at needing to acknowledge their mother's sexuality; sometimes adolescent girls become pregnant simultaneously with their remarried mothers. Parental sexuality can no longer be denied and, for many, sexual competitiveness results.

Teenage boys are concerned with identification with their fathers, and feel confused and unable to identify with stepfathers who are unlike their natural fathers. Tremendously ambivalent feelings occur during these years, feelings that many times simply get walled off because they cannot be expressed or worked through even with professional help.

Sexual feelings towards stepsiblings and towards stepparents occur almost routinely in stepfamilies where unrelated teenagers and new stepparents suddenly are expected to relate to each other. Therapeutic acceptance of these emotions is extremely helpful. In addition, explanation that the new living arrangements would naturally lead to sexual awareness is often reassuring to teenagers attempting to sort out and understand their emerging sexuality.

Adolescence is a time when children who have been living with their mother often wish to go to live with their father. Research is needed to provide adequate guidelines in this area to help stepfamilies and individuals working with stepfamilies. The reasons for the change of custody or living arrangements need to be assessed. Very often teenage boys are desirous of a closer relationship with the parent who can act as a role model. If the boy's mother has not remarried and there is no male figure in the home the change can be advantageous. Living with his father can provide an adolescent boy with an ongoing father-son relationship which acts as a positive role model. On the other hand, if the son experiences a stepfamily in which there is a good relationship between his mother and stepfather this can also provide him with guidelines and models for his own personal and sexual development.

If a teenage girl asks to move and live with her father, the request may signal a re-emergence of oedipal issues, and the move could be detrimental to the girl. She may attempt to "win" her father away from any female rivals and in the struggle stir up a hornet's nest for the stepfamily and retard her own psychological development. She may be so caught up in the struggle that she fails to move away from the family towards her own independent emotional involvements.

When children are older, they have had a longer original family history, they have usually been somewhat independent in their single-parent home, and they are further along in the developmental process of leading independent lives separate from their parents. It is a time of conflict for teenagers in all families as they struggle to assert themselves, needing to give up certain dependencies as they grow more independent.

In remarried families the adults are often insensitive to the teenagers' need for independence. If the stepparent attempts to become the "parent," the results can be open warfare. One counselor commented that when a teenage boy was required to call his stepfather "Dad," "he became psychotic over it."

Clashes with teenagers are common in intact families, and in stepfamilies the frequency and intensity of these interactions often becomes unbearable to all stepfamily members. These families usually come to the attention of mental health professionals through the acting-out behavior of the adolescent children. By the time children are this age many changes can be made by involving the children themselves in treatment even if their parents and stepparents will not participate.

Adolescents are able to see their needs as separate from the adult's needs, and with help they can often recognize that their parents' lives have been improved by the changes in their original family even though the teenagers would have wished to have it work out differently. As Dr. Kirk has commented, teenagers can get themselves out from between the adults, thus leaving the adults to work out their relationships independent of the adolescents.

Teenagers are able to recognize clearly the differences between homes, and therapists and counselors can be helpful in providing them with an opportunity to accept and come to terms with many of the differences. They can learn that it is possible to work within each structure and then choose which elements of each home to incorporate into their own lives. Indeed, many a stepfather and stepmother have provided much that the natural parents have not been able to give. As teenagers become able to acknowledge provocative behavior for which they are responsible and become willing to drop these behaviors they are often able to take advantage of the opportunities offered by their different home environments.

From a sociologist's point of view, the nuclear family is a new family structure, and one not found in many cultures. Since American nuclear families contain mother, father and children, this means that a few individuals are attempting to supply many divergent needs for the other family members. "Extended family" units provide a family system in which the burden of responsibility is shared among a larger number of individuals. This consideration underlies the impressions of stepfamilies outlined by Dr. William Ayres, a child psychiatrist. He commented that while he worked with many stepfamilies who were having difficulties, there were three stepfamily characteristics which he attempted to help the children utilize positively:

1. A stepfamily can resemble an "extended family" in which there are several sets of grandparents to meet various needs of the children.
2. Stepparents can provide the kinds of models, information, etc., that cousins and other relatives used to provide.
3. Children who have been having considerable difficulty with natural parents have the opportunity to relate to stepparents who may be very different from their natural parents.

As was mentioned earlier, teenagers do not readily accept individual or group counseling or therapy. If the idea of counseling or therapy is presented as being of benefit to the teenager rather than being a project designed to "shape them up so they will fly right," then adolescents can often develop therapeutic alliances which are very beneficial to them and to those with whom they live.

In summary, with adolescent children the basic task of the mental health professional is the task of helping adolescents attain an independent identity apart from their original nuclear family and from their stepfamily or families. This will enable them to join with the stepfamily from time to time as more self-sufficient individuals, in ways that are constructive rather than destructive to the family interactions.

DEATH OF A DIVORCED PARENT

While divorce rather than death accounts for the vast majority of stepfamilies in America today, there will always be situations in which children lose one or both parents by death. In intact families, the remaining parent or the relatives or friends who then become responsible for the children are also mourning the loss that has just taken place. For stepchildren the death of a parent may not lead to similar nurturance and understanding. When a non-custodial parent dies, children living with a remaining parent, or with a parent and a stepparent, who do not share the grief being experienced by the children, may feel very much alone. Even more tragic can be the situation faced by some children after the death of the custodial parent when they abruptly begin living with the non-custodial parent, where even the patterns of daily life are unfamiliar.

The following two cases illustrate such stepfamily situations. While there are differences, both represent situations in which stepchildren experienced divorce of their parents and then death of the parent with custody. This sequence of events does not occur frequently, but when it does occur separate attention may need to be given to the feelings of the children even if they are young. The children were not seen alone in these cases, and in retrospect the counselor considered that the children and the families could have benefited by the children having an opportunity to work through their grief away from the stepfamily context. While these stepfamilies do not represent the norm, they do illustrate in stark relief dynamics which can also occur in stepfamilies where there has been a divorce rather than a death.

Family B

Brad and his first wife were divorced when their two children, Beth and Bob, were preschoolers. Brad continued to see his children whenever possible, and after Brad's marriage to Susan the children regularly visited with their father and stepmother.

Three years before Brad and Susan were married, the children's mother developed cancer, and she died two years after her ex-husband's remarriage. At this time Beth was 14 and Bob was 12. The children's mother left their custody to her mother and to their father, Brad, and told the children that they could decide with whom they wished to live.

Immediately after their mother's death the children went to live with their grandmother, but within a few weeks they moved in with their father and stepmother and started the school year in a new and unfamiliar school. Susan, their stepmother, had not been married previously, and was about to have her first child.

Even though the structure of this stepfamily was less complex than many, tension began to build quickly and Brad and Susan sought professional help because of their concern about the two children.

The counselor reported:

I began meeting with the whole family at their house. Brad and Susan were particularly worried about Bob who was not communicating with them. They said that Beth was very helpful. Both Beth and Bob were very quiet and seemed sad. Brad was fairly quiet also, with Susan doing more of the talking. Susan indicated that the children had been very independent with their mother, especially as she became more ill, and Susan felt that her cooking for them and trying to clean their rooms was not appreciated. I sought to let Beth and Bob know that feelings of great loss would be natural for them. I also encouraged Susan to be accepting of their sorrow.

Brad and Susan's son was born after the first joint session and was a welcome addition to the family. Both Beth and Bob were helpful with him. Sessions continued for several months except when Brad was out of town on business. During these family sessions I encouraged active listening, "I messages," brought out how they all seemed to have a difficult time expressing feelings, and arranged for Beth and Bob to get pictures of their mother. Standards of cleanliness and food habits continued to be areas of disagreement although Susan became slightly more relaxed about letting them handle their own rooms. Susan criticized Beth's food habits as being unhealthy, but did praise Bob for some work he did in school shop. When Brad came out of his quietness to criticize he did so in such a way that the children were frightened. This was nothing new but had been that way for many years.

The children went to their grandmother's during Christmas vacation, and Susan called me in January to say that they were worse since their return and there was no reason for me to visit the family. Specifically, their grandmother had assured Beth that she did not have to do anything Susan asked her to do. Beth told Susan this and talked of getting a lawyer if necessary and moving out when she was 18 years old. I assured Susan I was available if she wanted to meet again.

In February Brad called to say their family life was miserable and asked if he and Susan could come to see me. Once there Brad explained that he had been away on business a good deal and Susan was being too harsh with the children He lectured Susan about how she should not treat Bob and Beth so strictly. When I asked Susan how Brad's criticism

made her feel, she walked out. I told Brad how Susan could
have easily felt belittled and suggested that he had forgotten
to tell how *he* was feeling. Brad calmed down and agreed to
bring the children to see me.

When they came, Beth and Bob talked of how Susan was
screaming and yelling at them all the time. They indicated,
however, that they were not particularly bothered by this
and they did not plan to leave. They personally did not care
to have better relations with Susan, and Bob said he never
had liked her because she tried too hard to be nice in the
beginning. The family dropped contact with me at this point.
Later Susan let me know that they had just taken Bob to a
child psychiatrist who happened to look like his grandmother,
and they were hopeful he was opening up to her. I praised
Susan for her continuing concern for Bob and Beth, and I
asked her to let me know if I could be helpful to the family
in any way.

In times of crisis intact families have numerous emotional conflicts. Adding a crisis to the complexities of stepfamily interactions
produces conflicts which many stepfamilies find impossible to cope
with alone. In this situation:

1. Beth and Bob had experienced their parent's divorce and
   so they knew that each parent had rejected or been rejected by the other parent. Thus when the children lost
   their mother they went to live with two people who could
   not feel their loss: a father who had rejected their mother,
   and a stepmother who was to take their mother's place
   and who was trying to be better than their mother.

2. The children's mother had left them the power to decide
   between their father and grandmother, and these individuals were rejecting of each other. The children heard
   their mother and grandmother being criticized by their
   father and stepmother, and also heard their grandmother
   criticizing their father and stepmother.

3. Due to their mother's single parenthood and later her
   illness, Beth and Bob had become quite independent in
   caring for themselves. Indeed, they may have been slightly
   neglected, and seemed to feel that affection was not important.

4. Susan had not been married before and she had very high
    standards of housekeeping; her expectations of children
    and parents were exacting. She was also very concerned
    that the children like her and upset when she thought
    they disliked her. These expectations of the children came
    at a time in their lives when adolescent rebellion also
    added to the other emotions the children were trying to
    handle.

5. Brad did not feel that the children's grandmother could
    take proper care of Beth and Bob, and so he was anxious
    for them to choose to live with him. Brad was out of town
    regularly which left Susan with the responsibility for the
    children a good deal of the time, and when Brad was at
    home Susan sometimes felt jealous of the time he spent
    alone with his children rather than with her and their
    infant son.

Brad felt torn between letting Beth and Bob do as they pleased
so that they would continue to live with him, or supporting Susan
in her wish for an orderly house and well behaved children thus
possibly losing the children to their grandmother.

The sorrow, the rivalries, and the fear of more loss are themes
found in many stepfamilies, and are highlighted here because of
the death of the children's mother.

Family T

Tom and Rose lived together for a number of months and then
were married for a year prior to seeking help for their stepfamily
situation. Rose had a daughter, Rachel, from a previous marriage
who was 14 at the time of the remarriage. Rachel had been an
infant at the time of her parents' divorce and, although her father
did not contribute financially to Rachel's or her mother's support, Rachel did visit with her father at irregular intervals.

Tom and his first wife had been divorced when his children,
Theresa and Timmy, were eight and five respectively. When Tom
and Rose were married they knew that Tom's first wife was dying
of cancer and that the children would move in with them when
she did die. Theresa and Timmy's mother had remarried and the

children liked their stepfather very much. A few months after Tom and Rose were married, the children's mother died, and Theresa, now 13, and Timmy, now 10, came to live with their father and stepmother.

It was Rose who made the therapeutic contact. Her analysis of the situation was that the biggest problem was that she did not love her stepchildren and was too harsh on them. Rose believed that she should love her stepchildren and treat them the same as she loved and treated her own daughter. Rose felt sorry for Theresa and Timmy because of their mother's death and because they had also lost a stepfather whom they liked. Rose reported that the children had not been permitted to attend their mother's funeral and that they did not seem to be very sorrowful. Rose felt that the children's mother had been too permissive with Theresa and Timmy but she was careful not to criticize her in front of the children.

The three children got along well together and Rachel was delighted to have a "full-time" father, something she had never known. Rose felt upset when 13-year-old Theresa would come and sit on her father's lap, and Tom had responded to his wife's feelings by having Theresa sit next to him rather than on his lap. Tom and both his children had a good relationship, and Tom was willing to do many things for them that Rose felt would be an imposition for her to do; i.e., taking them to doctor's appointments and swimming practice. Indeed, Rose felt more comfortable not having Tom support her child, and not feeling obligated to support his children. For this reason Tom and Rose, who were both working, contributed proportionately to the household account.

Rose attended a class for stepparents and gained a great deal from the group interaction. She recognized that it was acceptable for her not to love her stepchildren the way she loved her daughter, and that she would be wise to be flexible as Theresa and Timmy mourned their mother's death and learned new standards of living.

Rose realized that she had had a number of years of being single and independent with only herself and Rachel to care for, and now she had more than double the number of people to live with. Thus it would be natural that she would need a period of adjustment to these changes.

Rose's mother loved and adored her new stepgrandchildren and Rose could accept the fact that her stepchildren had therefore gained even if she never loved them. Basically, Rose was encouraged to be less harsh on herself for being the way she was and to ask Tom for help with the many new situations she faced.

Again, as with Family B, Theresa and Timmy were suddenly living with three people who did not share their loss—their father, Tom, who had been divorced from their mother, their stepmother, Rose, who wanted them to change standards held by their mother, and their stepsister, Rachel, who still had both parents plus a stepfather. In this family, Theresa and Timmy had not only lost their mother but also a stepfather whom they liked a great deal. The counselor involved with these two stepfamilies summarizes by saying:

> Although there are characteristics unique to each of the stepfamilies mentioned and to any that may be encountered in counseling, two facts would appear to be constant. One is that the children know that their parents could not live together and therefore the children are denied the experience of grieving the loss of a parent with the other parent, since the other parent has not lost a spouse. Secondly, instead of adjusting to the absence of a parent only, the children must also adjust to a stepparent's doing the dead parent's job. Children whose parents are divorced and have stepparents can recognize that the parent of the same sex does things differently from the stepparent, without being reminded that a parent is dead.
>
> In analyzing my counseling experience and considering the dynamics involved when stepchildren have experienced divorce of the parents and then death of the parent with custody, I would recommend grief counseling with the stepchildren. This could be in addition to, instead of, or before counseling with the entire stepfamily and/or couple. It is too easy otherwise for the stepchildren to deny their grief. After all, the bereaved children are surrounded by those who have not lost someone important to them, people who are busy

with their lives, are adjusting themselves to an increase in family size, and may feel uncomfortable with seeing the children grieving, even if they are not telling the children they have a parent replacement or that it is time to finish grieving.

In both of the two families discussed the children lost a mother and then changed homes. The situation of losing a father and changing homes is less likely but not impossible. While there are numerous variations on this arrangement, one salient characteristic is that when the children move back with the mother, if the father has remarried the children may have developed a strong attachment to the stepmother who they also lose at his death. Such a move can be unfortunate for the children since the stepparent has lost a spouse and might then be able to help the stepchildren with their grieving. If the children also had stepsiblings, loss of these peers could also cause sorrow.

Ideally, of course, all adults, and especially a parent, stepparent, and any stepsiblings, would be understanding with children who have lost a parent. However, since the reality is sometimes quite different, counselors can expect to encounter at some point people whose parents divorced and then one parent died while the person was a child. If the counselor meets these people as children he or she can help the children grieve, assist the other stepfamily members in accepting the necessity for grieving, and aid them all in becoming a successful stepfamily. The process may be very difficult but necessary, for if bereaved children go without an understanding stepfamily or counselor, I believe they will become adults who will need counseling to finish this grieving.

12

Stepfamilies

It is a complicated task to make "blended" families from the men, women, and children experiencing the mixture of feelings outlined in previous chapters. Many remarried families or stepfamilies do achieve family unity and happiness. With increased awareness and with understanding and acceptance of new family structures, it is likely that many more stepfamilies will be able to achieve realistic and satisfying goals.

It is difficult for a society to shift quickly. New family forms emerge while old family concepts linger. Dr. Lucile Duberman, (Flaste, 1977), a sociologist from Rutgers who has studied many remarriages, comments, "There's still that traditional idea of a family sticking together from the first and walking hand in hand into the sunset. But I think eventually the dominant form of the American family will be the remarried family."

As originally stated, the term "stepfamily" is used here to include all family systems in which at least one of the couple is a stepparent, a family system in which at least one of the couple has a child by a previous marriage. The child may visit or live with the couple. This definition is broader than the "stepfather families" of Bohannan and Erickson (1977) or the remarried families of the Census Bureau. The broader designation seems essential in meeting the mental health needs of these new families since the families who seek help take many different forms, including many families with stepchildren who are not considered to live with the couple.

One stepmother commented that she liked the term stepfamily because it gave her the feeling that everyone was in it together, rather than singling out certain individuals as being "step" individuals. Others prefer "blended" or "reconstituted" families, while others dislike these terms. It is unlikely that the coining of terms is over, and it is impossible to say at this point whether or not "step" relationships will acquire a familiar and comfortable emotional tone, or whether some other term will become the accepted choice. Whatever the name, the structure and system characteristics can be recognized and are important considerations.

The major task of the new family is to develop some feeling of wholeness. This is difficult to achieve because of certain characteristics of stepfamilies which make for specific problems, because of the escalation of difficulties found less frequently and less violently in intact families, and because the adults are sometimes trying to create a family more perfect than their families of origin or than the family of their failed marriage.

The major structural elements that need consideration are:

1. The "permeability" (Messinger et al., 1978) of the stepfamily boundaries.
2. The presence of stepfamily members with interpersonal bonds predating the present couple relationship.
3. The presence of at least two individuals who have experienced a rupture of spousal and/or parent-child bonds.
4. The presence of the other natural parent with power outside the restricted stepfamily boundary.

Given these structural elements, what is a realistic goal for stepfamilies? From minimal research data and clinical impressions it appears that one stepfamily goal which leads to healthy growth for all the individuals is the achievement of strong couple bonding. A strong coalition between the adult couple has been determined by Lewis et al. (1976) to be a primary characteristic differentiating the psychologically most healthy intact families from less well-functioning intact families. Its importance may be even greater for smoothly functioning stepfamilies. In addition, in many stepfamilies there needs to be less cohesiveness between the adult couple and the children, and between the children themselves, than seems optimum in intact families. In other words, there are less intense interpersonal involvements.

A strong and psychologically healthy bond between the couple can provide the foundation upon which is built a well-functioning family, whether or not it is a first or a subsequent family. In stepfamilies secure couple bonding needs to be accompanied by flexibility of roles and acceptance of a somewhat loosely functioning family unit. This structure can provide real advantages for both adults and children. Couples most frequently rate their main stepfamily satisfaction as deriving from the couple relationship, and children can benefit from the lessening of stepfamily cohesiveness as compared to nuclear family bonding. The benefit comes from the fact that this looseness allows the children to mature as separate individuals more easily than if there are tight interpersonal connections. This increased personal space is important for children, and seems to be a characteristic of many well-functioning stepfamilies.

It is difficult for many stepfamilies to attain the goal of strong couple unity together with space for the children to move easily within the complicated stepfamily structure. Difficulties arise primarily from problems adults and children experience in their attempts to deal with the four structural elements outlined below.

PERMEABLE STEPFAMILY BOUNDARIES

Many times individuals in stepfamilies and persons outside stepfamilies do not agree on where the family boundaries lie. This is because of ties to a former spouse when there are children of that marriage. As previously stated, these ties result in what Messinger et al. (1978) term "permeable boundaries." Since there are no cultural rules regarding how to deal with these more permeable boundaries, stepfamilies may have numerous difficulties in this area. A good illustration of difficulties in attitude with resulting consequences for the children involved is given by Messinger et al. (1978):

> One woman recounted that when her child was hospitalized following an accident, only "family" was permitted to visit the child. Because of the remarriage there were several role duplications among the visiting family members: two mothers, two fathers, four grandmothers, and a large number of siblings. In this case, the recognition and acceptance of the wider family boundaries produced by the remarriage appeared to give the child an extended world of love and support.
>
> In contrast, another example showed the effect of a restricted view of family boundaries:
>
> A noncustodial parent said his ex-wife refused to allow him and his partner to visit his child in hospital, despite the fact that both of them maintained a relationship with the child, who visited with them on weekends and during vacation periods (p. 267).

Clinical observation suggests that the way in which the majority of stepfamilies are now dealing with permeable boundaries is to consider that the children are members of two family units. If the adults in the two families are willing to acknowledge the rights of the children and of the adults in the two families, then boundary problems are minimal. If a child is in the hospital, for instance, then both families are "family" and hospital visiting rules apply to the members of both families.

When one or more members are "cut off," then restrictions occur and stepfamily problems multiply. Frequently, a custodial parent may attempt to cut the child off from the other natural parent, or remarried parents may cut off contact with an ex-spouse or both ex-spouses. Usually this is done because it appears to alleviate difficulties and make the family situation less emotionally complicated. However, in many cases such a solution is not the best solution for the family.

Children who are the only contact with ex-spouses have a very powerful position in the family which often works to everyone's disadvantage. In many stepfamilies where a parent and child are cut off from each other there is considerable emotional pain and suffering. If the adults can work together and not become competitive or fight their adult battles with the children as the targets, their children can gain rather than lose as the adults seek personal satisfactions in their new marriages.

"Boundary" disputes also flare up over special holidays and the rights of custodial and noncustodial parents. And many times several sets of grandparents become involved. When there is little contact or lack of clarity the children have many opportunities to "play one group against another group." For example, at Christmas time children often use some variation of "Is this all there is? Just wait till I see Dad this afternoon—he'll have a lot more for me." Or grandparents vie with other grandparents and stepgrandparents to form "blocs" and exclude other individuals.

Custody arrangements are also related to boundaries. Many parents in stepfamilies like the idea of avoiding the word "visit" and using the word "live" in reference to when children are with them. "My children *live* with me on the weekends," or "my children *live* with their father and stepmother during the summers, and *live* with me and my husband during the school year" are examples of exchanges that reflect a feeling of belonging.

More commonly, noncustodial parents consider that their children simply visit with them, and the children are half-guest/half-family and no one is clear about where they fit into the family structure. Noncustodial parents also worry about the quality of the contact they do have with their children, and often feel guilty in considering the children to be stepfamily members rather than guests to be entertained. Or the opposite reaction occurs, and noncustodial parents try to instill all their family values in their children during the limited number of hours they have together. In these stepfamilies the children usually rebel at the constant pressure. Noncustodial fathers and mothers may feel helpless and wish that they could relate to their children more spontaneously and on a less contrived and organized schedule. Wives of noncustodial fathers, or "remote control stepmothers" (Simon, 1964), may also feel helpless and out of control when the children are with them.

Many parents and stepparents are deeply concerned about the children's future lives. They try extremely hard and often feel very frustrated in their attempts to shape the future destiny of the children. The research studies of Bohannan and Erickson (1977), Duberman (1973) and Wilson (1975) are helpful to these couples, since the studies indicate that children are able to cope with stepfamily situations and grow into adults with similar positive characteristics as children from nuclear families. George Vaillant's book, *Adaptation to Life* (1977), is another source of comfort since his study of normal adult males again gives an optimistic picture of human flexibility and adaptability.

INTERPERSONAL BONDS PREDATING THE COUPLE RELATIONSHIP

The existence of parent-child bonds is the basis for the existence of permeable stepfamily boundaries. There are preexisting bonds in nuclear families in the attachment between the two adults and their family of origin, and many times unresolved difficulties in these relationships spill over into the marriage and cause problems. In stepfamilies, however, not only do the adults have bonds to their parents, but they may also have unresolved relationships with ex-spouses. And to complicate the scene even further, the children also have alliances with biological parents who are no longer legally related to one another.

Throughout this book there has been discussion of the feelings resulting from these preexisting bonds. Parents may feel guilty in making a primary commitment to a new spouse because this seems like a betrayal of the earlier commitment to their children. And children may view the new couple commitment as a betrayal of their other biologic parent by the remarried parent, as well as a personal betrayal of the children. Jealousies and rivalries are next to impossible to avoid, and many times painful choices are made by the adults as they attempt to preserve the existence of the present couple relationship. Children also make painful choices as they attempt to preserve stability in their lives.

Nancie Spann (Spann and Spann, 1977) talks of a choice made after her divorce:

> I, too, had a painful decision to make when I sent my Chris to live with his father several months after our divorce. Chris' behavior, in his confusion and frustration over the family's breakup, was taking its toll on the two younger siblings. Peter emulated his brother's negativism. They fought constantly. Even Ashley, as small as she was, was developing cranky habits. I was working long hours, running a household, trying to be a mother to a zoo act. Something had to change. So I sacrificed one child to save two.
>
> No, parenting is not easy. The scars run deep for many of us (p. 61).

This decision was made during the middle phase of the divorce-single parenting-remarriage process. Similar decisions may be made soon after a remarriage. The chaotic relationships between stepsiblings, stepparents and stepchildren, or between the spouses in relationship to the children, all can produce such unbearable tensions that one or more children are sent to live with the other natural parent.

Occasionally children are shifted back and forth between two parents a number of times, either at the insistence of the children or the wish of the parents. In either case, these children usually become disenfranchised children who are in need of help so that they can develop a sense of self-esteem and an ability to have close relationships with other people.

In all families there may be difficulties with what system theorists call "triangles" (Bowen, 1966). In stepfamilies, because of the many different coalitions, there is the possibility for many more triangles to occur, with more permanency to the existing triangles. For example, father and daughter may bond together against wife/stepmother, or the new couple may find stability in joining together against an ex-spouse. When this happens there is little or no direct communication between each dyad. The ex-spouses do not communicate directly, and the parent-child or step-parent-stepchild do not communicate directly. Breaking apart these triangles and establishing direct communication between sets of people can do much to enhance stepfamily functioning. Instead of a mother feeling "in the middle," interpreting her husband to her child, and vice versa, allowing husband and stepchild to work out their own relationship does much to develop stepfamily unity. As one mental health worker put it, "Stay out of the relationships that aren't your line." Let people relate to each other directly.

Messinger et al. (1978) describe another common situation where direct interaction creates resolution rather than problems.

> One woman reported that she had felt she should protect her children from their father's lack of dependability. At first she made excuses when he didn't turn up as planned. When she stopped this, the children reacted to their father's lateness by saying, "That's what Dad is like." They accepted him as he was, not needing their mother's protective interpretation of the reality of father's limitations, and not personalizing his behavior as rejection of them (p. 268).

Because stepfamilies are "instant" families with all individuals having former bonds and family histories, many value systems and ways of doing things must be negotiated. Unlike nuclear families in which the parents slowly evolve a family pattern with certain values and traditions, all individuals in stepfamilies come complete with family values and traditions. It is impossible for family patterns to be identical, and suddenly facing the fact that "givens" are not really "givens" can be a shattering experience. Differences come out in such small things as a "home cut" Christmas trees versus a commercially cut tree, tinsel versus no tinsel, opening presents Christmas Eve versus opening presents Christmas morning.

Many differences disappear as stepfamilies develop their own traditions. This, however, takes time, and in the beginning all members of the stepfamily, no matter what their age, need input into the decisions. Stepfamilies usually require negotiation and re-negotiation to survive with any level of comfort.

Because of the previous ties, there are difficulties around balance or accounting problems. You have three children—I only have one; my ex-husband gives me less than you give your ex-wife;

Dad spends more time with his stepchildren than he does with us. There are "ledger" difficulties in intact families, but the degree and possibilities for such accountings are magnified in stepfamilies, and usually run along blood lines. The question of fairness becomes an entangled and complicated matter.

Ex-in-laws or grandparents, and new in-laws or stepgrandparents are important to the stepfamily. All too often stepfamilies lack the usual community support systems, and sets of grandparents can be particularly valuable supports. Children are accustomed to having two sets of grandparents, and as a result they can more easily accept added grandparents than additional parental figures. This means that children can often work into new step-relationships gradually by relating first of all to stepgrandparents.

Unfortunately, some grandparents are unable to accept the remarriage of their children after a divorce or the death of the spouse. They make a point of ignoring the stepparent and any stepgrandchildren, using their influence for harm rather than for good as far as the reorganization of the stepfamily is concerned.

RUPTURE OF SPOUSAL AND/OR PARENT-CHILD BONDS

Stepfamilies contain at least two individuals who have experienced a disruption or loss in primary relationships, losing either a spouse, a parent, a child, or a spouse and child. The disruption may be a permanent and total loss following a death, or a partial loss following divorce.

Stepfamily cohesiveness is hampered by the incomplete mourning of different individuals in the family. As has been indicated previously, the children are less likely to have completed the mourning process at the time of the remarriage, and even if the death or divorce has been accepted, to the children the remarriage usually seems like another loss rather than a gain. Divorce, single-parent family, remarriage are blurred together for many children. Counselors and therapists report that children talk about the divorce and remarriage with little ability to distinguish between the two events. And adults who were stepchildren when they were young continue to relate divorce or death and remarriage in their conversation many years later.

After a death of a spouse, children are the link to the dead spouse; for some parents, even after a remarriage, their mourning process is not completed until the children leave home and are on their own. Often the parent becomes depressed at this time because the link with a dead spouse has become weakened as the grown child becomes independent.

Stepfamily relationships usually appear to be more difficult when a number of individuals in the stepfamily have experienced loss, and when the number and finality of the losses are greater. Even when the mourning process has been completed, the individuals are aware of the possibility of loss, and they are often wary of new close relationships. If children still believe that their angry wishes or bad behavior caused the original loss, they may feel anxious and guilty whenever they discern tension between the new couple. Since much of the stress in stepfamilies is connected with issues involving the children, even if the children carry little or no guilt in regards to the previous divorce or death, the children often become fearful of causing a another break as they experience the focus of attention on their behavior.

Statistics from the 1940s indicate that successive remarriages become shorter and shorter in duration (Walker et al. 1977). Recent national figures are unclear in this area. For many children involved in the multiple marriages of their parents, withdrawal from close interpersonal relationships becomes their way of coping with these successive losses.

The adults in stepfamilities often experience a sense of failure as well as loss after a divorce, and in their need to keep the subsequent marriage together they may attempt to negate personal needs and differences. In some stepfamilies the adults fear that their spouse will leave if they do not love their stepchildren, and the impossibility of "instant love" produces conflict and anxiety. The need to deal with losses in a psychologically healthy way becomes of prime importance for individuals involved in remarried families. This is one area in which working with a counselor or therapist can be extremely beneficial for these children and adults.

ANOTHER PARENT OUTSIDE THE SPECIFIC STEPFAMILY UNIT

In stepfamilies the boundary problem and the problem of who is in charge are related and cause numerous tensions. Stepfamilies look like a family unit long before they feel like a unit. All members may go skiing together, go to the movies together, or have a picnic at the beach together. To the outsider watching the group, they may appear to be a family on a weekend outing. To the stepfamily individuals it may feel totally different. Visiting children may stick close together, feeling strange and missing the parent with whom they live; the "live in" children may feel intruded upon by their stepsiblings; and the couple may be feeling helpless and angry because an ex-spouse refused to let one child join the group because of an appointment considered important by the ex-spouse.

In an intact family it is clear who the members are, and who has the power in the family. If the coalition between the couple cannot be eroded by the children, the family usually can function in a healthy manner (Lewis et al., 1976). In these families decisions can be made and implemented with little or no outside influence. Family roles are defined and recognized by adults and children alike.

In stepfamilies it is important for the couple to form a primary alliance so that the balance of power can rest with these adults. Too often a parent and natural children form a power bloc, or the boundaries are wide and the natural parents control the situation while the stepparent stands back feeling helpless and angry. Role definition is much more difficult because more individuals have to be fitted into the system, there are at least two adults with similar functions in regards to the children (e.g., father and stepfather), and the necessary roles can vary greatly. In an intact family children want a mother and a father, while in a stepfamily, a child may want a mother and a stepfather/friend, if the natural father is also providing nurturance. On the other hand, if the natural father has disappeared, this child may want a mother and "second father." The couple in a stepfamily have more chance for success and a reduction of tension if they are sensitive to the child and to the role most appropriate for the stepparent. This role can also shift as the stepfamily establishes new interpersonal bonds and shared traditions.

Another shift in role expectations in stepfamilies often occurs because the marriage follows a time of single parenting. For many women, this period when they have been on their own, often supporting themselves and their children, has given them the opportunity to be independent in a way not previously experienced. In addition, many women have felt at the time of the death or divorce that their former dependency on their husbands left them in extremely vulnerable positions. As a result, in subsequent marriages many women wish to play an equal role with their husbands in regards to family decisions involving finances, role definitions, etc. Openness and negotiation between the couple seem essential, difficult as they may be.

Because of the permeable boundaries and the powerful position of other natural parents who are outside the specific stepfamily unit, there is ambiguity for the adults. There is also ambiguity for the children as they go back and forth "from Jupiter to Mars," as one social worker put it. There are two subsystems within a larger system of relationships, with the children having an overlapping membership since they belong to both subsystems. Devoid of emotion such a structure is certainly manageable. With the strong conflictual feelings involved, such a structure often becomes complicated beyond reasonable imaginings. Individuals with little tolerance for ambiguity find the lack of control in many stepfamily situations particularly difficult.

If "visiting" children can have space that is theirs alone they can feel rooted in the more unfamiliar household. Even a drawer with clothes and toys can help, so they do not need to arrive suitcase in hand like a distant relation coming for a visit.

If the couple is clear and united in their requirements, the children will also experience less ambiguity and will learn to cope with the situation. And if all the adults directly concerned with the children are able to work together with some degree of cooperation in their various parenting tasks, it will be easier for the children to make the necessary adjustments.

The issue of control is a thorn in the side of many remarried parents. Many times both natural parents, custodial or not, feel stripped of power, and become very angry as they experience a strong sense of helplessness. In many cases ex-spouses use the courts in an attempt to gain some control, but there are many subtle ways to thwart court orders, and such court battles often fan the flames of anger rather than put out the smoldering fire. The courts are beginning to recognize that cooperation rather than litigation is sorely needed, and in some states conciliation rather than adversary proceedings are being introduced.

In the book *Beyond the Best Interests of the Child* (Goldstein et al., 1973), it is suggested that when natural parents cannot agree, the power needs to be in the hands of the custodial parent. This presupposes that the custodial parent will be the parent who can make the best decisions in regards to issues involving the children. Simplification and resolution are sorely needed, but noncustodial parents who already feel in a "one down" position do not react positively to being stripped of further power! Much more study needs to go into this complicated and important issue.

When the adults involved are willing to cooperate and share power, the children are able to accept the authority in each household more easily, and are not placed in a conflictual no-man's land as they go back and forth between their natural parents. Anne Simon (1964) comments on the need for a lack of competitiveness:

> A sensitive stepparent will skirt areas staked out by the child's own parent if he listens with the hearing aid of conscious respect for the other relationship. To him "Dad says he will teach me to sail" is not a signal for stepfather to dash to the closest shipyard, but a directive to stay in dry dock (p. 135).

Too often, however, hostility between the adults stands in the way of cooperation. One parent illustrated the extent of the difficulty when he said, "You'd think we could at least figure out hair cuts." Emotional wounds resulting from the divorce may still be raw, giving rise to personal insecurity and distrust of the ex-spouse.

Very often parents fear that they will lose their children because the custodial parent will move away to a more distant geographic location or the noncustodial parent will seek custody. An individual may become depressed and feel "replaced" when an ex-spouse remarries. When it is the noncustodial parent that remarries, the ex-spouse may also fear that the custody of one or more of the children will be changed.

This insecurity that parents feel may make it difficult for them to cooperate. Nothing seems to go smoothly for anyone. The nicer the stepparent may be, the more threatened the same-sexed natural parent may be, and the more conflicted and upset the children may be. It is difficult for adults and children alike to accept the fact that children can respect and/or love more than two parental figures just as parental love is not restricted to a set number of children.

A major problem for stepfamilies is that they feel out of control and attempt to control what they cannot control, neglecting to consider the control which they do have. If you cannot count on an ex-spouse bringing the children at an agreed time, you can chauffeur the children yourself or make plans that do not require a prompt arrival. If telephone calls are a disaster, you can restrict most communication to letters. If ex-spouses telephone at bedtime you can make arrangements to return the call the next day.

Because of their dual membership the children in stepfamilies are in a position that can easily become more powerful than is advantageous for the family. As in any family, all members need to have power in their own lives, with privileges and responsibilities commensurate with their maturational development. The adults, however, have special functions and are responsible for family management. If the adults give this responsibility to the children, disastrous results can follow.

In one stepfamily, for example, seven-year-old Susan held the power. Susan lived with her mother and stepfather and spent weekends with her father. There was almost no direct communication between the adults in Susan's life, and she carried tales and messages back and forth. When she was with her father, Susan would often complain that she had broken a favorite toy and that her mother and stepfather would not buy her another. Susan's father would then rush out and replace the toy. At other times Susan would be scheduled to be with her father and she would cry and say she didn't feel well and she didn't want to go. Susan's mother would comfort her daughter and say, "That's alright, dear, call your father and tell him you're sick and you can't come today." Then Susan's mother would cancel the plans she and her husband had made for the day or the weekend, and she would stay home with her daughter. When Susan recovered quickly, her stepfather recognized the manipulative quality of Susan's illness. The adults all suffered and felt helpless—Susan's father because the anticipated time with his daughter evaporated, Susan's mother because she felt she had to give up her time with her husband, and Susan's stepfather because he felt unable to communicate to his wife how he viewed the situation. The relationship between the new couple became strained, and a very vicious downward spiral developed for everyone.

Susan was fanning the competitive feelings between her natural parents, and between her father and stepfather. She also wished to have her father and mother together again, and she was behaving in a manner that separated her mother and stepfather. Susan was a whiny, unhappy child, and deep down she did not enjoy the powerful position she was in. She needed the adults to stand firm and set limits for her. With therapeutic help, direct communication between the adults was established, and Susan no longer found herself to be the pivotal point around which the adults orbited. Her first reaction was to have temper tantrums and complain about severe headaches, but when the adults went ahead with their plans anyway, Susan slowly settled down and became a much happier little girl. The relationship between Susan's mother and stepfather also improved markedly, as all the adults regained needed power in their lives.

Even when they have considerable control, because of the permeable boundaries in stepfamilies individual members need flexibility and a tolerance for ambiguity. Since all members come with a family history, and decisions need to be made instantaneously, negotiation and re-negotiation become the modus operandi. Many stepfamilies manage to do this without outside help. Others need the support and understanding of a counselor or therapist to achieve satisfactory stepfamily reorganiaztion.

13

Working with

stepfamilies

A question raised in various contexts is, "Are stepfamilies any different from intact families?" Most members of stepfamilies would answer with an emphatic "Yes!" Individuals who have not experienced the milieu of a stepfamily tend to negate or underestimate the differences, and many stepfamily members are unaware that the problems they encounter may have something to do with the complexities and ambiguities inherent in this family pattern.

In many stepfamilies much of the feeling of "differentness" and alienation is psychologically based. Roles are ill-defined, friends and neighbors seem to never understand the situation, institutions are not geared to handling more than the two biologic parents, and pervasive myths color the thinking, expectations and perceptions of stepfamily members and individuals outside the stepfamily circle.

There is also a structural basis for the feelings of "differentness." There have been recent losses of interpersonal relationships for virtually every member of the stepfamily, all members come together quickly and must somehow deal with the fact that every person of every age has a "family history," as well as interpersonal alliances, predating the creation of this family unit, and the boundary of the family is blurred because the children usually have another biologic parent not living under the same roof.

It is indeed true that interpersonal situations similar to step-family patterns occur in intact American families. A mother-in-law may live in the home, there may be a weakening of the couple bond because a parent in the family has not sufficiently severed emotional ties to his or her family of origin, or strong alliances may exist between a parent and one of the children. In intact families highly disruptive manifestations of such patterns are the exception, whereas in stepfamilies disruption due to simi-lar patterns is to be expected because of the nature of stepfamily structure. In other words, such disruptions in intact families suggest intrapsychic difficulties and are usually considered patho-logic in character. In stepfamilies, on the other hand, such diffi-culties arise from external factors impinging on individual psy-chology and can usually be expected, given the present structural characteristics of American stepfamilies.

Unfortunately, subsequent marriages can be burdened with even more unrealistic expectations than are first marriages. Many individuals in first marriages attempt to recreate their original family pattern if they considered their upbringing to be positive; or, on the other hand, the marriage may be an attempt to create a family pattern very different from the family of origin if early family experiences were negative. When this marriage fails the subsequent marriage and family may then be invested with an even greater expectation that it will meet the unfulfilled needs of the first marriage. Therapeutic assistance can be helpful to stepfamily members in sorting out their expectations and in com-ing to terms with realistic stepfamily goals.

The techniques employed in working with these families may be similar to those used for working with other types of families. The goals, however, may be somewhat different, and the combina-tions of individuals involved in the therapy or counseling will be more varied, because of the complexity of stepfamily structure. The issues raised will at times be similar in content to those raised with intact or with single-parent families, but there will also be dissimilar content arising from the psychological and structural differences of stepfamilies.

GOALS OF STEPFAMILY THERAPY OR COUNSELING

At the present time information from observation and research indicates that a stepfamily functions more effectively when there is a strong caring alliance between the couple, together with less cohesiveness than is optimal in intact families as far as the children in the family are concerned. More cohesiveness is possible with younger than with older children. Because of the ambiguous, permeable stepfamily boundaries, the children usually need freedom and independence to move freely in and out of two different living situations. The combinations of involved individuals possible in stepfamilies are legion compared to intact families, and the degree of freedom and of cohesiveness will depend on the particular stepfamily structure.

If a parent has died or disappeared, the children will need less freedom of movement than they will need in stepfamilies where the children spend time with each natural parent. Even in cases of disappearance, however, psychological space is needed for children to come to terms with the parental loss, so that the children can see the disappearance as resulting from the needs of the parent who disappeared, rather than a response to the unloveableness of the children. In this way, the children can in fact separate from the parent who is gone, and at the same time retain an emotional link with that biologic parent even as they accept the nurturance and caring in their present stepfamily.

Achieving stepfamily reorganization with good couple bonding and freedom of movement for the children can be a difficult task. There can be the pulls on the couple relationship, both internal and external, that have been discussed in Chapter 8. For adults and children there are also many conflictual emotions, including fear of more loss, guilt, anxiety, competitiveness and jealousy, anger, rejection, sorrow, and the problem of divided loyalties. As one father and stepfather said, "I feel I have four guns pointed at me—one from my wife, one from my ex-wife, one from my children, and one from my stepchildren."

The particular stepfamily pattern also affects the goals. If a man or woman without children has become a stepparent, this person has joined a going concern and needs help being integrated into the organization. If both adults have children, there can be more understanding of the feelings of the others, but the necessity of negotiating two cohesive family patterns into a third stepfamily pattern may become an important goal. If both natural parents play an active part in their children's lives, achieving cooperation between the adults in each of the child's households can be a very important goal, and perhaps the hardest one of all to approximate. Frequently cooperation between the adults can never be worked out, and the task for the children then becomes one of getting enough distance and independence so that they can function effectively despite the continued conflicts between the adults.

Many times couple education or a few individual therapeutic sessions for an adult or child in a stepfamily can offer enough assistance to shift unproductive stepfamily functioning to a satisfactory and acceptable level. For other stepfamilies a more prolonged and more family-oriented approach is needed. Counselors and therapists have many possible therapeutic combinations of individuals from which to choose and, while the ultimate goal may be to involve the stepfamily unit in sessions together, care needs to be taken especially in the initial stages to respect the feelings of the individual stepfamily members. Since the stepfamily couple has not had a time together before children were a part of the family picture, it makes theoretical sense to give them this opportunity in therapy before including other stepfamily members. Which other members will be included, and when, will depend on the issues involved, the availability and willingness of the individuals, and the goals that are acceptable to the stepfamily. At times a family may be asking to have its carburetor fixed while the therapist or counselor believes that a motor overhaul is in order. Pushing for unacceptable goals may deprive the stepfamily of help that would be beneficial, albeit incomplete.

As one family therapist stated, "In stepfamilies cross-generational coalitions are set in motion by the particular structure of stepfamilies. Stepfamily structure lends itself to these coalitions so that intact family processes become exaggerated and produce pathological behavior." There may be a coalition between parent and child which often makes it difficult for a stepparent to be assimilated. For this reason many stepfamilies seek help because of difficulties stemming from parent-child coalitions.

In some stepfamilies the natural parent-child bond has become so intense that the stepparent and stepsiblings (if any) cannot find a place in the system. At other times the parent may be seeking gratification from the child that the new spouse is not supplying. For example, a new couple is not speaking as a result of tension over disciplining the children. At such a time it is easy for a parent to seek approval from a natural child and the alliance between these two grows as the closeness between the couple decreases.

At times a noncustodial parent has been "pushed out" by the custodial parent, or the noncustodial parent has disappeared volitionally. The children may be rejecting of a stepparent and the stepfamily is focusing on the "desertion" of the other parent as the cause of the difficulties. Or the parents may say that behavior of the children is the cause of the stepfamily disturbance. Or the behavior of the stepparent or of the ex-spouse is the presented problem. The task of counseling or therapy in each case is to move from looking at a particular family member or subsystem to helping the stepfamily view itself as a total unit with individual input from each person interacting to produce a stepfamily pattern. As individual members are able to take responsibility for their own feelings and actions and see the stepfamily interactions as being a shared responsibility, unproductive patterns can shift to more productive functioning.

WHOM TO INCLUDE

The complexity of stepfamily structure makes many subgroupings possible.

1. *Stepparent couple*

The couple is the most common subgroup seen by counselors and therapists. Because of the need for a good couple bond it seems advisable to offer the opportunity for couples to perceive their need for unity before adding other members to the family group. In addition, since it will be the adult couple who make the decision to maintain a therapeutic contact, the establishment of trust in the counselor or therapist is important and may be achieved best without the need for dealing with the feelings of other family members.

For some couples who see a child as the source of the problem, the therapist or counselor may need to see the child at least once, thus meeting a need of the couple so that the adults will continue to make therapeutic contact. In most instances both members of the couple are seen as a part of the subgroup when adults are included.

2. *All adults involved with particular children*

This may mean seeing a father, a mother, and a stepmother together. When ex-spouses are seen as part of the therapeutic process, the focus needs to be on working together for the child's benefit.

One advantage that can materialize from meetings with the couple and ex-spouses is that it may become evident that patterns of behavior thought to be the result of the new marriage were manifested in the earlier marriage as well.

For example, a husband is hurt by what he sees as his wife's neglect of her "mothering" and "stepmothering" responsibilities. In joint meetings with the couple and her ex-spouse it becomes clear that she has never been an active and involved mother. This enables the husband to perceive his wife's behavior in better perspective. No longer need he measure her affection for him and his children by her attention to household duties and the children's school activities.

Many times an ex-spouse is seen as the source of the stepfamily difficulty. If this person is willing to meet with the other adults there is an opportunity to take the focus off of him or her and have the adults work more as a unit.

The usual content of such meetings involves visiting and custody arrangements, as well as negotiation of differences in child-rearing practices between the two households. Resolving former relationships is not the reason for meeting together.

3. Ex-spouses

When ex-spouses are seen by the counselor, the goal is to improve communication for the benefit of the child. Obviously old feelings will surface, but if the therapist or counselor is not clear in structuring the meetings these feelings may escalate, the meetings may become unproductive, and usually, there will be no improvement in regards to the child. This combination is probably the most infrequently encountered, and probably has the potential for being the most volatile. Even when several sessions between ex-spouses are productive, continued meetings with these two individuals can lead to problems between the new couple, as the new spouse becomes insecure and feels left out.

A time when such a meeting might be in order is where there has been little or no contact between ex-spouses, and the feelings about the remarriage on the part of the ex-spouses are so strong that having the new spouse present would preclude any profitable discussion about the child. Major content areas are visitation and custody issues, which need to be clearly defined.

4. All adults and all children

A major value in this combination is that the children see that their parents and stepparents can talk together without anyone getting killed! The value of this should not be minimized. Children tend to feel caught in the middle and protective of a natural parent, or of both natural parents.

With all adults present the children have the opportunity to relate directly to each adult in the presence of the others. Many uncommunicated feelings can be verbalized, and cooperation can be worked on. Since all are present, the children are not able to play one adult against the other, nor are adults able to blame absent parents.

5. *Various groupings of adults and children*

These groupings will depend on the issues which need attention, and how best to address these issues. At times the presence of grandparents is important. Inclusion of older children who are no longer in the home may also be important for unresolved problems with these children may be affecting younger children still in the home. At times a dead parent has become idealized and the remaining parent and children may need to get in touch with the human qualities of that parent.

One troubled stepfamily had a 23-year-old son who had become delinquent and eventually served a jail sentence. He was no longer in the home, but family therapy began to point to the need for resolution of issues involving him. His mother had died and it became clear that his difficulties centered around his relationship with his two natural parents. He and his father were seen together and the problems worked through. Subsequently he did not need to be included in the family group, and the rest of the stepfamily made good progress in resolving the here and now details of their living together.

6. *The couple and the children*
(visiting or living in the household)

When family therapy is indicated, the ultimate goal is to effect good stepfamily reorganization. The presence of all members facilitates direct communication between the individuals, and cuts down on indirect triangular communication. For children, being part of the process can lead to less feelings that things are going on behind their backs. Therefore they experience more control and mastery in their lives.

Individuals and families, as well as therapists and counselors, have many goals and ideals that are unattainable. Fortunately, human beings are able to adapt to a less than perfect world. The ideal of satisfactory communication between all children and all adults who have had or now have meaningful relationships is a goal that very few stepfamilies achieve. If a therapist conveys the message that there is a narrow range of healthy stepfamily functioning, this may bring a sense of discouragement and failure to many individuals in stepfamilies who otherwise might find satisfaction despite tensions, cut-off relationships, and less than optimum stepfamily reorganization. Different stepfamilies are satisfied with very different goals.

FAMILY WORK WITH STEPFAMILIES*

When all of the members of a stepfamily are seen conjointly and evaluated as a system, problems will present themselves in unique ways. Although classical defenses, resistances, distortions, avoidances, and impasses will manifest themselves, the opportunity to observe them "firsthand," as they actually occur, exists in the context of conjoint sessions. Actually seeing, hearing, and feeling how a family functions generally facilitates an understanding of the family dynamics in a way that verbal descriptions and the making of inferences which occur in non-conjoint therapy do not permit. On the other hand, direct observation presents such a wealth of data, with many inherent complexities, that the therapist may become overwhelmed, even to the point of immobilization. The expanded numbers of possible interactions and their intricate influences on the system become readily apparent in family therapy. This specific therapy approach is, therefore, not a simplifying modality for the therapist, but, rather, broadens and expands the application and relevance of the psychotherapeutic experience. In certain ways to be discussed, the family therapy "orientation" does make the therapist's task easier and adds an efficiency and economy to the experience for both the therapist and the stepfamily.

The stepfamily generally presents one of its stated desires in therapy as "getting along better together." The conjoint setting allows a psychologically safe setting for learning about, trying

* This section is adapted from an unpublished report by Marjorie Daehler, R.N., and Robert Daehler, M.D., family therapists at the Family Psychiatric Center in Phoenix, Arizona. We gratefully acknowledge their assistance.

out, experimenting with, and practicing new ideas and behaviors with the beneficial aid of a skilled therapist. Many of the problems in stepfamilies of getting along together are exaggerations of problems in intact or nuclear families; other problems are unique to stepfamilies.

In observing how and in what ways the stepfamily is getting along, the application of systems-information theory and communications theory in understanding and intervening with stepfamilies is invaluable. Simply stated, what is dysfunctional in one part of the system affects the other parts and therefore the whole in some manner. For example, a stepfamily may have an increased number of connections to other persons not directly involved in its system. Often these "outside" persons may briefly move into the system (on visitation or for a probationary attempt at living together), forcing very rapid adaptations in the stepfamily system, which are often followed by another rapid change. In very disruptive systems, often with marked communication difficulties, adaptations are often handled in a reflexive manner rather than as a planned thoughtful response to a difficult situation. It is helpful to teach the family alternative behaviors that may be preventive of having to make "reflexive" decisions and could strengthen the system rather than disrupt it.

For the stepfamily, the fact that the family is meeting together at the insistence of the parents is often the reassurance the family needs that their system is worth working to preserve. Another advantage of family therapy is the diluting of the focus on any person or subgroup within the family as the identified patient. Once the focus is taken off a "symptom bearer" and re-focused on the system, the identified patient can improve. Sometimes, parents bring in a child as the "symptom bearer" when therapy for their part in the problem is too threatening. Later, when a therapeutic alliance has been established, they may feel safe enough to focus on their own contribution to the problem.

Theoretical Considerations

In our experience, family therapy allows for the application of different theories either singly or eclectically. In order to maintain an organization to one's evaluation and therapy plan and avoid a "hit-or-miss" application of techniques or therapeutic approaches, we have found it useful to consciously and repeatedly refer to four basic conceptual frameworks (Lazare, 1973):

1. *The Biologic or Medical Model*—considers the disorder from its etiology, signs and symptoms, course, differential diagnosis, specific medication and/or psychotherapy and prognosis. This allows for genetic and physiologic considerations as they may be relevant to the dysfunction.

2. *The Psychologic or Psychodynamic Model*—considers such issues as developmental fixations or regressions, early deprivations and their effects, distortions in behavior and communications, and therapeutic alliances.

3. *The Social Model*—focuses more concern on the types and quality of relationships, forms of bonding, significant changes and the effects within one's life space; less concern is focused on intrapsychic conflicts and on psychopathology.

4. *The Behavioral Model*—considers the symptoms themselves to be the problem and, therefore, the behavior to be treated or changed. It takes into account the specific behavior to be modified, the situations in which the behaviors are manifested and perpetuated, and the relearning plan.

Any combination of these may be used as appropriate in an eclectic approach or they may be used singly.

Orientation to Family Therapy

There are specific and unique tools and theories and applications which have been described as family therapy (Bowen, 1978; Satir, 1967; Minuchin, 1974; Guerin, 1976; Ackerman, 1966; Jackson, 1961; Haley and Hoffman, 1967; Bell, 1975; Boszormenyi-Nagy and Spark, 1973). Our major "orientation," however, is that family therapy looks at the whole family system as well as its individuals and seeks ways to most beneficially and practically influence the persons involved to make therapeutic, positive growth changes for the well-being of all. Thus, a family therapy orientation as we view it may involve some individual therapy, or therapy with subgroupings of the family, but with an attempt to understand how this may affect the system as a whole. It also includes working towards conjoint therapy at some point for the family as a preferable way of dealing with many of the issues it is trying to solve.

Family System Evaluation

Once the decision has been made to use a family therapy orientation, an identification and assessment of the needs of the system should be made. We have found that all of the following issues are important to be considered and evaluated by the therapist. Their consideration in the evaluation phase of therapy will then allow the therapist to negotiate with the family their goals and priorities for work. They will also provide the understanding needed for the choice of therapeutic tools to be used in an eclectic approach.

Problems, needs, and goals. The problems presented by the family when they first approach therapy are usually sketchy and ill-defined. The parents may come in with a statement such as, "We need to get along better," or "All we do is fight, the children have no respect for me as a stepmother, and I don't even think anyone cares about anyone else." What the system needs is a clear definition by each member of how they see their problems, what their own needs are and what they would like to change. It is difficult if not imposible to try to respect your stepmother when you don't even know what she means by respect. Family members are usually adept at telling each other what they should do, but defining their own needs is much more difficult. If needs are not known then goals will be unclear or incorrect. A definition of goals should include both those for therapy and immediate change and a direction for the future. The most important aspects of this focus is that each member has a chance to hear how each one defines and feels about these areas to allow for an understanding of each other and eventual negotiations for change.

Evolving systems similarities and differences. It is important for the family as well as the therapist to gain some understanding of the similarities and differences of the different family systems that have merged in the formation of the stepfamily. These will include differences in the way things are done in the family, such as the celebration of holidays or the importance of special days like birthdays. It will include how affection is shown, how anger is tolerated, what form of discipline is used, and who is head of the household.

Role definitions. The system needs to define and understand the role of each family member and how that has changed or evolved through each of the family stages. They need to explore together not only how they see their own role, but how each other member sees their role, and what they want their role to be. What is it like to change from father to stepfather, or from a single person to instant parent, or from only child to middle child?

For example, Ted, a boy of 12, was the youngest child and the only boy in his family of three children in his original nuclear family. After the divorce of his parents he went to live with his father, became an only child in that system (except for absent sisters) and was constant companion (more "pal" than child) to his father. After his father's remarriage to a woman with an eight-year-old boy, Ted was again placed more in the role of a child as his stepmother became the major companion to his father. However, this time he was the older child and one of two boys. Had his sisters come to live with them he would have then been a middle child and still not the only boy. Because he was older, his father and stepmother now expected him to be the more responsible of the children and an example and a help to his younger step-brother. This is almost an opposite role to that which he originally had and with which he was familiar. In the past it had been expected that his older sisters would carry many of the responsibilities in the family. Later, when he lived alone with his father, he was usually on his own. After the remarriage he was expected to be the responsible, caring older brother. If you add an expected amount of regression based on the many significant changes Ted has gone through, and some sadness and anger at the seeming loss of his father as constant companion, it becomes apparent why the parents now describe him as "a sullen, irresponsible boy."

Alliances and loyalties. These are strong forces within a stepfamily. Deciding how the family wants to strengthen, dilute or change the existing alliances and loyalties is critical for relationship development. These factors may be quite obvious or may be subtle or covert. An obvious and expected alliance would be that of the members who come from the same original nuclear family.

In one stepfamily a biologic mother was seen to be protective of her boy and girl from the firm disciplining efforts of the stepfather. The children continued to relate to her for their needs as they had in the transitional family and developed only a superficial relationship with the stepfather. A more subtle influence on the stepfamily system became apparent after six to seven sessions with Mr. T. and his stepfamily. Mr. T. had never been very involved with his stepchildren or even his own biologic son born to him and his second wife. This was a real disappointment to Mrs. T. who had married Mr. T. with the thought that he would not only be a good spouse, but a good father for her children. Mr. T. had left his first family, which included two children that he loved dearly. He had seen how destructive the parents' constant fighting was on the children, and he felt they would be better off without him. He had never visited them after leaving and never spoke of them to his new family. However, later in therapy he said, "I also felt I was depriving them of a father and how could I give to someone else's children what I was depriving my own children of?" His alliances and loyalties had remained with his first family even though they did not benefit from them; as a consequence, he deprived himself and his second family of himself and what he could give as a father. He and his second family later decided together that he should visit his biologic children and invite them to visit him. After that Mr. T. was able to see how his avoidance of his second family had not helped his biologic children. He later chose to dilute those loyalties and to strengthen those to his second family.

Stepfamily myths and "skeletons in the closet." A number of the important myths which affect stepfamilies have been discussed in earlier chapters. Helping the stepfamily dispel these myths and offset the effects which they have had on the family can be accomplished through open discussion. In stepfamilies, "skeletons in the closet" may be just as significant as in any family. They may stem back to a parent's childhood family experience and history or they may be of more recent origin. Alcoholism, incest, extramarital affairs, suicides, concealed illegitimacies, and child abuse are a few of the more common "skeletons." They are not talked about but may seriously influence behaviors or be acted out.

For example, Mrs. H. had been married to a man who beat their children with a belt when he "disciplined" them. Frequently, severe welts and cuts from the buckle were visible. It was one of the reasons that led to divorce. Her new husband was not aware of this history. His intentions were to share in the disciplining rather than "leave it all up to their mother." Both parents had expressed their wish for this sharing of responsibility. Although Mr. H. never physically harmed the stepchildren, he would shout in his interactions with them. Mrs. H. would become fearful that an abuse might occur and would take the side of the children and reverse or modify the stepfather's punishment. Finally, Mr. H. gave up attempting to share in the discipline of the children. The children became more unmanageable and unruly. When the stepfather could no longer tolerate this, he would verbally explode. The children responded as fearfully as if they had been hit, and Mrs. H's feelings that she couldn't trust her husband to help with the discipline were reinforced.

This situation illustrates a "skeleton" of child abuse that was contained by displacement of the reactions onto the new father; the presence of the actual abusing parent in the new system was not a requirement for the potent influence of this psychological "skeleton" in this family. Again, open discussion of the previous experiences of child abuse made all the family members' behavior understandable, and they could then rationally make decisions about what discipline was needed and how to implement it.

Family rules and value systems. The rules that the family lives by and its values will affect most of the other parts of the family system. They may be the basis of the alliances and loyalties that develop. Mr. T., in the case history above, was unable to dilute his loyalties to his biologic children and thus was unable to give to his stepchildren. His value system, which he had probably learned from his own childhood family, was that your first and most important loyalty was to your nuclear family and biologic children.

Many of the family system similarities and differences that will occur and often be in conflict will be in the area of family values and rules. In one family there may be a strong value placed on physical affection; in another no physical affection may be shown. There may be a family rule from one segment of the stepfamily that on birthdays a cake and many packages are given from the other family members, while the other segment of the stepfamily has entered the family with a rule that birthdays are celebrated with only one package and no major fanfare. Unless these differences in the family rules are worked out and understood as differences, conflicts and upset feelings will very likely occur.

Communication skills. It is important to determine the family's level of communication skills, both verbal and nonverbal, and if their verbal and nonverbal communications match. Are they able to fight productively, and give appropriate feedback of their wishes, feelings and needs? When they say they are angry, do they look angry? If they say they love or care for another family member, do they also show it?

Logistics of family functioning. There are many system needs around the logistics of family functioning. These would include such things as how and on whom money is spent and from whom that money comes, visitation rights, discipline, and the celebration of holidays and special occasions.

Tension level. The level of tension of the family, as well as of each individual, needs to be determined. It will include the amount of anger, fears, anxieties and hostilities present among family members. It may also include feelings towards or generated by outsiders, absent family members, and the extended family. We see frequent examples of tension generated from external sources. One is when the absent parent requires the children to call his (her) new spouse "Mother" (or "Father"). Another would be when the grandparents (parents of the absent parent) continue a close relationship with their grandchildren, but use it to tell the children how bad or how much to blame their parent was for the divorce. A third tension from outside the system can result from frequent court battles over money, visitation, or whatever.

The level of tension, whether from internal system problems, intrapsychic problems, or from a source outside the family will probably be the most significant factor in determining the approaches taken in the beginning phase of therapy.

Feeling or emotional expression. Many of the problems the family faces are related to how feelings are dealt with. A variety of feelings are involved and may differ depending upon whether the breakup of the original nuclear family was due to divorce or death. Some of the important feelings to be worked with include:

1. *Anger*—There may be anger with a child for not adjusting to the new family that the parent has attempted to provide. There may be anger experienced by the child towards the parent for leaving (through divorce or death) or for upsetting the security of the original nuclear family. There may be anger with the stepparent for "taking away" the special relationship a child had with his parent in the transitional family system, or for preventing, through marriage, the fantasied restitution of the original nuclear family. There may be anger with the spouse for including the children as part of a "package deal" with the marriage.

2. *Love*—Love may not occur instantly or even with much effort between the stepparent and stepchildren or between stepsiblings. Love for the estranged parent and the accompanying loyalty may prevent relating to, working with, or even agreeing with the values, limits or rules of the new stepparent. Any new alignment with the stepparent may be perceived as showing less love for or loyalty to the biologic parent.

3. *Guilt*—Guilt may be felt by either parent or child around being the real or imagined cause of the family breakup. There may be guilt for not being able to love the stepparent or stepchild.

4. *Loss and mourning*—When the breakup of the nuclear family is due to death, feelings of mourning and loss are expected. When the breakup is due to divorce a sense of loss also occurs. There may be feelings of loss of the original family system and what that represented, including loss of a parent or children or siblings. There may be a sense of loss or mourning for not being able to fulfill the anticipated role of super-parent or super-child in the new stepfamily. This can occur when the stepparent observes the needs of an abused, neglected, or hurting child and hopes to be better than the original parent. It can also occur when a child attempts to be a super-child as a way to hold together the family system or to gain the love of a stepparent.

5. *Fears*—Children often show fears around the fact that they have experienced the loss of a parent or the breakup of their family. Their fear is that it will occur again. Stepparents and stepchildren often fear non-acceptance in the new family. A stepparent may fear that he or she will not be as good a parent as the biologic parent.

Phases of therapy

Beginning.—The beginning phase of therapy is primarily concerned with involvement of the family in therapy. The tension level may be so high that the stepfamily does not want to risk sitting in the same room together for a therapy session. Some of the tensions arising from fears or anxieties may be lessened once the family gets to the office and actually starts its work with the therapist. On the other hand, when anger and hostility are too great, as evidenced by serious, destructive interactions that continue even when a therapist attempts to intervene, it may be contraindicated to continue with conjoint sessions in this early involvement phase.

Sometimes preparatory therapy is needed before initiating conjoint work when one or more family members have intrapsychic problems which make it impossible for them to engage in the family group process or which may be too disruptive to the group process itself. Another factor suggesting the need for preparatory work is when there is a strong need for the couple to strengthen their relationship. The couple bond may not have been formed prior to marriage or may have been seriously disrupted secondary to the stepfamily discord. Specifically, development of some basic parenting skills might be one focus.

At times, we have known a family to withdraw from further therapy if the parental request that a specific child be seen is not responded to or is too strongly challenged. Frequently, seeing the child alone for an evaluation may be adequate for meeting this request and the parents may then be able to hear the recommendation for family therapy. Some parents are fearful about coming in for therapy and need an "identified patient" to keep the focus off of them. It also can occur when the family has become so disrupted that the parents have no sense of their own potency as heads of the family system. Their attempts to control what happens in therapy may be their attempt to regain some of this potency. Once a positive therapeutic relationship has developed the parents are generally able to broaden their view and consider the total system needs and the usefulness of conjoint family therapy.

A family which reflects a number of these considerations is that of the A's. Pam, the 15-year-old daughter, was identified as the problem because of her poor academic performance and thwarting of teachers' authority. Her relationship with her father and stepmother was very conflictful. The hostility level was so great that threats of "getting rid of her" were close to being realized. Pam was about five years old when her biologic mother suddenly left home. Pam's unresolved grief was strongly apparent. Her rage at her stepmother further contributed to an impasse as well as serving to keep the parents apart. Father protected his daughter and could not feel love for a stepmother who couldn't accept Pam.

After one conjoint interview, it was apparent that further work would require subgroupings. Pam was seen with an older sister. The two sisters were able to look at several of the sources of Pam's anger and lack of acceptance of the stepmother. The parents were seen together to work on their needs for one another and to strengthen their position as leaders in the family. The stepmother also worked on some of her long-standing intrapsychic insecurities.

With both of these subgroups, ground work was established for applying their gains in a conjoint effort. When conjoint sessions were reestablished, rapid strides were made in several directions by all family members and they moved into the "middle phase" of therapy.

This stepfamily example is also relevant to the following points. The early strengthening of the couple relationship is critical. Not only in their preliminary marital subgroup work, but also later in the conjoint setting, the parents were allowed to define and establish themselves as the united functioning heads of the family. Their developing support of each other lent strength to their stated desire and commitment to work towards resolution of the family problems. This united parental position did not negate the family as a group which together could determine their goals and needs. It did serve appropriately to weigh the parental position of leadership and responsibility for the family. This sent a message of stability to the family system that all were needing.

The above family example also demonstrates how the decision to meet in subgroups can facilitate an aspect of therapy which we feel is important. This aspect is the early modeling of the ability to separate from the family as well as to come back together to benefit from and contribute to a strengthened family system. This concept promotes not only the goals of individual growth and self-confidence, but also the ability to find strength and enjoyment from healthy interdependence and mutuality within the group. In families that lend themselves to direct entry into conjoint work, subgroupings later in therapy may be useful as a way of developing this concept and strengthening the individual members, especially when the children are older adolescents.

Middle. During the middle phase of therapy, when the major changes occur for the family, we see the family all together in conjoint therapy. At the same time we continually evaluate whether there is a reason for a "side trip." If so, we see either an individual or a grouping of individuals such as the parents or the children. Once conjoint therapy has begun, a "side trip" can occur at any time either the therapist or the family feel it might be necessary and all concerned agree upon this "side trip" as a necessary step in the therapeutic process. After the "side trip," which usually lasts not more than several sessions, the general content of the sessions is briefly stated to the conjoint group. This is preferably done by the persons making the "side trip." A father might say, "Your mother and I needed some time to work out some of the problems between us. We feel we have done that and now are ready to get back to the problems that involve all of us."

One of the purposes that conjoint family therapy serves is the elimination of fantasy. One area where a great deal of fantasy occurs is around the split in the nuclear family, which each member may remember differently. Frequently, the parent has never discussed it fully with the children or the new spouse, and all have only fantasized what really happened. These fantasies can lead to an idealization of the absent parent, a distortion of the feelings of the remaining parent, or questions by the children as to whether or not it was their fault. Sometimes they fantasize that if they are not "good," it will occur again with their present family.

One mother felt very inadequate because her husband did everything better than she—the housework, raising his children, etc. The children had fantasized that she was lazy or uninterested, or was forcing the father to do most of the housework. They felt inadequate for different reasons but had no idea she had such feelings. Another child imagined his stepmother hated him when in actuality she avoided him because she didn't know how to respond to him. She felt he didn't want her to relate to him. In both cases the family members had only to state what they were really feeling to see that they were acting on the wrong assumptions. Almost any problem in the family will have its fantasies that surround it. The important thing for the family to do is to get the facts out in the open where they can be realistically seen, struggled with and dealt with.

Another purpose of conjoint family therapy is to provide knowledge of how to negotiate and gain understanding of the problems faced by the family. Families need to learn to negotiate the usual things such as the division of chores, curfews, bed times, and allowances. A stepfamily must learn that when parts of two or more families come together (especially when the children are school age), they are trying to mesh many differences in some way that works.

When feelings are expressed in conjoint family therapy, a "commonality" may occur which is similar to that experienced in group therapy. This will occur between different family members at different times, but its effect is that of increased understanding among family members and a bonding together of relationships. The children mentioned previously who were surprised to share feelings of inadequacy with their stepmother are an example. One of the children, the one who had had the most conflicts with her stepmother, was having a lot of problems in school and in relationships. She had little to feel confident about. Just hearing that her stepmother had similar feelings of inadequacy, even if for different reasons, gave them one of their first areas of bonding. They both became more understanding of each other and each attempted to meet some of the other's needs. This in itself gave each more confidence because they began to feel lovable.

Getting feelings out in the open, even when a shared commonality does not occur, is important because when those feelings are known they can more easily be dealt with and understood. When the level of tension is excessively high due to overwhelming feelings, the individual as well as the family may become immobilized.

In one stepfamily the stepfather had risked a lot of his innerself in one session. He told the family how lonely he was, how he really did not feel a part of the family and how he needed some interaction with other members in order to feel he belonged. When no one acted on his requests during the following week, he was so angry with everyone that the whole family severely regressed not only in their relationships but in their functioning outside of the family. After ventilating his anger for a good part of one session he was again able to focus on how to negotiate in order to have his needs met. The family heard his anger, began to respond to his needs, and improved in their relationship with him.

Parents and children need to hear how each individual hurts, what feels good or fair or lonely. Success in developing a new system will depend on no one person totally rejecting all of any other person's previous system. Each person has incorporated a part of his or her past system. If there is nothing of value accepted from one's own past family system, then a part of oneself becomes unacceptable.

When it is felt that the important issues in this phase of treatment have been dealt with, consideration should be given to termination.

Termination. In family therapy, as in any type of psychotherapy, the termination phase is extremely important (Hiatt, 1965). Stepfamilies generally have so much business to "get on with" that they are eager to discontinue therapy as soon as possible. There are some that "drop-out" (prematurely) when the tension level has lessened to a degree that is tolerable to the members. This is usually premature because there has been inadequate time to focus on basic process and content issues. For these families, reduction of the tension level may allow them to relate acceptably but not ideally from the therapist's perspective. For those families that remain in therapy to do more complete work, there will generally be an eagerness to terminate once the defined goals have been achieved. This attitude usually should be looked upon as a favorable sign and may be an early indication of readiness for termination. It may be a way of serving notice that the family has dealt adequately with its problems and can now turn its attention to other concerns.

There may be significant issues that could be worked on further by a family or by individual members. If these were not identified in the early phases of therapy as appropriate therapeutic goals, it is best to not focus on them at length. In our experience, it has been most useful to call such issues to the attention of the family or appropriate member and recommend that they give consideration to dealing with this in future therapy. The most important consideration here is that the family work be viewed as completed and terminated. Otherwise, the members may feel "up in the air" about their work and not have a sense of having reached their objectives.

When there are a number of significant areas of "unfinished business," the therapist may need to negotiate an agreement to terminate with the family. It is appropriate to note these areas with the family and recommend as well as give permission for them to continue to work on them outside of therapy. They also need to hear that further therapy work may be indicated in these areas (or in newly defined ones) and that it is appropriate to return for further work. If the family leaves without some degree of acceptance by the therapist that the termination is satisfactory, then return for further work, especially with that therapist, will be much more difficult.

Alerting the family to the likelihood of relapses and advising them how to handle these can be useful. Frequently, this concern is brought to attention as termination approaches. The family or the early symptom bearer may briefly demonstrate a repetition of the behavior which initially prompted the family to seek therapy, causing fear within the family that they have been working in vain. Reassurance that this is usual in therapy is helpful and generally adequate. We have also found that it is helpful for the family to have a sense of how therapy was beneficial to them and what they worked on and accomplished.

During the period the stepfamily is "going it alone" (i.e., not meeting as frequently in therapy), scheduling sessions once every month or two may fill an important function. These sessions will give support as well as provide the opportunity to work out the small problems and deal with the uncertainties that occur during this phase. Sometimes brief telephone contacts are useful and economical at this phase of therapy. A finalization of therapy occurs when the stepfamily and the therapist can say "goodbye."

MULTIPLE FAMILY THERAPY WITH STEPFAMILIES

The Family Group Institute in San Francisco not only works with stepfamilies as a single family group, but sees a few families together as a multiple family group. Two therapists work with a maximum of four families at once, with a maximum of 16-20 persons involved.

This clinic on the average sees 50 percent intact families, 34 percent single parent families, and 16 percent stepfamilies. These figures are roughly proportional to the numbers of such families reported nationally (Population Reference Bureau, 1977).

At the Institute families are not immediately offered multiple family groups. Individual families are seen first at the clinic, and only if the staff then feels that a multiple family group might be beneficial to the family is the referral made. If the family agrees, all members of the family are seen in the multiple family group setting. If it appears that a family has needs that might be incompatible with the multiple family group process, they are seen for continued individual family meetings.

An interesting observation at the clinic has been that many members of stepfamilies have been unaware that it may be the structure of the stepfamily that is causing a problem. For example, a boy may be viewed as acting out in school because of intrapsychic problems, where in fact he is reacting to losing a defined place as oldest child in the family after the remarriage of his mother.

Generally all family members living under the same roof are the individuals included in the group. At times even babies may be included since they can illustrate important aspects of family functioning.

Multiple family groups meet for two-and-a-half-hour sessions once a week for three to four months. Setting a definite time limit can be helpful because it clarifies the boundaries and lets the participants know that they have a certain time limit in which to work. At the end of the agreed upon time renegotiation can take place and another time limitation set if this is the wish of the group.

The therapists act as models for the group as well as facilitating group process and communication. At the beginning of the first session exercises are usually given to break the ice and clarify the direction of the group. Such an exercise might consist of asking each member to fantasize the way in which he or she would ideally like their family to be. Such statements create the goals towards which each family may work. This process also sets the stage for the direction the group will go by creating an ideal model which may in fact not be totally realistic.

Early in the group history the group may be divided into two subgroups for a session or two with the adults being in one group and the children in the other group. This division can help to create stronger bonds among the children and among the adults, and at times it facilitates the sharing of material that cannot be discussed when the adults and children are together in the one larger group. During the weeks when the families are meeting in a group a family may also be seen individually if such a meeting seems valuable. In other words, different therapeutic combinations are used as they seem useful to a particular family.

In the early sessions the meetings begin with some structuring of the basic goals for that meeting. As the group members become more familiar with each other the sessions can be less structured.

During the sessions the basic problems in interpersonal relationships become clarified. It becomes clear that not all needs and wants can be met, that no person is perfect, and that there are many different ways of doing things. Understanding and acceptance of these limitations are extremely valuable for members of stepfamilies since satisfactory stepfamily functioning usually requires considerable negotiation of needs and tolerance for differences.

During the months they meet together, group members become very supportive of each other, acting as a support network or extended family. Many times members can accept feedback from peers that would be unacceptable from professionals. Participants also begin to recognize that they react in similar ways to individuals inside and outside their family. A stepfather may be uptight with all teenagers, not just with his own teenagers. Recognizing the universality of these feelings and behavior makes the reactions less personalized so that shifts become more possible. Some families meet together socially outside of the therapy meetings.

After official termination, groups sometimes choose to continue meeting on their own, thus continuing the support network they have found to be valuable to them. The therapists are willing to act as consultants if the group so desires, and from time to time groups will meet with a therapist-consultant. No longer do the families see themselves as "pathological families"; they are simply families dealing with common family problems.

In some settings stepfamilies are seen in groups with intact and single-parent families, while in other settings stepfamilies are seen in groups containing only stepfamilies. At the Family Group Institute in San Francisco, stepfamilies are seen in groups containing other types of families, while at the Clarke Institute of Psychiatry in Toronto, Canada, Lillian Messinger (Messinger et al., 1978) works with groups of stepfamilies only.

MIXED FAMILY INTERACTION GROUPS

A program for families of teenage alcohol offenders (Glines and Byrd, 1978) has successfully utilized a method of "mixed family interaction" in which members from different families interact together in a group setting for a set number of sessions. Such an approach might be helpful for stepfamilies.

In this alcohol abuse program there are five sessions. The sessions consist of an initial 30 to 45 minutes of didactic material followed by one-and-a-half hours of group discussion. After the didactic presentation is made to the entire group of 35 to 40 people, the group is broken into three groups for the discussion period. Each group contains mothers, fathers, and adolescents but family members are separated so that no family members are in the same discussion group. In this way adults and teenagers can communicate, but without the heavy emotional interactions that could occur among family members.

For the final session the entire group is given a specific task before breaking into the small discussion groups. At the end of the shorter-than- normal discussion period, the small groups meet together again to share and discuss the small groups' response to the assigned task.

In the case of this alcohol abuse program, the designated task involves arriving at small group consensus in answering these hypothetical letters written to "Dear Addie" in which some conflict involving teenage drinking is outlined. For stepfamilies the hypothetical letters to be answered would be concerned with common stepfamily problems. For example:

Dear Addie,

I've come to the end of my rope. I married my husband four months ago after living together with him for two years. After getting married his two sons from a previous marriage came to live with us. I have never been married before and these boys are driving me crazy. Ted is 9 and Bob is 11 and I spend all my time cleaning up after them, and cooking for them and they never leave my husband and me alone and let us have any time to ourselves. My husband says I'm over-reacting and the two of us are getting into terrible arguments every night. We can't talk about anything else except Ted and Bob, and my husband says I've turned into a real witch. When there were just two of us everything was wonderful, but now I just feel like a servant with no days off. What can I do?

Overworked and Unappreciated

Dear Addie,

I'm 12 years old and I have a big problem. My mommy and my daddy got divorced two years ago and now my mommy has married another man called Charles. She wants me to call him "Dad" and this makes me cry inside because I already have a daddy.

I try to be very good but whenever my new sister Ann comes over to visit us she gets everything she wants even when she's being bad. Her daddy, Charles, and my mommy both are very nice to her and give her special things. I feel all alone and if I start to cry and go to my room I get slapped and scolded. If Ann cries everyone is good to her. I feel very sad and I don't know what to do.

Laurie

Since the alcohol program is limited to five sessions, the discussions are concerned with improving communication and understanding, but issues requiring a longer, more therapeutic approach are not dealt with. Group facilitators lead the groups, and there is a mix of families with youth who are in minor difficulties, together with families where the youthful offender has significant problems with the law. There is a comprehensive study of the Utah program (Glines and Byrd, 1978) in which a recommendation is made to concentrate on families in which the adolescent is in serious difficulties. James Bradley, coordinator of the program, also considers that the less well functioning families can use the more functional families in the program as models for differing and more adaptive modes of interaction (Bradley, 1978).

The Utah program evaluation finds a 50 percent reduction in traffic accidents and recidivism compared to the control group. Such reductions are also found in a similar program for juvenile drug or shoplifting first offenders. Thus the effectiveness of such an approach for these difficulties has been demonstrated.

Many adolescents in stepfamilies engage in similar acting out behavior, or have a variety of school related problems. Even when there are other stepfamily difficulties, having the opportunity to relate to other adults and children would also seem beneficial. In the case of stepfamilies, since one difficulty is the formation of a bond between the adults, it might be advisable to keep the adult couple together in the small discussion group, but separate adults and children who are in the same family. In this way participants might be able to hear the messages from other adults and children that they would not be able to tolerate from their own family members, and, at the same time, cohesiveness between the couple might improve.

Further evaluation of such groups for stepfamilies is needed to determine whether or not it is indeed better to separate the couple as in the Utah program or have them participate together in the same small discussion group.

Interaction among family members has been found to improve after participation in such groups (Glines and Byrd, 1978), even though the family members are not seen together. Such skills are practiced outside the group sessions, while group process with the same small group membership takes place during the five-week program.

In addition to using such a model stepfamilies might continue after the five sessions with more therapeutically oriented, longer-term group programs. In this way, the mixed family interaction approach combined with the multiple family group approach might increase the number of stepfamilies receiving therapeutic assistance. Such an approach appears to be worth serious consideration.

14

Overview

Divorce rates continue to rise, but this trend does not signify that marriage is outmoded in American society since eighty percent of divorced persons remarry. Since sixty percent of these individuals have children, many remarriages create families in which there are children from a previous marriage either living in the household or visiting at regular or irregular intervals.

Many of these "remarried," "reconstituted" or "step" families are able to reorganize with little debilitating stress. For many individuals, however, being a remarried parent, a stepparent, or both, is a difficult adjustment. Individuals who have previously enjoyed being a parent find unexpected problems, while individuals who have not been parents previously often find themselves ill-equipped to deal with the complexity of this type of family. There are a myriad of strong feelings in stepfamilies which are internally and externally determined emotional responses to complex realities.

Marriage and parenting require skill and understanding to be successful. There are rewards and "occupational hazards" in all types of family structures, and knowledge of difficulties helps minimize the problems and maximize the satisfactions. Only recently has attention been given to the structure and characteristics of stepfamilies, and therefore many individuals are finding themselves in remarried situations with little preparation or understanding of what to expect. Little research on remarriage has been done, and much is needed to clarify issues and provide sound guidelines. In the meantime, clinical observation and experience are providing insight and understanding that can be helpful to therapists and counselors, and to stepfamilies in general. This book has presented material from available research and clinical impressions, together with more theoretical formulations. It is hoped that this information will enable therapists and counselors to have a better understanding of and appreciation for stepfamily dynamics. In this way mental health professionals will be able to better assist the stepfamilies who seek their help and will be more familiar and comfortable with this new pattern of family life.

While the emotions felt by members of stepfamilies are the same emotions felt by members of intact families, the structural differences in the two types of families produce differences in degree, complexity and interactional elements. It is valuable for stepfamily members to realize that parenting problems and decisions arise in all families; sibling rivalry and competition arise in all families; love and hate, joy and sorrow, satisfactions and dissatisfactions are present in all families. Many stepfamily members also find it important to understand that they have unique problems, and that they have tasks to accomplish for which most individuals have had little preparation. In most stepfamilies the emotional climate is intense, thus making the necessary tasks very difficult to accomplish. With knowledge, understanding and support many potentially defeating situations can become valuable growth experiences. This paves the way for satisfactions and rewards to emerge as the individuals become more self-confident in their ability to master their environment.

Therapists and counselors ask and are being asked about the unique characteristics of stepfamiiles. While the techniques of working with individuals, couples, and families may be similar with intact families, single-parent families, or stepfamilies, goals, common problems and specific interventions may be quite different. It is important to be aware of the differences because most stepfamilies sense quite clearly that there is a difference.

A stepfamily is born of loss. It is the last phase in a process beginning with a disintegration of a relationship due to death or divorce. For many the separation process is painful and unfinished. When adults have had a child together there is a biological link that does not end with physical or psychological separation. The child is part of both parents and because of this will benefit immeasurably if there is cooperation between the adults. Remarriage is usually experienced as a gain to the new adult couple, while many children view it as still another loss.

With a remarriage individuals who may still feel a sense of loss are often attempting to relate to each other. Indeed, individuals in the stepfamily may be asked to relate to persons whom they feel are fully or partially responsible for their loss and pain. For example, children may consider their mother or father responsible for the divorce, or their stepmother or stepfather responsible for the fact that their parents are not getting back together again. Interactions between these individuals then can produce anger or withdrawal and result in many tense interactions.

After a divorce, and to an even greater extent after a remarriage, many individuals experience the insecurity of sharing children and sharing parents. Compassion and understanding can lessen the hurt, and aid the healing process. Individual growth can then occur, bringing with it an interpersonal warmth and a deep understanding of other human beings.

Mental health professionals can be extremely helpful in assisting both adults and children with their mourning for a lost person or for a lost ideal. Even adults in stepfamilies who have never been married before often need help in recognizing and accepting that their dream of marriage may be a dream of youth which cannot materialize except in a first marriage. Trying to force subsequent marriages into the mold of first marriages leads to misery for many people.

Stepfamilies have permeable boundaries and this characteristic produces many conflicts. The bond between the new couple can be attacked from within and without the stepfamily. There are bonds between adults, between children, and between adults and children that precede the new couple bond.

Because of the length of time they have been in existence and because of the bonds, more "triangles" exist in stepfamilies than in nuclear families, and therapists who consider "de-triangling" as a goal in family therapy will be dealing with an increased number of exceedingly rigid triangles when working with a stepfamily.

Community recognition may be slow to develop, in-laws and ex-in-laws may be rejecting, and the new relationship flounders in its insecurity. Children may wish for renewal of the old boundaries in which they knew their place and felt secure, while adults may fear even further loss as they face withdrawal by their children or feel that the children may want to live with the other parent. Ex-spouses fight over money, visitation, and the upbringing of the children. Too often the children become pawns in a struggle which is in reality a struggle born of fear and guilt and anger.

Counselors and therapists can provide important support in validating the deep need for a primary couple relationship. Couples frequently need help in finding ways to nourish this relationship, and they need to know that the importance of this relationship is not a betrayal of the earlier parent-child bond. Indeed, strong couple unity provides a framework which can allow for flexibility, the forming of other important bonds (e.g., between stepparent and stepchild), and a tolerance for the ambiguity created by the existence of another important parent-child relationship outside the permeable stepfamily boundary. A strong couple relationship also acts as a positive model for the children as they begin to form their own primary adult couple relationships.

Because of the blurring or permeability of the boundaries, working with an ex-spouse as well as with the new couple is at times the treatment modality of choice. Sometimes all may meet together, while at other times this is not possible because of the reluctance of one or more of the individuals involved. In some instances it is important to involve the children as well as the adults in counseling, particularly when the children are junior high or high school age. Seeing them all as a group or with other stepfamilies can provide an opportunity for them to work together within the ambiguous stepfamily boundary. When combinations of individuals include adults and children it is necessary for the counselor or therapist to structure the meetings around specific issues involving the children. Working on old or new adult relationships is not the task of such meetings.

All individuals, children as well as adults, enter the new stepfamily carrying a family history from the past. Unconscious "givens" are no longer "givens," and there is usually considerable turmoil generated by an infinite number of small details as well as around larger more serious issues. Where does the TV go? Who feeds the cat? Is dessert a reward for good eating habits? Are snacks between meals allowed? Can jeans be worn to school? Who takes care of the bills? The list is endless and the answers are varied, and many involve all members of the stepfamily. Compromise is necessary in all families; negotiation, renegotiation, and more renegotiation seem essential in stepfamilies. Frequently considerable therapeutic intervention is required to assist in this process. Helping the stepfamily members accept that there are many ways of doing things and that the different family "givens" are not right or wrong may take considerable time. If this concept can be accepted, then negotiation becomes possible, new stepfamily traditions have an opportunity to develop, and children can move more freely between households.

Research indicates that children are in a better position if they maintain a relationship with both parents, provided that the parents are able to handle the situation reasonably well. Children then are dealing with two sets of rules and two sets of people. Therapeutic time with these children can be well spent in helping them realize that they can care for more than two adults, and that caring for a stepparent does not need to mean disloyalty or lack of caring for the same-sexed parent. Helping children come to terms with different sets of rules helps them out of the bind of needing to choose between "right" and "wrong" ways of doing things, thus facilitating their functioning to their own advantage in both family situations. It will also lessen the time the children need to go through transition periods as they go from living under one roof to living under the other roof.

New children born into a stepfamily often bring cohesiveness to the family and help solidify relationships between stepsiblings as well as between the couple. Adoption and living with the other biologic parent are options open for children in stepfamilies that are not options for children in nuclear families. The issues are complex and mental health professionals are often called upon by the court or by the families to help with the decision-making in these areas.

Adoption by stepparents is a delicate issue and one that often leads to heartache when there is a second divorce. Very little has been written on the subject and research investigation of the advantages and disadvantages is lacking. In *The Half Parent* Brenda Maddox outlines various opinions on the advantages and disadvantages (1975, pp. 167-172) of adoptions by stepparents, which she summarizes by saying, "One holds that adoption is desirable because it gives the stepchild the nearest approximation to the secure status of a child living with his two natural parents. The other holds that a child's identity is derived from his real kin, that it is his unique biological and cultural inheritance that should not be taken away."

The question of a change of custody is raised frequently in stepfamilies. Many times the stepparent is upset with the step-family situation and considers that the solution is to have the stepchildren live with the other natural parent. At this point the custodial parent, seeking a solution to increasing family tension, usually feels torn by guilt, but also feels relieved; the children sense the tentativeness of their living arrangements, and may react negatively. A downward spiral of negative and conflicting emotions is underway.

Therapists and counselors are often asked to give advice at this point. Like all solutions to complex family problems, there are many aspects to be considered. A proposed solution is simply one avenue to be explored, with more than the usual number of emotional ramifications. Changes of custody are disturbing and need to be made carefully and not with the thought that they can be shifted again quickly. Children need the security of knowing where they belong. Hopefully, present studies of various custody arrangements will result in valuable information to help with the decisions, but few guidelines are now available.

Satisfactory reorganization is the major task of a stepfamily. Available information indicates that this goal involves stepfamily integration, the development of a loving and secure bond between the couple, and the creation of a caring space for the children so that they can relate comfortably to both natural parents, as well as to stepparents.

Provided that the stepfamily couple has been able to make a primary commitment to one another and has nourished that relationship, there will be a stability and a future for the stepfamily unit. Resolving the hurt of past relationships is not always possible, and therefore many stepfamilies are not able to provide comfortable space for children to relate easily to both parents and to stepparents. Children, nonetheless, can adapt to discomfort and when they become adults be independent in their choice of family relationships. It is then that meaningful and warm bonds between stepfamily members may develop from earlier casual or strained relationships.

Even though stepfamilies tend to be more stressful than intact families, many adults and children find special satisfactions in this type of family. Adults often speak of their awareness of the deep meaning of their interpersonal relationships. Because of the earlier disruptions they are conscious that relationships are precious and not to be taken for granted. The complexity of the stepfamily can forge an emotional commitment as the couple works together to solve the problems that arise. Thus they gain much personal satisfaction from a rich opportunity for individual growth and human involvement.

An adult stepchild may speak for many children as she looks back on her experience growing up in a stepfamily and expresses herself this way:

> The men I went out with always were somebody very straight, and then somebody very radical, and then somebody

very straight. It think it's taken me longer to decide who I am, and who I wanted to marry. So I'm a different person and a more complicated and richer person from having different types of people in my family. I think it was more confusing putting it together, but I think it was richer. For me I think that I resented having to share, and lots of other things too, but I think that there has been so much more that is positive that I've gotten from having a stepfamily.

I've been struck this year by a sign which says something to the effect that the greatest gift a father can give to his children is to love their mother. The meaning I took from this is that the degree to which the children sense a lack of commitment between the parents, to that extent their insecurity increases. With no model of a close, effective, parent-couple, the children will be less able to establish close marital relationships themselves in later years. I'm glad I saw Mom and my stepdad's close relationship to one another.

Probably the most significant gain for the members of a stepfamily is the opportunity to rekindle a faith in close interpersonal relationships as they experience and share in the remarriage of two adults.

Appendix A.
Guidelines for
stepfamilies

1. It is difficult to have a new person or persons move into your "space," and it is difficult to be the "new" person or people joining a preexisting group. For these reasons it helps to cut down feelings involved with "territory" if families can start out in a new house or apartment.

2. Parent-child relationships have preceded the new couple relationship. Because of this, many parents feel that it is a betrayal of the parent-child bond to form a primary relationship with their new partner. A primary couple relationship, however, is usually crucial for the continuing existence of the stepfamily, and therefore is very important for the children as well as for the adults. A strong adult bond can protect the children from another family loss, and it also can provide the children with a positive model for their own eventual marriage relationship. The adults often need to arrange time alone to help nourish this important couple relationship.

3. Forming new relationships within the stepfamily can be important, particularly when the children are young. Activities involving different subgroups can help such relationships grow. For example, stepfather and stepchildren might do some project together; or stepmother and a stepchild might go shopping together.

Appendix A and Appendix B may be reproduced for teaching and therapeutic purposes, with full credit to the source: From Visher, E. B. and Visher, J. S., *Stepfamilies: A Guide to Working With Stepparents and Stepchildren.* New York: Brunner/Mazel, Inc., 1979, pp. 261-267.

4. Preserving original relationships is also important and can help children experience less loss at sharing a parent. So at times it is helpful for a parent and natural children to have some time together, in addition to stepfamily activities.

5. Caring relationships take time to evolve. The expectation of "instant love" between stepparents and stepchildren can lead to many disappointments and difficulties. If the stepfamily relationships are allowed to develop as seems comfortable to the individuals involved, then caring between step-relatives has the opportunity to develop.

6. Subsequent families are structurally and emotionally different from first families. Upset and sadness are experienced by the children and at times by the adults as they react to the loss of their nuclear family or to the loss of a dream of a perfect marriage. Acceptance that a stepfamily is a new type of family is important. It is also very helpful to recognize that this type of family pattern can provide the opportunity for children and adults to grow and mature and lead satisfying lives. Many upsetting behaviors may result from these feelings of insecurity and loss.

7. Because children are part of two biological parents they nearly always have very strong pulls to both of these natural parents. These divided loyalties often make it difficult for children to relate comfortably to all the parental adults in their lives. Rejection of a stepparent, for example, may have nothing to do with the personal characteristics of the stepparent. In fact, warm and loving stepparents may cause especially severe loyalty conflicts for children. As children and adults are able to accept the fact that children can care for more than two parental adults, then the children's loyalty conflicts can diminish and the new step-relationships improve. While it may be helpful to the children for the adults to acknowledge negative as well as positive feelings about ex-spouses, children may become caught in loyalty conflicts and feel personally insecure if specific critical remarks are made continuously about their other natural parent.

8. Courteous relationships between ex-spouses are important, although they are very difficult for many adults to maintain. If such a relationship can be worked out it is especially helpful to the children. In such instances the children do not get caught in the middle between two hostile parents, there is less need for the

children to take sides, and the children are better able to accept and utilize the positive elements in their living arrangements.

Direct contact between the adults can be helpful since it does not place the children in the sometimes powerful position of being message carriers between their natural parents. Although it may be strained, many ex-spouses are able to relate in regards to their children if the focus is kept on their mutual concern for the welfare of the children.

9. Children as well as adults in a stepfamily have a "family history." Suddenly these individuals come together and their sets of "givens" are questioned. Much is to be gained by coming together as a stepfamily unit to work out and develop new family patterns and traditions. During these "family negotiation sessions" the feelings and ideas of all members are important, regardless of age. Many creative solutions can be worked out as a family.

Even when the individuals are able to recognize that patterns are not "right" or "wrong" it takes time and patience to work out satisfying new alternatives. Values (the underlying approach to life in general ways of doing things) do not shift easily. Within a stepfamily different value systems are inevitable because of different previous family histories, and tolerance for these differences can help smooth the process of stepfamily integration. Needs (specific ways individuals relate together, individual preferences, etc.) can usually be negotiated more quickly than can general values. Having an appreciation for and an expectation of such difficulties can make for more flexibility and relaxation in the stepfamily unit. Negotiation and renegotiation are needed by most such families.

10. Being a stepparent is an unclear and at times difficult task. The wicked stepmother myth contributes to the discomfort of many women, and cultural, structural and personal factors affect the stepparent role. Spouses can be very helpful to one another if they are able to be supportive with the working out of new family patterns. Stepparenting is usually more successful if stepparents carve out a role for themselves that is different from and does not compete with the natural parents.

While discipline is not usually accepted by stepchildren until a friendly relationship has been established (often a matter of 18 to 24 months), both adults do need to support each other's authority in the household. The natural parent may be the primary disciplinarian initially, but when that person is unavailable it is often necessary for that parent to give a clear message to the children that the stepparent is acting as an "authority figure" for both adults in his or her absence.

Unity between the couple is important to the functioning of the stepfamily. When the couple is comfortable with each other, differences between them in regards to the children can sometimes be worked out in the presence of the children, but at no time does it work out for either children or adults to let the children approach each adult separately and "divide and conquer." When disciplinary action is necessary, if it is not kept within the stepfamily household many resentful feelings can be generated. For example, if visitation rights are affected, the noncustodial parent is being included in the action without his or her representation. Such a punishment, then, may lead to difficulties greater than the original behavior that caused the disciplinary action.

11. Integrating a stepfamily that contains teenagers can be particularly difficult. Adolescents are moving away from their families in any type of family. In single-parent families teenagers have often been "young adults," and with the remarriage of a parent they may find it extremely difficult or impossible to return to being in a "child" position again.

    Adolescents have more of a previous "family history" and so they ordinarily appreciate having considerable opportunity to be part of the stepfamily negotiations, although they may withdraw from both natural parents and not wish to be part of many of the "family" activities.

12. "Visiting" children usually feel strange and are outsiders in the neighborhood. It can be helpful if they have some place in the household that is their own; for example, a drawer or a shelf for toys and clothes. If they are included in stepfamily chores and projects when they are with the stepfamily they tend to feel more connected to the group. Bringing a friend with them to share the visit and having some active adult participation in becoming integrated into the neighborhood can make a difference to many visiting children. Knowing ahead of time that there is going to be an interesting activity, stepfamily game of Monopoly, etc., can sometimes give visiting children a pleasant activity to anticipate.

Noncustodial parents and stepparents often are concerned because they have so little time to transmit their values to visiting children. Since children tend to resist concerted efforts by the adults to instill stepfamily ideals during each visit, it is comforting to parents and stepparents to learn that the examples of behavior and relationships simply observed in the household can affect choices made by all the children later in their lives when they are grown and on their own.

13. Sexuality is usually more apparent in stepfamilies because of the new couple relationship, and because children may suddenly be living with other children with whom they have not grown up. Also there are not the usual incest taboos operating. It is important for the children to receive affection and to be aware of tenderness between the couple, but it may also be important for the couple to minimize to some extent the sexual aspects of the household, and to help the children understand, accept, and control their sexual attractions to one another or to the adults.

14. All families experience stressful times. Children tend to show little day-to-day appreciation for their parents, and at times they get angry and reject their natural parents. Because stepfamilies are families born of loss, the mixture of feelings can be even more intense than in intact families. Jealousy, rejection, guilt, and anger can be more pronounced, and therefore expectations that the stepfamily will live "happily ever after" are unrealistic. Having an understanding and acceptance of the many negative as well as positive feelings can result in less disappointment and more stepfamily enjoyment.

15. Keeping even minimal contact between adults and children can lead to future satisfaction since time and maturity bring many changes. With some communication between stepfamily members satisfying interpersonal relationships often develop in the future when children become more independent in their relationships with both natural parents and with stepparents.

Appendix B.

References for

stepfamilies

ATKIN, EDITH and RUBIN, ESTELLE. *Part-Time Father*. New York: Signet Edition, 1977. Highly recommended as a book on divorce and remarriage for fathers.

BAER, JEAN. *The Second Wife*. New York: Doubleday, 1972. A book of personal experiences and interviews by a journalist writer.

BOHANNAN, PAUL J. and ERICKSON, ROSEMARY J. "Stepping In," *Psychology Today*, January, 1978. An excellent account of research on stepfather families in the San Diego, California area.

GARDNER, RICHARD A. *The Boys and Girls Book About Divorce: With an Introduction for Parents*. New York: Bantam Edition, 1971. An excellent guide for children dealing with parental divorce.

KRANTZLER, MEL. *Creative Divorce*. New York: New American Library, 1975. A popular presentation of the subject of divorce with a chapter on new commitments.

MADDOX, BRENDA. *The Half-Parent*. New York: Evans, 1975. A popular book dealing with the problems of stepparents, particularly from the point of view of stepmothers. Now available in paperback edition.

MAYLEAS, DAVIDYNE. *Re-wedded Bliss: Love, Alimony, Incest, Ex-Spouse and Other Domestic Blessings*. New York: Basic Books, 1977. A popular journalistic book which may be helpful for consciousness-raising purposes.

NOBLE, JUNE and NOBLE, WILLIAM. *How to Live with Other People's Children*. New York: Hawthorne Books, 1977. A how-to book on stepparenting.

REINGOLD, CARMEL BERMAN. *Remarriage*. New York: Harper and Row, 1976. Another popular account of stepfamily experiences.

ROOSEVELT, RUTH and LOFAS, JEANNETTE. *Living in Step*. New York: Stein and Day, 1976. An easily read account of the experiences of the authors and a number of persons they interviewed about stepfamily problems. Particularly popular with stepparents. Now available in a paperback edition.

ROSENBAUM, JEAN and ROSENBAUM, VERYL. *Stepparenting*. Corte Madera, Calif.:

266

Chandler and Sharp Publishers, Inc., 1977. A book by professionals with advice and guidelines for stepparents.

SATIR, VIRGINIA. *Peoplemaking*. Palo Alto, Calif.: Science and Behavior Books, Inc., 1972. Contains a chapter on blended families by one of the best-known authors and lecturers on families. Paperback.

SIMON, ANNE W. *Stepchild in the Family: A View of Children in Remarriage*. New York: Odyssey Press, 1964. Helpful for parents and stepparents in understanding the needs and reactions of children.

SPANN, OWEN and SPANN, NANCIE. *Your Child? I Thought It Was My Child!* Pasadena, Calif.: Ward Ritchie Press, 1977. A humorous account of the experiences of the authors in joining two families.

THOMSON, HELEN. *The Successful Stepparent*. New York: Harper and Row, 1966. An older how-to book on stepparenting which seems less applicable to today's families.

WESTOFF, LESLIE ALDRIDGE. *The Second Time Around: Remarriage in America*. New York: Viking, 1975. A book summarizing interviews with stepfamilies, for popular consumption.

References

ACKERMAN, N. W. *Treating the Troubled Family*. New York: Basic Books, Inc., 1966.

ARNOLD, EUGENE L. (Ed.). *Helping Parents Help Their Children*. New York: Brunner/Mazel, 1978.

ATKIN, EDITH and RUBIN, ESTELLE. *Part-Time Father*. New York: Signet Edition, 1977.

AYRES, WILLIAM, Personal communication, 1978.

BAER, JEAN. *The Second Wife*. New York: Doubleday, 1972.

BELL, JOHN ELDERHIN. *Family Therapy*. New York: Jason Aronson, 1975.

BERNARD, JESSIE. *Remarried: A Study of Marriage*. New York: Russell and Russell. First edition, 1956, Second edition, 1971.

BETTELHEIM, BRUNO. *The Uses of Enchantment*. New York: Vintage Books, 1977.

BOHANNAN, P. (Ed.). *Divorce and After*. New York: Doubleday, 1970. Anchor Books Edition, 1971.

BOHANNAN, PAUL J. and ERICKSON, ROSEMARY J. "Stepping In," unpublished manuscript, 1977.

BOHANNAN, PAUL J. and ERICKSON, ROSEMARY J. "Stepping In," *Psychology Today*, Jan., 1978.

BOSZORMENYI-NAGY, I. and SPARK, G. *Invisible Loyalties*. New York: Harper, 1973.

BOWEN, MURRAY. *Family Therapy in Clinical Practice*. New York: Jason Aronson, 1978.

BOWEN, MURRAY. "The Use of Family Theory in Clinical Practice," *Comprehensive Psychiatry*, 7:345-374, 1966.

BOWERMAN, CHARLES E. and IRISH, DONALD P. "Some Relationships of Stepchildren to Their Parents," *Marriage and Family Living*, 24:113-131, May, 1962.

BRADLEY, E. JAMES. Coordinator, Juvenile Alcohol Offenders Program, Salt Lake City, Utah. Personal communication, 1978.

BURCHINAL, LEE G. "Characteristics of Adolescents from Unbroken, Broken and Reconstituted Families," *Journal of Marriage and the Family*, 26:44-51, Feb., 1964.

CANTON, CARLENE. "When a Marriage Becomes a Family Affair," *Palo Alto Times*, Wed., May 11, 1977.

CARTER, H. and GLICK, P.C. *Marriage and Divorce: A Social and Economical Study.* Cambridge, Mass.: Harvard University Press, 1970.

DRAUGHON, MARGARET. "Stepmother's Model of Identification in Relation to Mourning in the Child," *Psychological Reports*, 36(1):183-189, 1975.

DUBERMAN, L. "Step-kin Relationships," *Journal of Marriage and the Family*, 35: 283-292, May, 1973.

DUBERMAN, LUCILLE. *The Reconstituted Family: A Study of Remarried Couples and Their Children.* Chicago: Nelson-Hall Publishers, 1975.

EGLESON, J. and EGLESON, J. F. *Parents Without Partners: A Guide for Divorced, Widowed, or Separated Parents.* New York: Dutton, 1961.

FAST, IRENE and CAIN, ALBERT C. "The Stepparent Role: Potential for Disturbances in Family Functioning," *American Journal of Orthopsychiatry*, 36:485-491, April, 1966.

FAST, I. and CHETHIK, M. "Stepparents and Their Spouses," in *Helping Parents Help Their Children.* L. E. Arnold (Ed.). New York: Brunner/Mazel, 1978, pp. 292-303.

FISCH, RICHARD. Personal communication, 1977.

FLASTE, RICHARD. "Family Life Poses Poignant Problems for the Stepparent," *New York Times*, April 8, 1977.

GARDNER, RICHARD A. *Psychotherapy with Children of Divorce.* New York: Jason Aronson, 1976.

GARDNER, RICHARD A. *The Boys and Girls Book About Divorce: With An Introduction for Parents.* New York: Bantam Edition, 1971.

GLICK, P. C. and NORTON, A. J. "Frequency, Duration and Probability of Marriage and Divorce," *Journal of Marriage and the Family*, 33:307-317, May, 1971.

GLICK, P. C. and NORTON, A. J. "Perspectives on the Recent Upturn in Divorce and Remarriage," *Demography*, 10(3):301-314, August, 1973.

GLINES, STEPHEN W. and BYRD, ROY N. Report DOT-HS-6-01487 (I-2) 3/1/78, Evaluation of the Utah Juvenile Court Alcohol School, available to the public through the National Technical Information Service, Springfield, VA 22151.

GOLDSTEIN, JOSEPH, FREUD, ANNA, and SOLNIT, ALBERT. *Beyond the Best Interests of the Child.* New York: The Free Press, a Division of the Macmillan Publishing Co., 1973.

GOODE, W. J. *The Family.* Englewood Cliffs, New Jersey: Prentice-Hall, 1964.

GUERIN, P. *Family Therapy.* New York: Gardner Press, 1976.

HALEY, J. and HOFFMAN, L. *Techniques of Family Therapy.* New York: Basic Books, Inc., 1967.

HETHERINGTON, MAVIS, COX, M. and COX, R. "Divorced Fathers," *The Family Coordinator*, Oct. 1976, p. 417.

HERMAN, ROBERT, Personal communication, 1978.

HIATT, HAROLD. "The Problem of Termination of Psychotherapy," *American Journal of Psychotherapy*, 19(4):607-615, Oct., 1965.

JACKSON, D. D. and WEAKLAND, J. H. "Conjoint Family Therapy: Some Considerations on Theory, Technique, and Results," *Psychiatry*, 24:30-45, 1961.

KELLY, JOAN B. and WALLERSTEIN, JUDITH S. "The Effects of Parental Divorce: Experiences of the Child in Early Latency," *American Journal of Orthopsychiatry*, 46(1):20-42, 1976.

KIRK, E. WALTON. Personal communication, March 30, 1978.

KRANTZLER, MEL. *Creative Divorce.* New York: New American Library, 1975.

LANGNER, T. S. and MICHAEL, S. T. *Life Stress and Mental Health.* New York: Free Press, 1963.

LAZARE, AARON. "Hidden Conceptual Models in Clinical Psychiatry," *New England Journal of Medicine*, 288:345-351, Feb. 15, 1973.

LEWIS, JERRY M., BEAVERS, W. ROBERT, GOSSETT, JOHN T., and PHILLIPS, VIRGINIA AUSTIN. *No Single Thread: Psychological Health in Family Systems*. New York: Brunner/Mazel, 1976.

LUNDE, DONALD T. Personal communication, 1978.

MADDOX, BRENDA. *The Half Parent*. New York: Evans, 1975.

MAYLEAS, DAVIDYNE. *Re-wedded Bliss: Love, Alimony, Incest, Ex-Spouse and Other Domestic Blessings*. New York: Basic Books, 1977.

McCLENAHAN, CAROLYN. "Group Work with Stepparents and Their Spouses," unpublished paper, 1978.

McCORMICK, M. *Stepfathers: What the Literature Reveals*. La Jolla, Calif.: Western Behavioral Sciences Institute, 1974.

MESSINGER, L. "Remarriage between Divorced People with Children from Previous Marriages: A Proposal for Preparation for Remarriage," *Jounal of Marriage and Family Counseling*, 2:193-200, 1976.

MESSINGER, LILLIAN, WALKER, KENNETH N., and FREEMAN, STANLEY J. J. "Preparation for Remarriage Following Divorce: The Use of Group Techniques," *American Journal of Orthopsychiatry*, 48 (2):263-272, 1978.

MINUCHIN, S. *Families and Family Therapy*. Cambridge, Mass.: Harvard University Press, 1974.

MOLINOFF, DANIEL D. "And Now . . . Equal Rights for Father," *San Francisco Chronicle*, Friday, June 3, 1977.

MOWATT, M. H. "Group Psychotherapy for Stepfathers and Their Wives," *Psychotherapy: Theory, Research and Practice*, 9 (4):328-331, 1972.

NADLER, JANICE HOROWITZ. Unpublished doctoral thesis on psychological stress of the stepmother, 1976.

NATIONAL CENTER FOR HEALTH STATISTICS. "Children of Divorced Couples: U.S., Selected Years," 1970, *Vital and Health Statistics*, 21(18), Feb., 1970.

NOBLE, JUNE and NOBLE, WILLIAM. *How to Live with Other People's Children*. New York: Hawthorne Books, 1977.

NOLAN, J. F. "The Impact of Divorce on Children," *Conciliation Courts Review*, 15(2): Dec., 1977.

NYE, IVAN F. "Child Adjustment in Broken and in Unhappy, Unbroken Homes," *Marriage and Family Living*, 19:356-361, Nov., 1957.

Parade Magazine, "Middle Age Divorce—The Family Time Bomb," Sunday, March 5, 1978.

PFLOGER, JANEL. "The Wicked Stepmother in a Child Guidance Clinic," *Smith College Studies in Social Work*, 17: March, 1947.

Population Reference Bureau, *New York Times*, Nov. 27, 1977.

RADOMISLI, MICHEL. From an unpublished paper presented at the American Psychiatric Association Annual Meeting, Atlanta, Georgia, May 11, 1978.

RALLINGS, E. M. "The Special Role of the Stepfather," *Family Coordinator*, 25(4): 445-449, 1976.

REINGOLD, CARMEL BERMAN. *Remarriage*. New York: Harper and Row, 1976.

RICCI, ISOLINA. "Where's Noah Webster Now That We Really Need Him," *The Single Parent News*, Nov.-Dec., 1976.

RICCI, ISOLINA. Personal communication, 1978.

ROOSEVELT, RUTH and LOFAS, JEANNETTE. *Living in Step*. New York: Stein and Day, 1976.

ROSENBAUM, JEAN and ROSENBAUM, VERYL. *Stepparenting*. Corte Madera, Calif.: Chandler and Sharp Publishers, Inc., 1977.

SAGER, CLIFFORD J., ET AL. Annotated Bibliography: The Remarried and Their

Families. Remarriage Consultation Service of the Jewish Board of Family and Children's Services, 120 W. 47th Street, New York, N. Y. Unpublished manuscript, 1978.

SARDANIS-ZIMMERMAN, IRENE. The "Stepmother: Mythology and Self-Perception," Unpublished doctoral dissertation and personal communication, May, 1977.

SARDANIS-ZIMMERMAN, IRENE. Personal communication, 1978.

SATIR, VIRGINIA. *Peoplemaking*. Palo Alto, Calif.: Science and Behavior Books, Inc., 1972.

SATIR, VIRGINIA. *Conjoint Family Therapy*. Palo Alto, Calif.: Science and Behavior Books, Inc., 1967.

SCHULMAN, GERDA L. "Myths that Intrude on the Adaptation of the Stepfamily," *Social Casework*. 49:131-139, 1972.

SIMON, ANNE W. *Stepchild in the Family: A View of Children in Remarriage*. New York: Odyssey Press, 1964.

SPANN, OWEN. Personal communication, 1977.

SPANN, OWEN and SPANN, NANCIE. *Your Child? I Thought It Was My Child!* Pasadena, Calif.: Ward Ritchie Press, 1977.

SPOCK, B. "The Stepchild," *Ladies Home Journal*, 32:35-36, 1962.

STEINZOR, B. *When Parents Divorce*. New York: Pantheon, 1969.

STERN, PHYLLIS NOERAGER. "Stepfather Families: Integration Around Child Discipline," *Issues in Mental Health Nursing*, 1 (2) :50-56, 1978.

THOMSON, H. *The Successful Stepparent*. New York: Harper and Row, 1966.

VAILLANT, GEORGE E. *Adaptation to Life*. Boston: Little, Brown, 1977.

VISHER, EMILY B. and VISHER, JOHN S. "Common Problems of Stepparents and Their Spouses," *American Journal of Orthopsychiatry*, 48(2):252-262, April, 1978.

Vital Statistics of the United States, 1974, Volume III—Marriage and Divorce. Washington, D. C.: U.S. Department of Health, Education, and Welfare, Public Health Service, National Center for Health Statistics.

WALKER, K. N., ROGERS, J., and MESSINGER, L. "Remarriage After Divorce: A Review," *Social Casework*, 58:276-285, May 1977.

WALLERSTEIN, JUDITH S. and KELLY, JOAN B. "The Effects of Parental Divorce: Experiences of the Child in Later Latency," *American Journal of Orthopsychiatry*, 46:256-269, April, 1976.

WARNER, JANE-LOUISE. "The Influence of Stepmotherhood Upon Attitudes Toward a Stepchild's Problem and Involvement in Help at a Child Guidance Clinic," Unpublished masters thesis, Boston, 1958.

WESTOFF, LESLIE ALDRIDGE. *The Second Time Around: Remarriage in America*. New York: Viking, 1975.

WHITE, ANNIE. "Factors Making for Difficulty in the Stepparent Relationship with Children," Abstract of a thesis. Illinois Institute for Juvenile Research, 1943.

WILSON, KENNETH L., ZURCHER, LOUIS A., McADAMS, DIANA CLAIRE, and CURTIS, RUSSELL, L. "Stepfathers and Stepchildren: An Exploratory Analysis from Two National Surveys," *Journal of Marriage and the Family*, 37:526-536, Aug., 1975.

WOOLLEY, PERSIA. *Creative Survival for Single Mothers*. Millbrae, Calif.: Celestial Arts, 1975.

WOOLLEY, PERSIA. *Child Custody Handbook*. New York: Simon-Schuster, Summit Books, 1978, in press.

Index

DATE DUE